# INFORMATION FILING AND FINDING

# INFORMATION FILING AND FINDING

## PAT F. BOOTH & M. L. SOUTH

 *ELM Publications, 1982*

First published 1982 by ELM Publications, 45 Park Road,
Buckden, Cambridgeshire PE18 9SL which company holds
the copyright on behalf of the authors — Pat F Booth and
M L South.

 British Library Cataloguing in Publication Data

Booth, Pat F..
    Information filing and finding.
    1. Information storage and retrieval systems
    ——Administration
    I. Title        II. South, M.L.
    025.5'24        Z699

    ISBN 0-9461390-0-8

(c) ELM Publications, 1982. Printed and bound by Biddles Ltd, Guildford,
Surrey. Production services by Book Production Consultants, 7, Brooklands
Avenue, Cambridge .

# ACKNOWLEDGEMENT

We acknowledge the stimulus provided by our colleagues Bob Burrows, Viera Horth, John Shinebourne and Alan Thomas, in the School of Library and Information Studies, Ealing College of Higher Education, in the course of many animated, intense and invigorating debates which have taken place on some of the topics treated in this book.


P.F.B.                                                    M.L.S.

## ABOUT THE AUTHORS


M L SOUTH, MA, FLA, PCGE

Mary South has worked in libraries within engineering, petroleum technology and broadcasting and, for the last ten years, has been a lecturer in information retrieval at Ealing College of Higher Education.

She is a graduate in Romance Languages and is especially interested in the relationship of linguistics to information retrieval.


P F BOOTH, MEd, BA, ALA, ACP, MIInfSc

Pat Booth has worked in a number of special libraries in private and nationalised industry, government and research organisations. From 1976 to 1982 she taught information retrieval studies in the School of Library and Information Studies at Ealing College of Higher Education.

# CONTENTS

# INTRODUCTION

This book is about 'information storage and retrieval'. The term is commonly abbreviated to 'information retrieval' and further abbreviated to 'IR'. We have, however, chosen to entitle this book 'Information filing and finding', partly because the title is descriptive of the activity of information retrieval and partly because in some usages (but not in ours) the term is exclusively associated with computer-held files (and often with large-scale computer-held files). We wish to emphasise our opinion that a small pocket diary on the one hand, and a computer-held file containing millions of records on the other, are essentially the same kind of system and that they are subject to the same 'laws' which affect their operations. We call *both* these systems 'information retrieval systems'.

Given this usage of the term, there can be few adults in a literate society who are not constantly involved in information retrieval activity, whether or not they are aware of the fact and whether or not they could describe and name the activity. We do not suggest that formal study of information retrieval is a prerequisite to the design and use of every system. It is not necessary to study higher mathematics in order to add up; it is not always necessary to study dietetics in order to provide a nourishing meal, nor to study law and accountancy in order to calculate personal tax returns. Similarly it is not necessary to study information retrieval in order to keep personal tax papers tidy and accessible; nor indeed is it necessary to do so in order to maintain small office files.

Nevertheless, formal knowledge of mathematics, dietetics, law, accountancy and so forth becomes useful and even necessary as the scale of an activity increases or as the constraints on the activity increase. For example, if nourishing meals are to be provided for a large number of people on a small budget, a knowledge of dietetics may become extremely useful.

Information retrieval is part of the core curriculum of librarianship/information science, in which area the study can be taken to a very high level. It is also an important component in computer studies. We are not aware of the subject being given such eminence in any other areas of knowledge. We are of the opinion, however, that information retrieval could usefully occupy a more prominent, though not necessarily pre-eminent, place in any studies relating to information flow and information systems; and that, in respect of particular occupations, training for those which entail the creation and maintenance of records (e.g. most office occupations) could usefully include a prominent component concerned with information retrieval.

Searching information retrieval systems is, moreover, a task not reserved for those professionally concerned with design and maintenance; and some instruction in both the principles and practice of searching, as given in some universities and colleges, is almost certainly beneficial. An information retrieval system, indeed, can be said to *include* the searcher and the search processes.

The book is intended for the following categories of reader:-

1. Students both at graduate and non-graduate level who are beginning formal studies of librarianship/information science.

2. Staff of library/information units who have 'moved sideways' into librarianship/information science. These staff may have relatively high qualifications

in other kinds of work (perhaps similar but not identical to information work), but need to formalise and extend their practical knowledge of information retrieval. Such staff may often constitute 'one-person bands' and have nobody easily accessible from whom to seek advice.

3. Students or staff who have an 'information filing and finding' content in their work, without necessarily being concerned primarily with library/information work.

The book is intended to be a foundation work, and it therefore includes discussion of theory as well as descriptions of practice. Detailed descriptions of particular techniques are obviously outside the scope of this work, but particular points of interest can be followed up by using the reading list at the end of the book. References relating to each chapter are given by using the numbers in the alphabetically arranged list (alphabetically arranged in order of author or title).

We would like to pay tribute not only to our colleagues with whom we have had personal contact, but to the many authors (past and present) who have contributed to the development of the science or art of information retrieval. Some (though not all) of these are represented in the reading list and, indeed, it has proved extremely difficult to make a selection.

This book is jointly the work of two authors, and we accept joint responsibility for the whole. The particular chapters were, however, written by us as individuals.-

|  |  |
|---|---|
| Chapter 1 | M L South |
| Chapter 2 | M L South |
| Chapter 3 | P F Booth |

| Chapter 4 | P F Booth |
| Chapter 5 | M L South |
| Chapter 6 | M L South |
| Chapter 7 | P F Booth |
| Chapter 8 | M L South |
| Chapter 9 | P F Booth |
| Chapter 10 | P F Booth |

Pat F Booth                                                    M L South

*October 1982*

# LIST OF FIGURES

## CHAPTER 1: BASIC DEFINITIONS

In this chapter some important terms will be defined and explained. The terms are, for the most part, familiar ones, but may be given special meanings within the context of this book which is the context of *information retrieval.*

The familiarity of the terms serves to indicate that information retrieval is itself a familiar and pervasive process. There can be few readers of this book who have not used an information retrieval system; and most readers will have designed one even if on a very small scale, and even if they were not aware of so doing.

The terms to be discussed in this chapter are grouped under the following heads:-

INFORMATION
DOCUMENTS
 Documents as physical artefacts
 Documents as communicatory artefacts
 Documents as intellectual artefacts
 Document uses and users
AUTHORS AND PUBLISHERS
WORKS, COPIES AND PUBLICATIONS
DOCUMENT REPRESENTATIONS
DOCUMENT LISTINGS
FILES AND INDEXES
INFORMATION RETRIEVAL
DOCUMENT COLLECTIONS

1

# INFORMATION

For the purposes of this book 'information' is any thought which is capable of being shared between two or more persons and which is capable of being recorded in documents (e.g. in books, periodicals, letters, pictures). Information has referents (i.e. information *refers* to something, or is 'about' something). The referents may be simple elements or combinations of elements (e.g. 'food' or 'food and drink'); or may be assertions, questions, commands about the elements (e.g. 'The *food* is ready'; 'Is the *food* ready?', 'Prepare the *food*'). Information may relate to facts or pretended facts or supposed facts (i.e. to facts or pseudo-facts), and is then 'factual information'; or it may relate to fiction (imaginings), to speculation and to opinions; and is then 'non-factual information'. Information includes the contents of a romantic novel as well as the contents of a driving licence, and of a forged driving licence.

The term 'information' has many though confusingly similar meanings according to area of discourse and in particular contexts, and the above definition represents only one of them. The specialist usage of communications theory gives the term a very wide scope and provides a useful basis for discussion of other usages. In communications theory 'information' is any event in the environment which causes a human, animal or any other thing to change state in however slight a degree. A shaft of sunlight is 'information' if it causes eyes to blink; the smell of food is information if it causes digestive juices to flow, and the sound of a voice saying 'food is ready' is information if it causes the hearer to think about food. The movement of a brake pedal is information if it causes the wheels of a vehicle to stop turning. Information can be received and transmitted by humans, animals and inanimates; and the processes neither entail nor do they exclude an element of conscious awareness.

General usage of the term is more restrictive. In general usage the 'change of state' entailed by the receipt of information is confined to changes in thought: to changes in awareness. Conscious awareness is an essential element in the receipt of information; so that in the above examples only the statement 'food is ready' would 'count' as information, and then, only if heard and mentally processed by a human. In general usage only humans receive information, and only humans actively transmit it, although humans can 'gather' information from the entire environment. In general usage it is only in humorous and anthropomorphic contexts that motorcars and dogs give or receive information.

General usage further differs from the usage of communications theory in that the former is referential. The shaft of sunlight is not itself information, although it may be a source of information *about* itself or *about* something else. The sound of the person's voice may be a source of information about the food (information consciously transmitted) or it might be a source of information about the speaker's voice, nationality, sex, state of health, not consciously transmitted but 'gathered' by the receiver.

It is obvious that the difference between general usage and the usage of information retrieval lies in the relationship of the term to 'external reality'. In general usage a single thought element would not count as 'information': something must be explicitly or implicitly asserted about the referent before the element becomes 'information'; and usually questions and commands do not 'count' unless an assertion is implied (e.g. 'Is the food ready?' implies that there is food in the course of preparation). In general usage, moreover, 'information' most commonly relates to facts or pseudo-facts, the facts being of a kind which are testable if means and evidence are available. The contents of a driving licence or of a forged driving licence are information; the contents of a romantic novel are not. The assertion 'the universe contains 22.234 billion stars' constitutes 'information' (unless presented as science fiction), because although the 'fact' is in practice

3

untestable it is of a kind which could be tested given the means and the evidence. The assertion '23% of the population believes that God is omniscient', is information about people but not about the omniscience of God; but the assertion 'God is omniscient' is not in itself information, because whether true or untrue it is by its nature not provable by ordinary rules of evidence. In general usage we have 'knowledge' of God but not 'information' about God. In general usage although the possession of 'knowledge' may imply a higher level of thought than the "mere possession of information", it does not seem to imply the same level of factual precision, so that paradoxically a dog 'knows' when its meal is ready, but does not 'have information' about the meal.

The above discussion of general usage does not imply the existence of prescriptive rules. There is no law which prevents clergymen 'imparting information about God', or which prevents dogs being said to 'request information', but both usages are unusual and would probably be perceived as expressions of irony. The factual and precise nature of information as the term is generally used could be shown by contrasting attitudes to the first chapter of Genesis. Fundamentalists believing this chapter to represent the literal truth, and a truth carrying its own authority and proof might suppose the chapter to carry 'information' about the beginning of the world. Non-fundamentalists who regard the Genesis story as a 'creation myth' might suppose the chapter to carry information about creation myths but not about the beginning of the world. Alternatively, they might not regard it as carrying information about anything.

Within the usage of information retrieval the first chapter of Genesis contains information on any count. Obviously the specialist usage of information retrieval is wider than general usage, although its referential character is maintained. Information can be categorised by a number of criteria of which the most important produces the difference between factual and non-factual information.

4

# DOCUMENTS

Documents are physical artefacts in which information has been purposefully stored for use beyond the immediate moment, and for the purposes of information retrieval both factual and non-factual information is stored in documents.

Information is stored in the brain for use beyond the moment. It is stored in the 'memory'; and in effect documents are external memories. (The term 'memory' is also used in relation to computers which are essentially information storage and handling devices). Documents include copies of romantic novels in readable print, in braille, on film, in sound and on videotape; they include handwritten copies of bank statements, the same statement in the form of a computer print-out as well as the statement as it is held in machine-readable form by the computer. Documents include stone-age cave paintings, and photographs of stone-age flints. They do not include stone-age flints themselves since these, although they may be used for the same information-gathering purposes as the photograph, were not created as sources of information. The information in documents is deliberately recorded and transmitted, albeit transmitter and receiver may be widely distanced in space and time.

For practical functional purposes associated with the transmission of information the distinction between documents and non-documents may not always be easy to maintain (as in the case of the flint and photograph of the flint); and by other criteria the distinction between document and non-document may be blurred. By the criterion of time a smoke signal is of doubtful status, although it almost certainly 'lasts' beyond the moment; and burial mounds are of ambiguous status since their purpose is both to conceal and to commemorate the dead.

5

The question of 'what is a document' may become of crucial importance in some situations, as for example in the administrative distinction between libraries, resource centres, and museums, (see below, *Document collections*). However, in this book we shall be dealing mainly with items of undoubted documentary status, and which are relatively easily portable and collectable (e.g. with photographs of smoke signals and burial mounds but not with the originals).

It is obvious that general and special usage of the term 'document' corresponds approximately to the general and special usage of the term 'information' as discussed above. In general usage documents store factual information, but there may be a further restriction to items which have a purposed evidential value. Thus driving licences are referred to as documents, chemistry text books less frequently so, and copies of romantic novels almost never. There is a slight variation by which any of the above become 'documents' if they are used for evidential purposes. The chemistry text book becomes a 'document' when used as evidence of prior publication in a patents case; and the romantic novel becomes a document when used by scholars to prove facts about its author. For information retrieval both factual and non-factual information is stored in documents and the term is applied irrespective of the document's evidential value.

Documents are physical, communicatory and intellectual artefacts, with varying intended recipients and end uses; and they must be created and distributed.

**Documents as Physical Artefacts**

As physical artefacts documents have weight, shape, size, colour, relative strength, brittleness etc. As physical artefacts they have three dimensions (although the 'message' may be recorded in two dimensions). These are their 'storage characteristics'. Terms representing types of documents by their physical or storage characteristics exclusively are non-existent. Even the term 'book' implies more than the physical artefact.

6

## Documents as Communicatory Artefacts

As communicatory artefacts documents must operate directly or indirectly through the medium of the senses. Visual (sight) documents include the present book, pictures, sculptures, handwritten letters. Audio (sound) documents include tape recordings and gramophone records; tactile (touch) documents include books with embossed writing such as Braille. Audio-visual documents include videocassette records and talking films. Audio-records and some visual records are not available other than through the medium of a machine. Although the term 'machine readable' is used in relation to computers, the principle of 'machine readability' applies as much to films, video recordings, sound recordings (including pianola rolls) and microforms (miniaturised documents requiring magnification). The term can also be applied to older forms such as settings of type and engravers' plates, the operation of which is similar to one computer mode: the production of secondary documents for which the machine readable document is the 'master'.

Documents must operate through the medium of symbols. A symbol is something which for referential but not for other purposes, stands in the place of something else. Thus a picture of a railway-train, or the word 'railway-train' spoken or written, stand in the place of the train for purposes of referring to it, but do not perform its function of providing transport. It can be argued that all communication and thought beyond an elementary level is heavily dependent upon the process of symbolisation. Whether this is so or not documentary communication is entirely dependent upon symbols. The symbols used are important characterising features of documents since their 'meanings' have to be learnt before the information becomes accessible. Representational pictures require less special learning than do verbal symbols, since the latter are almost entirely 'arbitrary' bearing no relationship of likeness to the thing symbolised. However, since all normal human beings learn to speak, and most humans in a literate society learn to write, it is possible that written and spoken (sound-

7

recorded) documents are accessible to more persons than - for example - musical notation, graphs, diagrams and maps which do have an analogical likeness to the things represented. It should be noted, moreover, that totally representational pictures of, for example, apples might be incomprehensible to persons who had never seen apples, and that words may be more efficient in explaining the unknown. Words (linguistic symbols) will be totally incomprehensible unless the particular 'linguistic system' is known i.e. unless the 'language' is known, e.g. English, French or German.

The term 'information-carrying media' is used to indicate the variety of documents distinguished by the use of different sensory channels and different systems of symbolisation.

## Documents as Intellectual Artefacts

Documents as intellectual artefacts are characterised by the different kinds of information they contain. As already stated, information can be categorised by a number of different criteria the most important of which produces the difference between 'factual' and 'non-factual' information. This dichotomy is not the same as the dichotomy 'truth and non-truth'. For example Keats' 'Ode to a nightingale' might be considered truthful without being factual. Between the extremes of factual and non-factual information, and the extremes of truth and non-truth, there is a vast intermediate area of questions, speculations, suppositions, opinion, guess work and fiction mingled with fact (as in historical novels and the so-called 'faction' of some television documentaries).

It is obvious that the fundamental criterion by which we classify information is its relationship to external reality. The fact/fiction and truth/non-truth dichotomies approximate to a third: information which is, or purports to be, an exact reflection of external reality, and information which carries its own reality. The assertion that each of the angles of a square is of 90 degrees is an extreme example of the first, and the contents of an 'abstract painting' or a piece of 'non programme music' extreme examples of the second.

All art forms, to a greater or lesser extent 'carry their own reality'. It is for this reason that in documentary classification they are not classified primarily by the 'subjects' to which they refer (e.g. nightingales or Grecian urns) but by their aesthetic form. Documentary classification distinguishes between 'subject classes' (e.g. chemistry, nightingales) and 'form classes' (e.g. poetry, music painting), which are classified primarily by their form and only secondarily (if at all) by their referents in external reality. Works of art, however, especially the less abstract such as novels and portraits can be used as sources of factual information, (for instance 'Nicholas Nickleby' is a source of information about the 19th century provincial theatre). Works of art can, moreover, themselves be the subject of information; and in libraries provision has to be made not only for the works of art (e.g. the novels of Dickens) but works about the works of art.

**Document Uses and Users**

Documents are created and used for many social and personal reasons: for example in support of education, recreation, social control, administration. It is difficult to envisage an advanced industrial society which did not make extensive use of documents (for example, even traffic signs are documents, as are income tax forms, and the daily newspaper). The immediate purposes of documents are, however, the preservation and transmission of information, whatever other functions documents may be made to serve further along the chain of purpose and motivation. In the context of immediate purpose, documents may be administrative documents or non-administrative documents with a blurred area in between.

Administrative documents are the result of an activity of which they form part. They are not 'free-standing' and may lose significance when they are disassociated from the activity of which

9

they form part. For example, in a household a note to the daily milkman saying 'No milk today' is part of the activity of controlling the supplies of milk, and the note is an administrative document which will obviously lose significance as 'today' becomes 'tomorrow', and the source of the note is forgotten. In a research laboratory, administrative documents might include laboratory notes, procedural manuals and correspondence with suppliers. In a household, administrative documents could include the note to the milkman, and a daily shopping list. Less ephemeral documents might include insurance certificates, property deeds, and copies of electricity bills.

Non-administrative documents are 'free-standing' and, although they might support an activity, are not part of or product of the activity. For example, in the research department copies of technical journals and reports of organisations might be needed to support the activities: as in a household 'bought-in' cookery books would help the household cook. Within the intermediate area are documents which, although not the result of an activity of which they form part, are treated as if they were. For example a published copy of a standard specification could become an adminstrative document if the specification is adopted by an organisation as a complete procedural 'law'.

Also in the intermediate area are documents which have ceased to have currency. These are sometimes called 'dead' documents, and they could include, for example, copies of customers' orders which have been dealt with and which no longer need be kept for either administrative or legal reasons. Archives (or archival documents) are administrative documents which, diverted from their original purposes, are used for historical research. The copies of customers' orders might be used for research into economic trends during a certain period; and mediaeval land registers are used for research into land tenure in the Middle Ages.

Another and common case of documents diverted from their first purpose is the use of popular recreational literature as a source of information regarding social attitudes and social conditions. For example, nineteenth-century popular magazine stories are a fruitful source of information regarding attitudes to women and to the working classes.

All documents have intended users as well as intended uses. The intended use may be explicitly announced as in 'Chemistry for third-year students of engineering'; may be implicitly assumed (as in much popular fiction); or may be deliberately concealed (as in some advertising). The intended user is part of the use and the user affects the content (obviously 'Jack and the Beanstalk' written for five year olds is different from the same basic work written for older children). In the case of administrative documents – especially correspondence – the intended user (the recipient) is in a way part of the content. Two seemingly identical communications may implicitly or explicitly include the assertion 'I am telling you, Mr Smith that. . . . ' or 'I am telling you, Mr Jones that . . . . '.

In documentary classification the term 'bias' is used (in a non-pejorative way) to indicate clearly - definable and explicitly expressed adaptations to specific user requirements; as for example ' "Alice in Wonderland" adapted for students of logic and mathematics'; or 'Theory of numbers written for 10 year olds'.

In the context of this book the term 'document user' will be employed as a generic term for what might otherwise be called 'reader' 'viewer' 'listener' 'audience' etc.

# AUTHORS AND PUBLISHERS

The term 'author' is generally understood to signify a 'writer'. Within librarianship (and in the context of this book) 'authors' include not only writers, but any other persons or organisations responsible in some degree for the information content of the document. Authors include writers, artists, performers, conductors (of music), film directors, cameramen, composers. Authors may be 'originators' or they may operate on other authors' originals as translators, adaptors, compilers, editors. Persons as authors are called personal authors. Organisations as authors are called corporate authors. An organisation is said to be the author if the information content in some way expresses the opinions of the organisation as such, or if the work is undertaken by persons on behalf of the organisation. For example, political parties are 'authors' of their manifestos; and a research report by John Smith as Chief Chemist of Jones Industries Ltd., has Jones Industries as its author. Documents may have more than one author, and the authors may be performing the same functions (as in this book) or different functions (writer/illustrator; original writer/translator). Documents may have both corporate and personal authors, the research report being a possible example.

Although all documents necessarily have *de facto* personal authors, they may be assumed to have only corporate authors if the personal author is non-significant (as in the case of the manifesto) or undeclared. They may be assumed to have no authors at all if the authorship is unknown or undeclared (anonymous works); or if it is considered non-significant. Within a particular issue of a daily newspaper many authors (named and unnamed) are represented, and they are working under the direction of an editor. But unless particular parts of the newspaper are being identified, the newspaper is usually deemed to be 'authorless', on the grounds that the creative function is diffused amongst too many persons, and that editors can change at frequent intervals.

12

A publisher (as distinct from an author), is the person or organisation responsible for making the document available to the public at the primary stage of distribution. 'Publishing' in a legal and in some other contexts, is to make known; so that a conversation between two friends can constitute publishing. In the context of documents, however, the term means 'to offer a document to the public' either *gratis* or for a price. (This usually entails creating multiple copies of the document. See next section *Works, Copies and Publications*). Administrative documents (however widely distributed) are not 'published' documents, but a set of 100 copies of a book of art reproductions, priced at £100 each, constitutes a publication, if offered without restriction to the public. 'Semi-publishing' or 'half-publishing' occurs when copies of a document are widely distributed but there is a technical restriction as who may receive copies. Fifty-thousand copies of a consultancy document sent to members of a trade union or political party might constitute a 'semi-publishing'. (It would not be difficult for non-members to acquire copies by legitimate means).

Authorship is significant in the identification and evaluation of documents, because authorship significantly affects the value of the documents, either fundamentally or as the value is perceived. The manifestos of two different political parties would be perceived differently, and would indeed be different, even if the contents were identical. The known authority of individuals may rightly affect attitudes to their work; and – particularly in the case of works of art – the 'creator' may be interesting *per se*. Lastly, authorship tends to be a recognisable and remembered feature of documents.

Corporate authors are often identical with publishers, e.g. the Institution of Electrical Engineers can be both the author and the publisher of a research report. This dual function is rare in the case of personal authors, and rare, in the case of 'commercial publishers', i.e. those which – unlike the I.E.E. – have publishing as their main business. Publishers as publishers are significant in

13

the evaluation and identification of documents although they are not often 'sought' for their own sake. Publishers are recorded in listings of documents because they may have authority and reputation for publishing particular types of document (e.g.Virago Press for feminist literature, Butterworths for scientific literature); and because the name of the publisher as primary distributor may be important for the process of obtaining the item.

## WORKS, COPIES AND PUBLICATIONS

Works are intellectual artefacts, the information content of communications whether or not embodied in documents. The contents of a letter or of 'Hamlet' constitute works; works are generally considered to be discrete creations characterised not only by their referents (nightingales for example), but by their form (poetry), and by the sensory and symbolic media of communication (a poetry recital, using words and hearing). In some cases a 'work' may be a compilation of other works (as for example an anthology of poetry). When issued in documentary form a particular work may vary in some degree from document to document. In organising a collection of documents, the essential identity of a particular work needs to be established, whilst the variants should be indicated. For example, 'Hamlet' translated into French is at once the same and a different work from 'Hamlet' in the original English. The following are ways in which works might vary:-

1. 'Textual criticism' — especially of older works — establishes alternative texts (particularly of musical and literary works).

2. Translations are made; and adaptations from one medium to another; adaptations for particular users (e.g. 'Gulliver's travels' for children). The extent to which any of these are considered to be the 'same' as the original varies from case to case.

**14**

3. Content is revised to bring it up to date. Such revisions may continue for so long (especially in the case of books of law), that although the title is retained the revisions are virtually distinct works.

4. The work is used with accretions in the shape of (for example) notes, illustrations, or glossaries.

A copy is the work embodied as a physical artefact. The term is used whether or not the document is 'original' and whether or not there is more than one copy. Most documents can be replicated to produce copies which — in their pristine state — are totally interchangeable. Any member of the set is 'the document'. Works can be distributed through several documents (as in serial stories), or conversely, several works can be included in one document (all the Brandenburg Concertos on one disc; the works of Shakespeare; Readers' Digest condensed novels). Documents which are published become 'publications'.

Works have authors (which may or may not be known), may have titles, were produced (though not necessarily published) at a certain time (which may or may not be known), and use some kind of sensory and symbolic channel for communication.

Copies in addition have physical characteristics (storage characteristics). In the case of books, for example, they have height and a certain number of pages.

Publications, in addition, may have publishers and a date of publication, (which may or may not be known).

In this book we shall use the term 'document content' or 'content' to indicate the content of a particular document, which may include one or more works or parts of works.

# DOCUMENT REPRESENTATIONS

Document representations are references to documents in recorded form, designed primarily for the purposes of identification, and secondarily for the purposes of quick evaluation by anticipatable criteria (e.g. length, date of publication). Document representations are used in document listings.

The *citation* gives the 'minimum identification information', which will vary according to whether only the 'work' is to be identified, or whether the document or publication is to be identified. The *description* gives further information which might help in the evaluation of the document. In some cases an abstract is included. An abstract is an indication of the information content. *Indicative* abstracts indicate 'what the item is about'; *informative* abstracts summarise the content. The term 'surrogate' meaning 'substitute' usually has a functional connotation, i.e. the 'surrogate' is able to perform some of the functions of the thing it represents. In this sense, only informative abstracts are surrogates to more than a limited extent and in this book we prefer the term 'representation'.

The following are examples of document representations:-

Citation: Southwell Borough Council. Road Traffic Committee. Report on traffic density at junction of Greenwich and Palomar Streets. August 1982.

Description: Southwell Borough Council. Road Traffic Committee. Report on traffic density at junction of Greenwich and Palomar Streets. Prepared with the assistance of the University of Southwell's Department of Transport Studies. August 1982. 78 p. 6 folding maps.

| Indicative abstract: | (Added to citation or description)

Describes traffic count at junction during week beginning August 2nd 1982. Makes recommendations regarding control and re-routing. |
|---|---|
| Informative abstract: | (Added to citation or description)

Describes traffic count at junction during week beginning August 1982. Highest density (500 vehicles per hour mean) Monday to Friday 8 am to 11 am. Recommends East/West one way system re-routing West/East traffic through Hurstmonceaux Street from High Street. Recommends traffic lights Palomar Street opposite School. |

## DOCUMENT LISTINGS

The term 'catalogue' is generally used for any inventorial listing of items which have an administrative connection (e.g. mail order catalogues, museum catalogues, publishers' catalogues and library catalogues). In this book it will be used for catalogues of document collections, as, for example, library catalogues. The term 'bibliography' is used for listings of documents which do not necessarily have an administrative connection, e.g. do not belong to any particular library or collection, but which may be associated by a common subject, authorship or other non-administrative factor. The term is etymologically associated with 'books', but is now quite commonly used for listings of all kinds of documents. (The term is also used for the study of books as physical artefacts, and for the total 'literature' of a subject or author, (as when it is said that the 'subject has an extensive bibliography').

17

Both catalogues and bibliographies consist of document representations. Catalogues (as in the case of library catalogues) have an obvious administrative function in the recording of items held in a collection, which may or may not always be 'in place'; and also act as a guide to the collection by making reference to the places where the original documents can be found.

The term 'database' is commonly used for bibliographies and catalogues held by computer; and the term 'databank' for items of information held by computer. For example a database produces the references to a document which might contain information; while a databank produces the information. In order to emphasise the essential similarity between computer-held and manual listings, we prefer to use the terms for both computerised and manual listings, specifying the computer or manual element when necessary.

## FILES AND INDEXES

A file is any collection of documentary items arranged for the purposes of searching. Files may include documentary items which are physically discrete, (e.g. a collection of books); or items which are included in one discrete document, for example, a catalogue consisting of document representations each of which is held on one card, or the same list printed in a book. The documentary items may be documents, document representations or recorded items of information. The following are examples of files:-

a — A shopping list arranged according to shops to be used.

b — The alphabetical subject index to a book.

c — A list of words in alphabetical order as in a dictionary.

18

d — An encyclopaedia arranged in alphabetical
order of subjects.

e — A list of a firm's personnel held on cards
(one name per card) in alphabetical order.
The same list held by computer.

f — An engagement diary held in a pocket book
arranged in chronological order of engagements.

g — A collection of letters held in a wallet arranged
in random order or in alphabetical order of
correspondents.

h — A collection of letters kept in filing cabinets
arranged according to subject.

i — Books arranged on library shelves by subject.

j — Bibliographies and library catalogues arranged
by author, subject or title held on cards (one
card per representation) or by computer or
book-type listings.

The term 'index' has a number of different meanings (in
economics, engineering and documentation for example), all of
them associated with 'pointing' or 'guiding'. In documentation
the term may be used as a synonym for catalogue and bibliography, and the term 'indexing' is sometimes used to relate to all
the procedures associated with information retrieval. In the
present book a more precise usage will be adhered to. A self-
indexing file is one arranged in a self-evident order (i.e. an indicative order) of which alphabetical order of the names of things
(people or subjects) is the most obvious example. Although all
files arranged in this way are 'self-indexing', the term 'index' will
be reserved for those files which include minimal information,
their function being to 'point' to the places where information

can be found. Examples include the subject index to a book (in alphabetical order and referring to page numbers); the alphabetical index to a library classification scheme, such as the Dewey system used in most public libraries. Some catalogues and bibliographies consist of more than one file of representations, one file under subjects and another under authors. Often in such cases, full information is given in only one file, and the file containing the briefer information is referred to as 'the index'. A typical public library catalogue might consist of:-

1. A file of representations arranged by subject according to the Dewey Decimal Classification, in which detailed information about each item is given.

2. An alphabetical subject *index* to the arrangement which simply 'indicates' where items on the particular subject can be found.

3. A file of representations arranged in alphabetical order of title and author, in which brief information about each item is given, plus an indication of where fuller information can be found. This is referred to frequently as the author/title index.

## INFORMATION RETRIEVAL

Information retrieval is the process by which documentary information is organised for the purpose of searching, and the processes by which the resultant information retrieval system is searched. In a sense every document is an 'IR system' but the term is usually reserved for those documents, parts of documents, or document collections specifically arranged for searching, e.g., for the alphabetical index to a text-book but not for the text-book itself. The creation of an IR system includes the process of arrangement and may include the process of creating document representations. Information retrieval systems include one or more files.

Information retrieval systems perform one or more of the following functions:-

*Reference retrieval.* The system produces references to documents in which information may be found (produces document representations). The answer to the question 'Where can I purchase an electric food mixer?' could be 'Directory of Electrical Goods suppliers, 1982'.
All databases (computerised and manual catalogues and bibliographies) are reference retrieval systems.

*Document retrieval.* The system produces the documents in which information may be found. The answer to the question 'Where can I purchase an electric food mixer?' is the production of a copy of the directory. Examples include the arrangement of books on library shelves, and of letters in filing cabinets. Library catalogues are part of document retrieval systems. 'Full text retrieval' is a development in computerisation which makes 'document retrieval' by computer a possibility.

*Data retrieval.* The system produces the information required without intermediary of either document or representation. The answer to the question 'Where can I buy an electric food mixer?' could be 'Electrical Supplies Ltd.'. Data retrieval systems include telephone and trade directories, dictionaries and encyclopaedias (alphabetically arranged), bank statements and engagement diaries, computerised air-line booking systems and some services provided by 'viewdata' type systems. Catalogues are data retrieval systems in so far as they provide information about the documents listed.

21

Data retrieval systems are sometimes called 'fact retrieval' systems. This is because computerised data retrieval is most commonly concerned with 'concrete"facts. In common with information retrieval in general, data retrieval has tended to be regarded as a development associated with computers totally different in kind from age-old processes of 'filing and finding'. In consequence the terms 'information retrieval' and 'data retrieval' are in some contexts exclusively associated with computers. However, although computerisation has considerably extended the possibilities of information retrieval systems, it has not altered their essential nature. In this book the term 'information retrieval' relates to both computerised and manual systems.


## DOCUMENT COLLECTIONS

This book is concerned with the organisation of files and it has already been stated that a file may exist within a document or comprise a number of physically separate units within a collection. Whilst it is technically feasible for particular purposes that a whole 'library' should be contained within the covers of one book, for most purposes inquirers will need to have access to a collection of documents. Document collections are referred to by various terms according to their purpose and nature of the documents, but terminology is idiosyncratic; the term 'library' – despite ambiguities – being the only standard term. This term seems to carry with it a connotation of 'systematic collecting and orderly arrangement in order to facilitate systematic searching and considered choice'. The term has been used metaphorically in this sense in the case of so called 'toy libraries' 'fabric libraries' and 'plant libraries'. In a non-metaphorical context, libraries tend to reflect the etymology of the term and are therefore associated with collections of books. However, there are probably few libraries which do not extend their scope to include 'non-book materials' (i.e. documents other than books and periodicals). Despite the proliferation of new communication media, the English language has not been prolific in the production of terms to signify collections of documents other than books. The term 'discothèque' (analogically from the French 'bibliothèque') does not signify a collection of gramophone records, and we have not 'filmoteches' or 'filmeries', nor 'mapperies', 'sound taperies' or 'videotaperies'. The only neologism which reflects the proliferation of new media is 'resource centre' which is short for 'learning resource centre', 'educational resource centre' and 'multi-media resource centre'. A resource centre is a collection of items of various documentary forms (e.g. films, sound tapes, overhead projector sheets), and often including non-documentary items (e.g. samples of clothes rather than pictures of clothes) used as sources of information. The resource centre often includes the apparatus necessary to use the items (e.g. videotape recorders) and for creating items (e.g. for making recordings or overhead projector sheets). Resource centres often exclude from the collection so-called 'library materials' (e.g. books and periodicals); but libraries are often closely associated with resource centres administratively and functionally, even if they do not form part of them. Resource centres have developed in order to support formal education, but there is no reason in principle why they should not exist outside the environment of formal education; and indeed many 'librarians' claim to be providing the facilities of a resource centre.

The designation of document collections (and of the places where they are kept) is usually related to the uses of the documents rather than to the type of media collected. The following is a list of types of document by use with suggestions as to where (in terminological terms) they might be kept.

> *Administrative documents derived from various sources* (e.g. correspondence).
> Kept in 'filing departments', 'registries', in the offices of the receiving and creating departments.
> Rarely in 'libraries'.

*Administrative documents created for purposes
of record* (e.g. membership or staff records;
fingerprint records; vehicle licence records).
Kept in 'records departments', 'registries',
qualified or not by function of parent department (e.g. Fingerprint Records Department).
Rarely in 'libraries'.

*Archival documents*
Kept in 'archives departments', 'record offices'
(e.g. County Record Offices, the Public Record
Office), and in 'libraries'.

*Non-administrative documents*
Kept in 'libraries'; but 'intelligence departments',
'information departments' and 'public relations
departments' are likely to have collections; and
the term 'information service' is commonly used
for services basing their activities on recorded
information from non-administrative documents.

In this book the term 'document collection' or 'collection' will
be used as a generic term.

## FURTHER READING

Items 12 and 44 from section B, p. 275 and 278.

# CHAPTER 2: FILE ORGANISATION: BASIC FACTORS

A file is a kind of store. All stores are created in order to fulfil one or more of the following functions:-

1. The prevention of loss through damage or deterioration. (The preservation function).

2. The prevention of loss through unauthorised use. (The security function).

3. The prevention of loss through dispersal (through not finding). (The search function).

This book is concerned primarily with the search function, and with the other functions in so far as they affect the search function. The functions are interactive. The operation of the security function, on the one hand, will tend to prevent damage through unskilled use and through over-use and, on the other hand, may prevent loss-through-dispersal by ensuring that items are not misplaced by unauthorised (or other) persons. The operation of the preservation function may demand that special kinds of equipment are provided for different physical forms, which conflict with the search function, which demands that items are arranged according to pattern of use. Grouping by pattern of use does not necessarily coincide with grouping by storage characteristics, whether or not the items to be stored are documents, clothes, food or engineering spare parts. In the case of documents storage characteristics relate to physical form while use characteristics are likely to relate to intellectual content. It is unlikely that all items on 'underground rivers of London' will be found together on library shelves, because some will be in the form of 'flat' maps, others in the form of large books, small books, microforms (miniature documents) and relief models. The flat maps are most likely to be found with other 'flat maps' dealing with streets of London or underground rivers of Wales.

Here the search function will be discussed, on the assumption that the materials are physically homogeneous. This is likely to be so in the case of letters in a correspondence file (differences in physical form being minor and irrelevant), in files of document representations, (whether in separable units or integrated in a 'book' type document) since in this case the items have been specially created for the purposes of filing; and in other files of specially-created items (e.g. personnel records).

A file (or any other store) organised for the purposes of searching must be capable of responding to one or more of the following types of search inquiry:-

1. *Search for an item (or group of items) which are already selected and which are known to be in the store:-*

    Examples: Find the jam, the copy of David Copperfield, the two research reports on X, the letter from Mr Smith, the brochures on holiday camps.

2. *Search for items which are not known to be in the store:-*

    (a) To confirm that the items exist.

      Examples  Is there a pot of jam, a copy of David Copperfield, a research report on X, a letter from Mr Smith, a brochure on holiday camps?

(b) To confirm the non-existence of items.

Examples: Are we sure that there is no jam (etc)?
(This is to 'prove the universal negative', i.e. to
prove that something does not exist).

(c) To ensure that all items in a certain group are
found, or to find out 'how many' or 'how much'.

Examples: Is this all the jam; are these all the
research reports (etc)? (This is the 'complete
retrieval' question).

In all cases where more than one item is being sought, the ultimate
purpose may be to 'retrieve' more than one item, or it may be to
retrieve a group of items from which a further selection is to be
made. For example, if 'all the jam' or 'all Dickens's novels' are
being sought, the ultimate purpose may be to use 'all the jam' for
the dinner menu, or to choose 'the best jam' by criteria which
cannot be defined until the jam is seen. Similarly a student may
wish to read 'all Dickens' or dip into a selection of Dickens's
novels before making a final choice.

In the case of inquiries of type 2, the purpose of the inquiry may
not primarily be to find the items but to ascertain what action is
necessary or not necessary, such as ordering more jam, starting or
not starting research on X. The organisation of a store is *per se*
a source of information.

At an initial stage the store (the file) may be totally unorganised.
The items are in unfixed accidental order which may change every
time the store is used. In such a store it will be necessary to search
the store item by item until the items sought are found. In the
case of the 'complete retrieval' type of inquiry this will *always*
entail searching the whole store; and in the other cases it may
entail a comprehensive search. However, such a store is not
necessarily ineffective, and indeed it may be more cost-effective

than an organised store. If the items in the store are relatively few in number, if they are easily recognisable and distinguishable one from another, there may be little point in using time in organising the store, especially if the items are easily accessible (handleable and seeable). For example, letters in an office in-tray should not be very great in number, and are easy to ruffle through to find letters from Mr. Smith. A meagre domestic food store presents few problems, pots of jam are distinguishable from packets of butter, and the whole store can easily be scanned. In the case of a simple shopping list (which is a kind of file), provided it is on one page, special arrangement is not necessary.

There is a point, however, at which some kind of pre-organisation becomes necessary. This is the point at which 'searching the whole store' becomes an unreliable search procedure; or at which the repetitive effort (or cost) of searching the whole store becomes unacceptable; or at which the time taken to respond to the inquiry becomes unacceptable.

The point will be reached when the items in the store become relatively numerous or when they become in some sense 'inaccessible' (for example if a list is impossible to scan, or when the size of the collection makes access to all the items at one time impossible). The unreliability of a search process, when the items in the store are randomly arranged, is demonstrated in a search for a telephone number in a telephone directory arranged under subscribers' names, when only the subscriber's address is known. For the purposes of this search the items are randomly arranged; and the search may not only be lengthy, but the item is quite likely to be missed.

The extent to which it is desirable to pre-organise the file depends upon frequency of use, desired response times, and desired reliability.

Output effort, in terms of time, skills and money spent in searching, tends to go down as input effort (time, skills and money spent in organising the file) goes up; the output effort being repetitive, the input effort to a great extent non-repetitive. If the file is infrequently used, there is obviously a case for reducing input effort to a minimum, provided that when the file is used the response time is acceptable and the response is itself adequate. At an extreme, we can imagine a single, annual inquiry the answer to which is produced by six people 'searching the whole store' for six days. However, although this method might be suitable from an economic point of view, there is a likelihood that the six-day response time might not be acceptable, and a stronger possibility that the quality of the response might not be acceptable, since humans (as distinct from computers) are not very reliable searchers. (NB. A search by computer would, however, imply a fairly high degree of pre-organisation).

There are three situations in which a long response time is unacceptable. Firstly, when facilities (or staff) for searching are limited, long response times will reduce the number of inquiries which can be dealt with. Secondly, although an inquirer might be able to wait for a response, this wait might be inconvenient, and inhibit the inquirer's other activities. (E.g., until the correspondence from Mr Smith is found, the inquirer must wait before he can begin a particular job). Thirdly, there is the situation in which time is of the essence; when, if the material is not found immediately, it is useless. This is likely to be the case in commercial intelligence services and in newspaper offices, where action on information may need to be taken immediately or not at all (e.g., if the paper is going to press, or if an investment is to be made).

There are some situations, moreover, in which 'the fire station' approach is necessary. This is the situation in which there is a high level of investment in terms of labour, equipment and money, in order that there should be a very quick response to demands, although they may rarely be made.

Fixing the order will increase reliability and memorability ('jam is on the top lefthand-shelf; money in the drawer'). But except in small and highly personalised stores further measures will be required. These fall under three heads:-

1. Signposting the store.

2. Labelling the items.

3. Reducing the area of search by conforming to classificatory use patterns.

Signposting is the process by which searchers are led from 'where they stand' to where they want to go; and of indicating to them (fingerposting) not only their destination but their present position. In effect, this will entail arranging items in an indicative order or of providing an 'index' to the arrangement (see Chapter 1). An indicative order is a 'self-evident' order based upon principles which are easily applied and which are known to the user, without special learning of the filing system. Indicative orders include date order in diaries, and alphabetical orders of the names of the things. For example, libraries may arrange their books in alphabetical order of authors' names; and in office files correspondence may be arranged in alphabetical order of the names of correspondents. The signposting function of indicative orders is exemplified by the alphabetical index of place names appended to atlases. The searcher 'knows where he is' (knows the name of the place he is looking for) and is led by the index to what he doesn't know — the part of the map on which the place is represented.

Secondly, the items in the store can be labelled so that they are recognisable and the file thereby made more easily scannable. For example, in a card index file of student records in a college, arranged in alphabetical (indicative) order of student names, different coloured cards could be used to indicate different years of entry, so that several files are incorporated in one. Similarly, a collection of novels arranged alphabetically by authors' names and including items conspicuously labelled 'M' for mystery,

'W' for westerns, 'R' for romances and 'S' for science fiction, making it possible to pick out scattered examples of these well-defined categories. However, labelling systems which do not intrude upon order are of use only in small files and for limited categories, except in the case of computer-held files. (Computers, unlike humans, are capable of repeated acts of 'recognition' provided that the labels are machine-readable). In most other situations the labels are used not only to facilitate recognition but to fix the order. These are the two functions of 'headings' in card index files, and the spine labelling on books in libraries.

If items are arranged in indicative order and if they have been labelled, a prior decision has been taken as to *what* is being placed in order, and what the labels represent. The labels will be either 'non-class terms' representing individual items, and particular to the individual item; or they will be 'class terms' representing classes of things. The majority of labels in filing systems are class terms or incorporate class terms.

Classes are the result of the process of classification. Both in logic and in practice one-member and no-member classes are possible; but for the present it will be convenient to refer to *classification* as the process by which individuals are grouped according to their degrees of likeness; likeness consisting of the possession of one or more attributes in common. Individuals belong to the same class if they possess common attributes, and to that extent are 'the same' and interchangeable.

The principle of interchangeability is seen most clearly in the case of 'peas in a pod' or in the contents of a bag of nails, when the members of a class are so alike that no choice need be made between them. In other cases interchangeability is the basis of a hierarchy of choices, which in effect is a hierarchy of exclusions. Potential house-purchasers may, at an initial stage, regard all houses in a particular area as 'the same', having excluded from consideration houses outside the area. Within the group, however, further choices and further exclusions will be made. All houses

31

costing under a certain amount are 'the same', houses costing more than this amount being excluded. In filing terms these purchasers would be provided for by a file of house information grouped primarily according to area, and within the area grouped according to price. However, for poverty-stricken purchasers, relatively indifferent as to area, the order would be reversed, with primary grouping according to price.

Searches, whether or not in stores, and whether or not in documentary stores, tend to begin as searches for classes, i.e. as 'generic searches'. This is so whether or not the proposed end result is the choice of an individual thing and whether or not the particular class characteristic is required for its own sake. For example, police detectives may begin searches for 'red-headed men' not because red-headedness or masculinity are criminal characteristics, but because these class characteristics are ones by which 'John Smith, Burglar' can be recognised. They are reducing the area of search by excluding black-haired women. No different from the library user who asks for the 'red book', because that is the recognisable characteristic of the book required; or who asks for works by 'Lord Scarman' not because Scarman is of particular interest as an author, but because he is known to have been concerned with the particular report which is required.

Classification is a variety reduction process. A file of a hundred books is reduced to a file of ten groups of books. Assume that one of these groups comprises ten books on chemistry; then any search for a book on chemistry may be reduced from a one-by-one search of one hundred items to a one-by-one search of ten groups, plus a one-by-one search of a further ten items.

However classification is also an information-losing process, since, apart from 'peas-in-a-pod' the members of the class are alike only in some respects; and all of them will be members of other classes which are not recognised in the actual classificatory arrangement. (This applies in thought as well as in store arrangement. to call somebody a 'politician' may hide the fact that he is also a musician, a schoolteacher and father of a family). As was demonstrated above, the class 'mystery novels' was concealed or 'scattered' in an arrangement based upon authors. Similarly in telephone directories where information is classified according to subscriber, information regarding the inhabitants of Barchester High Street is concealed and scattered.

It is therefore important to make proper decisions regarding the criteria to be used in the creation of classes in a filing system. The following principles should be adhered to.-

1.  Things which are in some way interchangeable should be stored together (cups with cups, saucers with saucers; books on chemistry with books on chemistry). Alternatively, things which are to be used together should be stored together, (blue cups with blue saucers, London telephone directories with Surrey telephone directories).

2.  Classes should represent the subjects of the questions asked, rather than the information sought about the subject. For example "What is the telephone number of John Smith" is a question about John Smith, which should lead to arrangement of a telephone directory by subscriber. "Who lives at 21 Barchester High Street" is a question about Barchester High Street (the answer to which may be "John Smith"), and should lead to an arrangement by streets.

3.  The classes should be definable by objective criteria. 'Nice books' and 'nasty books' are real classes but they cannot be incorporated in main file systems except in highly personalised files, because essentially they are subjective classes.

4.  As far as possible 'ad-hoc' membership of classes should be avoided in main filing systems. The class 'books on current affairs' is a real class definable by objective criteria, but in common with the class 'nice books' membership of the class will frequently change, for external if not for subjective reasons. This class — when recognised — is usually the subject of ad-hoc arrangements and ad-hoc reading lists (e.g. in public and school libraries and in book shops). The class 'recent books' is of the same kind.

5.  Membership of classes should be small enough to allow for easy scanning; and to limit the choices which have to be made at each search to a convenient number. It is on this factor that the specificity of classes should depend. Whether or not it is necessary to divide books on chemistry into two groups dealing with organic and inorganic chemistry respectively, will depend upon the actual or potential size of the file.

The characteristics by which classes are defined, and about which questions will be asked, are called the 'sought' characteristics, whether or not these are sought for their own sake, or, (as in the case of 'blue and red books') represent 'recognition classes'. When these characteristics are turned into labels, they become 'sought terms', and, because the sought terms to a greater or lesser extent determine order (the way in which items are 'sorted'), they are also called 'sort terms'.

Any characteristic of a document can be a sort term and it follows that any document or documentary item can belong to more than one class (e.g. the class 'books by Agatha Christie' which includes detective stories; and the class 'detective stories', which includes books by P D James). In most systems it is necessary to limit the characteristics used in classifying items, and it is therefore necessary to determine which are the important characteristics, i.e. which are the characteristics about which questions are most likely to be asked. It is unlikely that questions will be asked about 'books with 364 pages' although the number of pages in a book may be important information once a group of books has been selected by other criteria. Preference should be given to classes which will be sought for their own sake rather than merely 'recognition' classes. Publishers, for example, are important features of publications but less frequently than authors form the subject of a primary question ('I am looking for books published by Butterworths'). When they are sought, it is usually as a recognition class'.

The most useful criteria for classing documents relate to the following -

1. **Content**
   Tigers; zoology; sales figures for the South-West.

2. **Criteria affecting content**

   **Authors**
   Authors, although individuals, represent class characteristics in respect of their works.

   Books by Dickens, Letters from Mr Smith.

   **Bias** (Recipients)
   Books for children. Letters to Mr Smith.

   **Media**
   Sound/Print.

   **Type of use**
   Quick reference books. Textbooks.

   **Date of issue**

Physical form *per se* is rarely sought, but it may coincide with media (e.g. gramophone records/sound recordings) and may be a factor in choice where special apparatus is needed for access (e.g. tapes/discs).

Files of books and correspondence are usually 'one-place files'. This is because even if there is more than one copy of the document it may be thought desirable to keep all the copies in one place. Files of document representations and files of items specially created for filing purposes (e.g. personnel records on cards) may be 'multiple entry files', because copies of the item can be made for grouping with each class (e.g. under authors and under subjects). However, in manual files, there is an economic limit to the number of entries that can be made, and for this reason it is rarely possible in a catalogue of books for example, to 'call up' all the books published by a particular publisher.

Computer-held files can produce listings grouped under any document characteristics provided the information is appropriately labelled (or tagged). If the computer is 'told' how many pages books have, it will, if appropriately programmed, be able to produce lists of books having 536 pages. The value of the computer in information retrieval, however, lies rather in its ability to deal with a variety of content approaches; in the classification of document content, most documents either deal with more than one subject, or deal with subjects which are susceptible to many different approaches.

When the classes in a filing system and the classificatory criteria have been exhausted, it is necessary to decide how the individual items should be arranged between themselves and how the classes should be arranged between themselves. If the membership of a class is small there is a case for treating the class itself as an 'unorganised store', but at the other extreme large libraries with many millions of volumes individualise each copy by means of a serial 'shelf number'. Assuming that a file of books is arranged first by content and then by author, the final class is a subject/author class. Within this class it would be possible to arrange the items by their 'proper names', e.g. in alphabetical order of titles, in numerical order of patent specification numbers, standard specification numbers, or research report numbers. These have the advantage of being memorable and may be asked for.

The classes between themselves may similarly be treated as an unorganised store. For example in a domestic filing system documents are stored in wallets, one for 'Mortgage repayments', another for 'Household repairs' etc. As there are not many of these wallets and they are self-contained, no particular order is necessary for their arrangement. In most cases however it will be necessary to fix an order, and in most cases a purely arbitrary order of classes is unsatisfactory.

There are two basic methods for arranging classes (other than random arrangement):-

(1) Systematic order of class inclusion.
This presupposes that there are classes within classes.

Music
Orchestral music
Scores
Gramophone records
Vocal music

(2) Indicative order; which in practice is an alphabetical order of the names of classes.

Gramophone records (Orchestral music)
Music
Orchestral music
Scores (Orchestral music)
Vocal music

It is obvious that where there are classes within classes, the alphabetical (indicative) order poses problems of scatter, as will be more obvious in the following list:-

(3)                    Aluminium
Chemistry
Ferrous metals
Inorganic chemistry
Iron

If there are no classes within classes alphabetical order presents few problems. For example a file of patients' records kept in a doctors' surgery in alphabetical order of patients' names, presents no problems if one patient is held to bear no relationship to another patient (for example the doctors do not wish to group them by age). Where there are classes within classes elaborate systems of referencing may be necessary, and this, combined with the physical scatter of items makes alphabetical orders unsuitable for all but the most compact files. (Running from 'Aluminium' to 'Zinc' in a search for 'all materials on non-ferrous metals' would be exhausting and possible ineffective. Systematic orders are more suitable for 'browsing' and are in consequence used to arrange books in 'open-access' libraries (i.e. libraries where the searcher selects direct from the shelf). Their disadvantage is that the order is useful but not self-evident, and it may even be arbitrary. For example in the music classification given above it can be supposed that a deliberate and non-arbitrary decision has been made to subordinate 'media' to subject or type of music (the users of this collection being versatile musicians to whom scores and sound recordings are 'the same'). The decision to place orchestral music before vocal music is however almost certainly arbitrary, involving no obvious principle.

It must be emphasised that any feature of a document or of

documentary information can be used as a basis for arrangement, and that in any document collection several systems may be in operation and that these might be independent or complementary. It may be neither necessary nor desirable to employ the same system for books, correspondence and periodicals. On the other hand some differing systems may be complementary. For example, a library could arrange its books on the shelf systematically by the Dewey Decimal system; provide an alphabetical index to the system; and provide a catalogue (file of representations) arranged in alphabetical order of authors, titles and subjects, with references to where on the shelves particular items are to be found. On the other hand the catalogue might itself be in systematic order, in which case an alphabetical subject index to the catalogue would be provided.

An advantage of representations files is that copies of each item can be made for filing in all appropriate places, and in consequence 'scatter' caused by the operation of the classification, or by the need to use different types of storage equipment, can be mitigated. This advantage can be seen further in the case of items arranged in fixed arbitrary order (mechanised by a numbering or lettering system), which can be represented or indexed in subsidiary files.

The contents and arrangement of the representation file is discussed in Chapter 3, and further in Chapter 4, where the classification of document content is treated, with particular reference to the labelling of classes through the medium of 'index languages'. Chapter 6 deals with approaches to documents other than the content approaches, and also discusses the problem of accommodating different physical forms.

**FURTHER READING**

Items 22 and 39 from section B, p. 276 and 278.

# CHAPTER 3: THE REPRESENTATION FILE: CONTENT AND ARRANGEMENT

It is first necessary to state that a file of document representations ('catalogue entries') may not be needed at all in some information environments. Some kinds of information need can be satisfied by the provision of an open-access browsing arrangement of the documents themselves; these, being in some kind of helpful order, give all the information required at the time. In some circumstances, even a random arrangement of documents is satisfactory — as in a 'recent publicity material received' or 'photographs of local interest' display. If inquirers are only ever interested in the documents which are 'in' and immediately available, there is no point in troubling to set up a file of document representations which can tell them about the total store of material held in the collection — a significant proportion of which is not available to them at that time.

In many situations, however, a representation file is essential for at least some, if not all, of the material in a collection, since it is not only administratively useful as a record of the stock, but may be the source of specific and, when required, very detailed information about each document, allowing its identification, selection and partial evaluation in relation to a particular inquiry, even when the document itself is temporarily absent from its usual place in the collection (being consulted by another inquirer, on loan, being photocopied, being repaired, on display, for example). In simple terms, the representation file can be said to be the key to the collection; in addition, if the documents themselves are arranged in a helpful order, the representation file and the document arrangement will complement and supplement each other, to give a multiplicity of access points or approaches. For example, the representation file may be in alphabetical order of entries filed under document titles, authors' names, series titles, and subject headings — giving easy access to any of these elements when known — and the document arrangement may be in systematic order, with subjects represented by notational symbols, such as 63 for 'agriculture' or QD for 'social work', so that documents on a particular subject are located in one place in the sequence, with documents on related subjects adjacent to them; or a file of correspondence may be in chronological order, with the representation files in alphabetical order of correspondent/addressee and of subject or project title. These are only two possibilities in the provision of files, making several different approaches available to inquirers and assisting them in locating the desired documents, whether they have in mind authors, titles, series, correspondents, project names, or a word or words representing a narrow topic or a broad subject area within which they wish to browse.

Some of the most important decisions to be made in relation to the representation file concern:

1) which documents are to be represented in it,
2) how much information is to be recorded for each document (how full the description),
3) how the file is to be arranged and
4) which access points are to be provided.

A number of factors influence these decisions: the type of access available for the documents (free public use, restricted to certain inquirers): the intellectual level of the documents (scholarly, newsy): the physical form of the documents (books, motion pictures): the type of information need shown by the inquirers ('fact-seeking', educational, recreational — these are overlapping categories): the abilities of the inquirers with regard to using files; and the proportion of inquirer use to information staff use.

42

# DESCRIPTION

The selection of documents for description is related to their potential usefulness to inquirers, their rarity, value, and intended or expected life in the collection. Some documents, such as holiday brochures, educational prospectuses and various other kinds of advertising and publicity literature, in a general library may be anticipated to have only a short life as far as reader interest is concerned and are therefore often not represented in the file, but left for the clientele to browse through, with no attempt made to keep the documents in any order or even to ensure that they are not taken away. In other situations, these same documents — and others of an even more ephemeral nature — are fully described and carefully stored, being of potential archival and historical interest. It is certainly not possible to list here, in a 'vacuum', all kinds of documents and to say which should and which should not, be represented in a file, this decision must always be determined in relation to the environment within which the collection is to function — as are the decisions on appropriate arrangements for documents 'on the shelves' and for representations in the file.

As to the fullness of the description, in some collections a very detailed entry — containing all bibliographical details, and including annotations or abstracts — may be necessary for all documents, in others a brief entry only, and in yet others full entries for some documents, brief for others. (Comparative examples are shown in Chapter 1). Much depends on whether the collection has open or closed access. In a closed-access situation, where the inquirers are spatially separated from the material and gain access to it by stating their requirements to the person in charge of the collection, there is a need for them to be able to identify precisely which document is needed before making a request. This is likely to be the case with fragile, rare or valuable documents which could suffer wear and tear in an open-access browsing situation (such as old maps, music manuscripts and diaries) and with materials requiring special apparatus for their use (such as cine-film, photographic slides and audio-cassettes). Many information environments consist of a combination of closed-, restricted- and open-access collections and may therefore require different levels of description and separate files of representations.

In a research or commercial organisation, whose staff produce a series of papers or reports for internal consumption, or for limited internal distribution (but not for full publication), there is likely to be a need for full description, giving not only title and date, but a complete listing of all authors, project numbers and titles, clients in connection with whom the work was carried out, a detailed statement of pages and illustrations, content, relationship to other papers and so on. This kind of 'in-house' record is unique, in the sense that such descriptive data is likely to be available to and needed in only one organisation. The descriptions of commercially-published materials, on the other hand, which are acquired by and stocked in a number of collections, appear in many files and, for this reason, it is now common for these descriptions to be produced centrally or on a cooperative basis and made available, either by sale or exchange, to those who ask for them. For public libraries and academic libraries, both of which are likely to have large stocks of commercially-published British and US documents, subscription to the centralised services of the British Library Bibliographic Services Division - BNB MARC and LC MARC (British National Bibliography MAchine - Readable Cataloguing and Library of Congress...) — can obviate the need for in-house compilation of descriptions for a large proportion of their stock, leaving only the so-called EMMA (Extra-Marc-MAterial) documents — those not included in the BNB and LC files, to be dealt with internally.

Other centralised services exist for such materials as British Standard Specifications and long-playing records and cassettes, and these may be of use to those with such collections. Cooperative systems, in which a number of organisations (not necessarily in the same area of the country, or even all in the UK) pool and share descriptions as they are compiled, usually on a computerised basis, are becoming more common; again, these are likely to bene-fit the larger libraries of the public and academic varieties. Seal (1980) has provided a guide to some of the automated cataloguing services — BLAISE/LOCAS, BLCMP, Oriel Computer Services and SWALCAP). For the great majority of smaller, more specialised information collections, however, whose material is related to their own very individual environments — in terms of subject content, physical form and points of access, there remains a need for descriptions to be prepared within the organisations them-selves.

Criteria for selecting documents for description and representation and rules for levels of description should be the subject of organ-isational policy decisions, to be adhered to by all those involved. Once the nature of the collection and its selection and acquisition practices are defined, it should follow that certain categories of material can be identified and their appropriate treatment agreed. Whether buying-in, or pooling and sharing, or compiling one's own descriptions, it is clearly necessary that descriptions are prepared according to an agreed standard, Preparing a description is not in most cases the straightforward task it is sometimes assumed (by the uninitiated) to be; it is not merely a question of 'copying from the title page', though the title page (if there is one — not all documents have one) is often likely to be the prime source of information. Take the following (fictitious) example: a single issue of a periodical which indicates that it is supplement number 1 to volume 14, number 3, September 1982, of the Journal of the Ealing Institute of Library Studies, and that it consists of the proceedings of the 7th Biennial Conference on Computer Applications in Information Retrieval, held at Ealing, London, in July 1982, is edited by M L South and P F Booth, and contains 20 papers by 25 different authors, plus discussion. In this case, by 'copying from the title page' six different catalo-guers might well produce six different (though all accurate) descriptions.

The need for a code of rules is therefore indicated, providing for consistency between those doing the describing (usually known as 'cataloguers' in libraries), between collections and between bibliographical services. The rules are required to specify what information is necessary for each document, in what order that information should be arranged, how it should be expressed (abbreviations, capitalisation, punctuation), and which points of access should be provided to the description in the file. For a collection consisting of items of the same physical form — such as photographic prints — a single specification may be drawn up and observed automatically once those responsible for description have become familiar with it; it could consist of (in this order): title of photograph, name of photographer, date of shot, film used, aperture size and shutter speed, size of print, black and white/colour, type of paper, and any annotation required about the subject of the photograph, special circumstances relating to its shooting and so on.

Many document collections consist of a variety of document types, and it is useful for a code to cater for more than one type. The best-known code among libraries in the UK (also used in several other countries) is the *Anglo-American cataloguing rules* 2nd edn 1978 (*AACR2*), a comprehensive and detailed listing of rules intended to provide for all kinds of document. The full list of materials catered for is:

> books, pamphlets and printed sheets;
> cartographic materials;
> manuscripts;
> music;
> sound recordings;
> motion pictures and videorecordings;
> graphic materials;
> machine-readable data files;
> three-dimensional artefacts and realia;
> microforms;
> serials.

The general introduction states that the 'rules are designed for use in the construction of catalogues and other lists in general libraries of all sizes. They are not specifically intended for specialist and archival libraries, but it is recommended that such libraries use the rules as the basis of their cataloguing and augment their provisions as necessary'.

There is clearly an advantage in documents in different collections being described according to the same set of rules; it makes searching easier, because of the standard layout and content of descriptions, it aids the exchange of descriptive data and the interlending of documents. *AACR2* is used by the BNB in its printed lists and the related machine-readable output of its bibliographic services, which means that the majority of public library collections are described by these rules. There are, however, other codes in use, some of them specially compiled for an individual type of collection, or category of document; those using them are easily able to justify them on the grounds that they are particularly suitable for their needs.

*AACR2* recognises that full descriptions are not always necessary for each circumstance and therefore provides for three levels of description (rule 1.OD). The fullest level is used by BNB, but even the briefest level of *AACR2* is more detailed than has been found necessary for some collections, and some organisers, therefore, may prefer to establish a briefer standard for their own purposes; it is, however, essential that there is a standard, and that all the conditions likely to be encountered in a particular collection are catered for. This is best done not by instructing 'For a film do this, for a technical report do that, for a conference proceedings do the other', but rather by identifying conditions such as single personal authorship, shared responsibility, and modified works, and by deciding on, for example, the most suitable form of authors' names to be used (full original, abbreviated, pseudonymous, changed), and, again for example, the detail in which the publisher or originator and date of publication or issue or production details are to be given. When these and other conditions are dealt with, then the particular requirements of individual physical forms can be considered — how best to indicate that a sound recording is in the form of two twelve-inch stereophonic discs with accompanying script and notes, for example, or that a flip chart is double-sided, one side coloured, the other black and white and measures 80 cm by 50 cm.

Even if it is decided not to use *AACR2*, an investigation into the principles on which it is based, and the conditions which it identifies, will prove invaluable in devising one's own set of rules. Hunter (1980) provides a number of examples illustrating the use of *AACR2* for a variety of document types — organisers can judge from this whether the result of applying this code is suitable for their purposes. In any event, the possible disadvantages of not using a standard code of one kind or another should be considered before compiling one's own home-made set of rules — those disadvantages being lack of searching compatibility with other collections, difficulty in the exchange and merging of data from different collections, as well as having to devise rules  for all the necessary conditions. Time spent in ensuring consistency at this early stage will repay when searching for information later.

There are three major components in the typical document representation:-

1) the description itself (produced by reference to a code of rules — as indicated above), ranging from brief to full, and containing such elements as title, author or originator, edition, publisher or producer, date, series, running number, number of pages or parts, and notes;

2) an indication of the subject of the document (produced by the application of an index language — see p.52 — using a word or words, or a notational symbol;

3) the heading (filing element, search term, sort term) being the name, title, subject word(s) or symbol under which a particular copy of the representation is to be located in the file.

Any one document, of course, may be required to be accessible from a number of approaches, and — depending on the physical nature of the file — will generate either several copies of the representation filed in different places (as in a card or microfiche catalogue) or a single entry with all appropriate elements 'tagged' so that the entry can be retrieved by specifying any tagged element (as in a computer-held file). At this point the reader may recall the particular virtue of the representation file as opposed to the document file; a document can be filed in only one place in the file, whereas copies of its representation can be located in, or available at, as many places in the file as are deemed necessary. A consideration of these access points shows up the multiplicity that may be required:-

an individual document may be identified by its

a) title: 'Proposals for departmental reorganisation'
'Green fingers: how to grow things'

b) authorship or other contributors:
'By H T Maples'
'Illustrated by F T Jameson'

c) edition: 'Revised edition', '3rd edition',
'Abridged edition'

d) publisher or producer: 'ELM Publications'
'Scherzo Records'

e) date of publication or issue: '1977', '17 July 1982'

f) extent, size: '250 pages', '22 by 16 centimetres'

g) physical form: 'folded map',
                       'tape/slide presentation'

h) illustrative matter: 'coloured illustrations'
                          'half-tone photographs'

i) relationship to another document: 'translation'
                                'supplement'

j) internal form: 'directory', 'bibliography'

k) intended readership: 'confidential to staff of
                      PCH Ltd'
                      'for children between
                      6 and 8 years'

l) membership of a named or number series:
                       'Technical report 47/A/82'
                       'Enterprise series No.6'

Some of these are unique identifiers, others examples of the 'recognition' classes mentioned in Chapter 2; used in combination with each other, they become more specific, such as title and author, title and series, author and date of publication and intended readership. Whatever the combination, it may be utilised in the search for a particular document. The file of representations, therefore, must attempt to provide for all these approaches, or whichever are appropriate for the particular information environment in question. The adoption of a code of rules will provide guidance on the compilation of descriptions which can contain some or all of the elements listed; this is not to say that each of these elements automatically becomes an access point. In the cards-in-drawers type of catalogue, for example, it is usual to find access by title, author and series — less so to discover entries under publisher, and rarely under date, edition, size or number of pages (approaches which, as indicated in Chapter 2, are less likely to be required — except in specialised situations); in a computer-held file the provision of additional approaches is easier and relatively cheaper so that access even by these less-used elements can be arranged.

A chapter on the choice of access points (Ch.21) is included in *AACR2*, giving instructions as to the choice of a) the main (principal) access point for a document and b) added entries to be made. These may satisfy the requirements of the majority of general collection organisers; special collection organisers may need to devise their own policy. For example, *AACR2* instructs that when more than three authors are named on a document, only the first is to be named in the description (rule 1.1F5); if these authors share equally the responsibility for the content of the document, with none of them being regarded as the principal author, then the principal entry for this description is to be made under the title of the document, and an added entry made under the heading for the first-named author (rule 21.6C2). Access is therefore incomplete — the excluded authors being 'unsearchable'. In a research, commercial or industrial organisation, where reports are frequently issued under the names of several people working in a team, this could be a distinct disadvantage. The implications, therefore, of formulating or adopting a particular rule must be carefully examined.

In any situation, rules regarding changes of name need to be established. Over a period of time, a particular author or contributor may use alternative forms of name on different documents: Tina Lorde (to her friends) may become Christina Wellington-Lorde on personnel and legal records, T.L. when she writes poems for the house magazine, and (when honoured for 'services to literature') Dame Christina Lorde; the rules for description must indicate how these different forms and changes of name are to be presented and connected in the file. In the same way, firms and other organisations change their names due to expansion, merger, take-over and so on — careful attention to these alterations is often vital.

## CONTENT REPRESENTATION

The subject content and (internal) form approaches are not dealt with by codes for description such as *AACR2*, which confine themselves to the recording of the kinds of element already mentioned. Subject representation is the function of a subject indexing system, of which there are many.

Frequently, inquirers do not have in mind an individual document, but seek for something related to a given subject (theme, topic) — for example, hang-gliding, or obstetrics, or the practice of psychiatry in the United States since 1950, or the effect of long-term solitary confinement on political prisoners, or the value of sales of video-recorders during a particular period of time in the UK. In these cases, it is possible that one out of a number of documents could satisfy the inquirer's need. Sometimes an inquiry is framed using subject, description and form features:   a set of colour slides on road safety suitable for use with primary school children, or a state-of-the-art report published within the last five years on the use of computers in small businesses in England and Wales, with accompanying statistical data. In these cases the full range of information provision of the file is brought into play.

The most common system used for the representation of subjects in the great majority of public libraries in the UK and in many others, is the *Dewey Decimal Classification* (currently in its 19th edn, 1979), which includes subjects from the whole 'universe of knowledge', and represents them by the use of numerical notation — 'railway engineering' by '625.1', for example. Other systems employ alphabetical notation — 'TXS' for 'marketing', others words (single words or combinations) — 'Hazardous substances', and 'Refrigeration equipment. Fishing boats'. The majority of indexing systems allow for the representation not only of the intellectual content (subject, theme, topic) but also of the internal or literary form of the document (illustrated survey, bibliography, historical presentation, thesis, research report, specification, letter, directory); in some kinds of document, indeed, it is the form which is more important than, or as important as, the subject — poems, for example, novels or plays — and indexing systems also allow for this approach.

The varieties of indexing system are described in detail in Chapter 4. It should be noted at this stage that if a notational index language is used for the formation and allocation of subject 'indicators' for document representations, then one produces at the same time 'shelf locations' for the documents, which may then be arranged according to these notational symbols, that is to say in systematic order. (This is the sequence encountered in the principal non-fiction sections of most public libraries — but it should be recorded that there are usually many separate sequences of documents in such libraries, each one supposedly appropriate to the nature of the documents and to the pattern of use anticipated for each kind).

The choice of index language must be related to the particular collection; merely because the Dewey scheme is the most familiar from contact with school and public libraries is not sufficient grounds to justify its application to all collections, indeed in many circumstances it is quite inappropriate. The evaluation of available systems and the significant features of those most used are dealt with in Chapter 4, and the construction of one's own scheme (necessary when existing published schemes do not suit) in Chapter 5. The use of, on the one hand, notational symbols and, on the other, words that can be recognised from everyday language, indicates that different sequences of representations can be established. A file of representations which is in alphabetical order, containing in one sequence entries filed under significant elements such as author, title and words indicating subjects, is known as a 'dictionary' file (Fig. 3:1). If subjects are represented

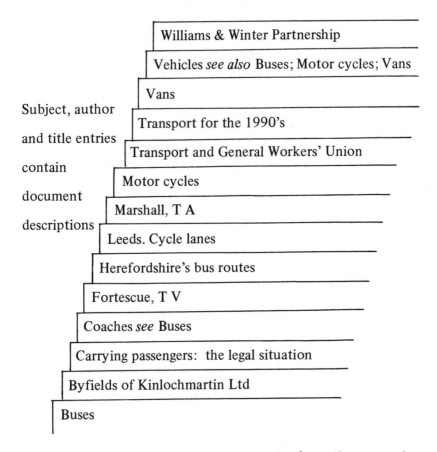

Fig. 3:1
*Dictionary file*

Subject, author and title entries contain document descriptions

- Williams & Winter Partnership
- Vehicles *see also* Buses; Motor cycles; Vans
- Vans
- Transport for the 1990's
- Transport and General Workers' Union
- Motor cycles
- Marshall, T A
- Leeds. Cycle lanes
- Herefordshire's bus routes
- Fortescue, T V
- Coaches *see* Buses
- Carrying passengers: the legal situation
- Byfields of Kinlochmartin Ltd
- Buses

The file includes (in one sequence) author/contributor entries; title entries; subject entries; synonym references; references between related terms.

If more convenient, subject entries and references may be grouped in one sequence, author/contributor and title entries in another.

54

by notational symbols, and entries arranged in notation order, then a systematic file results (Fig. 3:2) having a separate file or index for the author and title approach, and requiring an alphabetical subject index to lead inquirers from the subject which they name to the symbol employed for it in the file. The virtues and disadvantages of these files have been outlined in Chapter 2.

The 'simple', self-evident order of an alphabetical sequence is not without its difficulties; the precise nature of the alphabetical order has to be established. Most important, is it 'word-by-word' or 'letter-by-letter'? In the first, spaces between words are taken into account, in the second, they are not — a phrase or combination of words being treated as though it were one long word; two quite different sequences result from the application of these two principles, as indicated below:-

| *Word-by-word* | *Letter-by-letter* |
|---|---|
| Light at the end of the tunnel | Lightall, A.C. |
| Light haulage | Light at the end of the tunnel |
| Light in the window | Lighter-than-air craft |
| Light metals | Light haulage |
| Light vehicles | Lighthouses |
| Lighter-than-air craft | Lighting and design |
| Lighthouses | Light in the window |
| Lighting and design | Light metals |
| Lightships | Lightships |

Further instructions must be given regarding the filing of headings containing initialised abbreviations ('Z B G and Company'), punctuation symbols ('Meat, frozen', 'Meat — processing') and numerals ('3-star hotels', '125 Priory Avenue'); also for the integration of different kinds of headings — personal and corporate names, titles, subjects — into a single sequence. (In a computerised file, these instructions must be incorporated so that the sorting of the entries into their correct order is done automatically

**55**

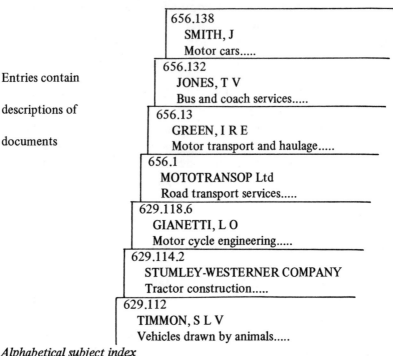

Fig. 3:2

*Systematic (classified) file*

Entries contain

descriptions of

documents

656.138
 SMITH, J
 Motor cars.....

656.132
 JONES, T V
 Bus and coach services.....

656.13
 GREEN, I R E
 Motor transport and haulage.....

656.1
 MOTOTRANSOP Ltd
 Road transport services.....

629.118.6
 GIANETTI, L O
 Motor cycle engineering.....

629.114.2
 STUMLEY-WESTERNER COMPANY
 Tractor construction.....

629.112
 TIMMON, S L V
 Vehicles drawn by animals.....

*Alphabetical subject index*

Classified file is
incomplete
without
this

Tractors. Engineering   629.114.2
Road vehicles. Engineering    629.1
Road transport services         656.1
Private cars. Road transport     656.138
Motor transport. Road transport 656.13
Motor cycles. Engineering      629.118.6
Motor cars. Road transport      656.138
Land vehicles. Engineering      629.1
Haulage. Motor vehicles. Road Transport  656.13
Coaches. Road transport       656.132
Cars. Road transport       656.138
Buses. Road transport       656.132
Animal-drawn vehicles. Engineering       629.112

An author/contributor and title index is also needed.

**56**

and with absolute accuracy). Guidance on alphabetical filing is given in the *ALA rules for filing catalog cards* (1968) and the *Specification for alphabetical arrangement and the filing order of numerals and symbols* (1969) of the British Standards Institution.

## PHYSICAL FORM OF THE FILE

It can now be seen that the final document representation in the file can be a highly informative record, giving the means of access by any one of a number of elements specified by the inquirer, permitting the identification and partial evaluation of the document before it is consulted, and complementing the arrangement chosen for its filing.

The file of representations may take one of several very different physcial forms and may be capable of being reproduced in large numbers (perhaps in different forms) for distribution to inquirers, even for publication and sale – alternatively, in certain situations, the file may be confidential to a small group of users and require protection and guaranteed security. Chapter 7 describes and evaluates the most common forms of file.

## PLANNING FOR CHANGE

Once the file of representations has been set up, it is tempting to regard it as a permanent and unchanging record, apart from the need for additions for new documents. It is, however, subject to change for a number of reasons. Organisations collectively, over time, change their interests, extend or concentrate their resources; inquirers individually move into new areas of activity. The kinds of document acquired and the uses made of them therefore change to reflect these modifications; it follows that the practice of description and representation may require amendment, to satisfy the new intérest profiles. This may involve changing to fuller (or briefer) description; being more (or less) selective; changing to a new cataloguing code; adopting a later edition of an index language; or changing to a different one.

In planning for the 'care and maintenance' of a file, resources must always be allowed for a certain amount of recataloguing and reclassification, in addition to the normal processes of addition, amendment, and withdrawal. Chapter 9 gives further information on the organisation of file maintenance.

## REFERENCES

*ALA rules for filing catalog cards*, (1968), Edited by Pauline A Seely 2nd edn, Chicago: American Library Association.

*Anglo-American cataloguing rules* (1978), 2nd edn. Edited by Michael Gorman and Paul W Winkler. Library Association.

*British National Bibliography*. British Library Bibliographic Services Division. (Weekly, with cumulations).

*Dewey decimal classification and relative index* (1979), Edition 19. Edited under the direction of Benjamin A Custer, Albany, New York: Forest Press.

Hunter, Eric J (1980), *Examples illustrating AACR2*, Library Association.

Seal, A W (1980), *Automated cataloguing in the UK: a guide to services* Bath: Bath University Library, Centre for Catalogue Research (BLRD Report 5545).

*Specification for alphabetical arrangement and the filing order of numerals and symbols* (1969), Rev. edn. British Standards Institution (BS 1749 1969).

## FURTHER READING

Items 6,17,20,27,31,32,34,35,46,56,57,66 from section B, p.274 -.

58

# CHAPTER 4: CONTENT APPROACHES

There are several different ways of representing the content of documents in an IR system; each has its own particular set of features which, when related to the needs of a particular information collection, may be recognised as a combination of merits and disadvantages. No subject indexing system can be said to be 'good' or 'bad' in the abstract (except that if its theoretical base is faulty, the system is likely to be poor); it must be related to a specific situation before a judgment may be made as to its suitability for that situation. The Dewey Decimal Classification has many features making it appropriate for use in a general open-access public library containing material on a wide range of subjects, but is less likely to find favour with the organiser of a collection of technical drawings, correspondence and publicity material in a civil engineering firm.

Clearly it is not possible to claim (with proof) that there is an overall best system. It is, however, essential that collection organisers should choose the best for their own collections. This requires organisers to have an awareness of:

a) the characteristics of the documents in their collections,
b) the characteristics and needs of their inquirers and
c) the theoretical bases upon which indexing systems are constructed.

Chapter 9 deals with the considerations involved in the design of an information retrieval system, including the identification of document and inquirer characteristics. The present chapter is devoted to identifying the types and describing the individual features of the main indexing systems available.

## INDEX LANGUAGES. NATURAL AND ARTIFICIAL

The component of the IR system used to represent the content of documents is known as the index language. This language may be either 'natural' or 'artificial'.

### Natural Index Languages

A natural index language is one which employs terms (e.g. words) taken from the title, or the title and text, of the document itself, without change, and files them in self-evident (alphabetical) order, so that an inquirer may then look up a particular term and find (depending on the nature of the file) the citation or description of the wanted document or the document itself.

A periodical article, for example, entitled 'The collection and recycling of glass containers' could be entered under all the significant' terms ('keywords') contained in its title – 'collection', 'recycling', 'glass', and 'containers'. Since this title is indicative the terms contained in it are likely to be useful as 'search terms' (terms employed by inquirers seeking information on this subject).

Another article, entitled 'Trailing clouds of glory? Carry on fuming!', being perhaps a personal account of living next to a major highway carrying continuous heavy traffic, is less likely to produce (from its title) search terms which will assist an inquirer towards this information. One of the requirements, therefore, for the successful use of a natural index language using title terms is that titles should give a fairly precise indication of the documents' contents, using the appropriate technical terms employed in the particular subject field, rather than be imaginative, flippant, pun-containing or allusive.

One method which uses title terms is known as KWIC (Key Word in Context) indexing. This is a very simple method, able to be performed by human or computer, and produces an alphabetical listing which may look like this:-

| Colour | Coding In Supermarkets | Tech. Rept. 13/74 |
|---|---|---|
| | Coloring In Food | Data Sheet. 1468 |
| | Colour Coding In Supermarkets | Tech. Rept. 13/74 |
| Coloring In | Food | Data Sheet. 1468 |
| Colour Coding In | Supermarkets | Tech. Rept. 13/74 |

The terms in the centre of the page are the search terms, arranged in alphabetical order, and the rest of the title is placed around the search term, with the citation of the source document following it. (Significant terms from two imaginary titles have been used in the example above).

The particular feature of a natural index language is that the terms are used in the form in which they are found in the title. In the example above, one of the titles is supposedly from a periodical published in the United Kingdom, the other from a US periodical; the result is that 'colour' and 'coloring' are used as search terms (British spelling of the word 'colour' and its derivatives differing from the American). If other titles from various sources were added, with the terms 'color', 'colouring', 'colorant' and 'coloured' included, it can be seen that there would be two sequences of entries, the first comprising the items with US spelling, the second those with British spelling.

In the use of natural index languages for searching, therefore, inquirers have to be aware of, and remember to look under, variant spellings and forms of words and also, equally important, under all the synonyms for (and related terms to) the search term they have in mind. For example, one title may refer to 'windscreens' (UK), another to 'windshields' (US), one to 'measles' (popular term), another to 'rubeola' (medical term), one to 'strawberries' (popular term), another to 'Fragaria' (botanical term) and yet another to 'soft fruits' (broader popular term).

In a natural index language, no reference will be made from one synonym to another nor from one related term to another; the onus is on the inquirer to think of all possible search terms, if a complete check of relevant material is required. For the reasons given above, this kind of system is most likely to operate success-fully in a field where not only are titles precise and indicative — as already stated — but the inquirers themselves are well-acquainted with the terminology of the subject field.

Alphabetical files produced by methods such as KWIC are often found in the form of 'current-awareness' indexing publications, which list titles of newly-published documents in an easily-scanned format, and serve the purpose of bringing new material to the attention of specialists in particular fields. These methods are useful also for the production of indexes to files of reports, data sheets, commercial papers and so on, issued for internal use in an organisation; the principal requirement is that the titles of the documents to be indexed are indicative of their content and employ terms which are likely to be used by someone searching for items on a particular subject. Frequently they are computer-generated, the only intellectual effort required by the indexer being to produce a 'stop-list' of common title words which are not to be printed in the search term position (e.g. 'in', 'a', 'the', 'of', 'at', 'by', 'with'). Care must be taken not to suppress in this way words having two meanings, one non-significant, the other significant, e.g.:-

Title 1: Microfiche can save you money

Title 2: Computerised operation speeds can manufacture

In the second title 'can' is a likely search term, in the first it is not; if these two titles were contained in the same KWIC file, both would appear under 'can', even though one of them would be irrelevant and unwanted, but the word 'can' must not be suppressed throughout the file, otherwise one would lose the useful title along with the unwanted one.

Another method similar to KWIC is KWOC (Keyword Out of Context), which sets out the search term at one side, as follows:-

    Catalog

        Catalog entries for microforms

    Catalogues

        A collection of trade catalogues and samples

Sometimes in KWOC the keyword is not repeated in the title, but replaced by an asterisk (*).

Double-KWIC combines features of KWIC and KWOC, as follows:-

    Catalog

        entries for microforms. Catalog
        microforms. Catalog entries for

    Catalogues

        Collection of trade catalogues and samples. A
        trade catalogues and samples. A collection of
        samples. A collection of trade catalogues and

All of these may be computer-generated.

The particular advantages of natural index languages are that they are speedy in application and, once the list of 'stop-terms' has been compiled, the final file is automatic to produce. The use as index terms of the terms used by the authors of the documents is also likely to lead to a high level of 'precision' in the results of the search. Precision is a measure of the efficiency of a search system, in terms of the number of documents which are relevant, out of all those retrieved. Precision will, of course, be lessened in those cases (as with 'can' above) where homographs (words with the same spelling, but different meanings) occur.

In order to remove, or at least reduce, the homograph problem, some indexers 'enrich' the titles when listing them, by the addition of context words indicating the specific meaning to be given to the word in each case, e.g.:-

> Cycles (Biological)
> Cycles (Economic)
> Modelling (Sculpture)
> Modelling (Fashion)
> Screens (Cinema)
> Screens (Furniture)

Another way of enriching the title (in cases where it is not indicative) is to add words from the text, in order to portray more accurately the content, e.g.,

> Sitting in the dark (Household illumination levels)

Words from the text may also be listed as search terms; thus, from the example above:-

Illumination

> Sitting in the dark (Household illumination levels)

The techniques just described are sometimes known as KWAC (Key Word And Context).

The activity of enriching, though valuable in providing more information and hence aiding searching, requires more intellectual input, takes time, increases the cost of production, and may delay the construction of the file. It is for the compiler to decide whether the benefits of enrichment are, overall, worthwhile.

## Artificial Index Languages

The disadvantages of the existence of synonyms, variant spellings and derivatives from the same root word in a natural index language may make this kind of language unsuitable for applications other than the current awareness lists and other quickly-compiled indexes mentioned above. In many situations, inquirers cannot be expected to know the synonyms, spellings and word forms in the subject area of their enquiry. In others, the need to identify *all* documents related to a particular subject requires that the index language used must be capable of leading inquirers to all the relevant entries, without them having to call to mind unprompted all the necessary terms. 'Artificial' index languages, therefore, may be constructed, in which levels of control are exercised on the appropriate vocabulary, with the result that one term is chosen to represent a particular concept, with references to that term from others with similar meanings, spellings or forms.

The problems associated with the use of language are dealt with in detail in Chapter 5. It is sufficient to remark here that artificial index languages aim to overcome, or compensate for, some of these problems. In so doing, they may of course generate other difficulties which themselves need resolution.

### Vocabulary control

The term 'vocabulary control' is applied to the processes of:-

    a) selecting from a number of similar terms the one which is to be used as an index term, (for example: from the synonyms and near-synonyms 'Blaeberries', 'Bilberries', 'Whortleberries' and 'Vaccinium myrtillus' one might choose 'Bilberries' as the index term or choose to represent them all by the notation LHV 1467 Ts, and from the different word-forms 'Spray', 'Sprays' and 'Spraying' one might select 'Sprays'), and

b) providing contexts for homographs (e.g. Cycles . . . . . as on p. 64.

It is also necessary to decide (in the case of index terms consisting of more than one word) on the most useful order of those words — 'Nuclear power stations' or 'Power stations, nuclear', 'Bathrooms. Design' or 'Design. Bathrooms', 'Medical research. United Kingdom' or 'United Kingdom. Medical research' or 'Research, medical. United Kingdom'. (It is usual for connecting words such as 'of', 'in', 'by', 'the', to be removed, except when the meaning of the term would be destroyed or made ambiguous by so doing).

A further step needed to make an index language using words more useful is to provide references between terms which are hierarchically related, e.g. 'Soft fruits' and 'Strawberries', 'Motor vehicles' and 'Lorries', 'Higher education' and 'Universities', 'Measles' and 'Infectious diseases', 'Ericaceae' and 'Vaccinium myrtillus', 'Taxation' and 'Capital transfer tax'. Inquirers are assisted in extending their searches by means of these signposted connections.

Such control activities have specific effects on the results of searches; the reduction of synonyms and word-forms increases 'recall' (another measure of efficiency in terms of the number of relevant documents retrieved out of all the relevant documents in the collection), and the clarification of homograph contexts increases the precision level ( see p. 64 ), while the provision of references between hierarchically-related terms can increase both precision (by enabling a search to be more narrowly focused) and recall (by prompting the inquirer to look at other terms under which relevant information may be found).

The application of a controlled index language using words (as opposed to notation) will produce an alphabetical subject file, a selection from whose sequence of headings might appear as

> Automobiles *see* MOTOR CARS
> BICYCLES
> > *see also* ROAD VEHICLES
> BUSES
> > *see also* ROAD VEHICLES
> Coaches *see* BUSES
> CYCLES (Business)
> > *see also* PRICES
> Cycling (Bicycles) *see* BICYCLES
> LAND PRICES
> > *see also* PRICES
> LAND VEHICLES
> > *see also* ROAD VEHICLES
> > VEHICLES
> LORRIES
> > *see also* ROAD VEHICLES
> Mopeds *see* MOTOR CYCLES
> MOTOR CARS
> > *see also* ROAD VEHICLES
> Motor coaches *see* BUSES
> MOTOR CYCLES
> > *see also* ROAD VEHICLES
> PRICES
> > *see also* CYCLES (Business)
> > LAND PRICES
> ROAD VEHICLES
> > *see also* BICYCLES
> > BUSES
> > LAND VEHICLES
> > LORRIES
> > MOTOR CARS
> VEHICLES   MOTOR CYCLES
> > *see also* LAND VEHICLES

Examples of homographs, differing word-forms, synonyms and hierarchically-related terms can be seen here. The terms in capital letters are those selected as 'index terms' (under which details of particular documents will be filed); the others are 'entry terms', which lead not to document descriptions but to the appropriate index terms which have been used.

There are two major ways of directing inquirers to other terms. The first, used in the example on p. 67, employs 'see' for linking synonyms, near-synonyms and different word-forms, and 'see-also' for connecting hierarchically-related terms. The second, used in the example below (with some of the same terms) employs 'use' instead of 'see' for synonyms and word-forms, and 'BT' (Broader Term), 'NT' (Narrower Term) and 'RT' (Related Term) for distinguising three different hierarchical relationships, instead of the all-purpose 'see also':-

> Automobiles *use* MOTOR CARS
>
> BICYCLES
> > *BT* ROAD VEHICLES
>
> LAND VEHICLES
> > *BT* VEHICLES
> > *NT* ROAD VEHICLES
>
> PRICES
> > *NT* LAND PRICES
> > *RT* CYCLES (Business)

This kind of structure (in which connections are provided between terms by means of 'see, see also' or 'BT, NT, RT' references) is sometimes described as 'syndetic' (i.e. connective). It is clearly essential that these connections are provided, since alphabetical order widely separates many terms which are related to each other ('Buses' and 'Road vehicles', for example) and makes it unlikely that inquirers will happen upon the whole set of possibly useful terms when searching.

*Systematic (classified) files*

This disadvantage of the alphabetical file (scattering of hierarchically-related terms) is to a great extent overcome by the kind of file which results from the application of an index language subjected to a more extreme form of vocabulary control, namely the substitution of notational symbols for words in the representation of document contents. The file thus produced is a systematic (classified) sequence, (as in Fig.3:2), in which those concepts related by their most significant characteristics are brought together, so 'Buses' and 'Road vehicles' might be represented by symbols such as 6J (for 'Road vehicles') and 6L (for 'Buses'), thus ensuring their close proximity.

This kind of indexing language depends upon:

1) the construction of a classification scheme (hierarchy, taxonomy) of the subject area, into which all concepts may be fitted, and

2) the application to those concepts of a set of notational symbols (alphabetical, numerical, or a combination of the two).

(The procedures for constructing such a language are detailed in Chapter 5).

It should not be assumed that by using the notation of a classification scheme to represent document subjects, one is freed from the problems of using words, as inquirers always start a search on the basis of words representing the subject of interest, and therefore will need to be referred from those words to the appropriate piece of notation under which relevant information is to be found, e.g.,

| | | |
|---|---|---|
| | Cycles (Bicycles) . . . | Gsv |
| | Cycles (Meteorology) . . . | Rts |
| or | | |
| | Soft fruits . . . | 85.14 |
| | Strawberries . . . | 86.1 |
| or | | |
| | Capital transfer tax . . . | HO 72 |
| | Taxation . . . | HO 7 |

## INDEX LANGUAGES: PRECOORDINATE AND POSTCOORDINATE

Another way in which indexing languages may be distinguished from each other is according to the level of concept coordination in them and the stage at which this coordination is performed (i.e. as part of the indexing procedure or as part of the search).

Many documents (as can be seen from previous examples) have subjects which are too complicated to be expressed in a single-word term like 'Imprisonment' or 'Butterflies' or 'Finance'; subjects like 'The influence of long periods of solitary confinement on political prisoners', 'A 20–year survey of variations in butterfly colouration in Suffolk' and 'A comparison of personal taxation regulations in European Economic Community countries' each contain a number of individual and separate concepts which cannot be compressed into a single word. Such subjects are capable of being sought by any of their constituent concepts and indexing languages must endeavour to provide for all these approaches. Precoordinate and postcoordinate systems do this in different ways.

## Precoordinate Systems

Precoordinate systems (which may employ either words or notation) provide for the combination (coordination) at the indexing stage, into a single index term of words representing all (or as many as thought necessary) of the concepts, e.g.,

Political prisoners. Solitary confinement.
(One index term, four words)

Butterflies. Colouration. Variations. Suffolk. Surveys.
(One index term, five words)

Personal taxation. Regulations. European Economic
  Community. Comparison.
(One index term, seven words)

174: 333.3.073
(One index term – two notational groups, divided by colons)

These four index terms would file, respectively, under 'Political . .' 'Butterflies . . ', 'Personal . . ', and '174 . . ', but with all the remaining words or notational groups showing in the heading and giving full representation of the subject.

Clearly, for inquirers searching under 'Colouration' or 'Suffolk', 'Solitary' or 'Prisoners', 'Taxation' or 'European' and '333.3.073', these single entries alone would not suffice. In some files (single-entry files) only one full entry of the kind shown above is made, and references are included from the remaining terms, e.g.,

Colouration. Butterflies.
    *see*   Butterflies. Colouration

Prisoners, political.
    *see*   Political prisoners

Solitary confinement. Political prisoners.
    *see*   Political prisoners. Solitary confinement

Taxation, personal
    *see*   Personal taxation

Estate agents. Professional ethics
    *see*   174:333.3.073


In this way, no matter which individual words are used by the inquirers, they are referred back to the single entries which give information regarding particular documents.


In other files (multiple-entry files) full entries are made under each sought word in the index term, e.g.,


Butterflies. Colouration. Variations. Suffolk. Surveys

Colouration. Variations. Butterflies. Suffolk. Surveys

Variations. Colouration. Butterflies. Suffolk. Surveys

Suffolk. Butterflies. Colouration. Variations. Surveys

Surveys. Butterflies. Colouration. Variations. Suffolk.

In multiple-entry files, the inquirer is likely to be more successful (in locating a reference to a document) at the first lookup, than in the single-entry type, but the latter is simpler and more economical to construct.

The exact form of these entries and references varies according to the indexing procedure being employed, as can be seen in Chapter 5. It is unlikely that a completely permuted set of entries would be produced for the example above; this would entail 120 separate entries (five words placed in every possible order in relation to each other: $5 \times 4 \times 3 \times 2 \times 1 = 120$) many of which would be unnecessary.

## Postcoordinate Systems

Postcoordinate systems, on the other hand, (which may also use either words or notation) divide such subjects up into their constituents and index them separately, not in conjunction, e.g.,

Butterflies

Colouration

Variations        i.e. 5 separate headings in the file

Suffolk

Surveys

each term leading to details of the relevant document(s). In order to retrieve references to documents on 'variations in butterfly colouration in Suffolk', therefore, an inquirer puts together (coordinates) the references under the four index terms and knows that any which appear against all four terms are relevant.

One characteristic of language which affects such systems is that words when placed together without their usual connecting words may have more than one meaning, e.g. the terms 'Birds', 'Pests' and 'Control' could be used for 'control of birds *which are* pests', 'control of pests *on* birds' and 'control of pests *by* birds', and if these terms were  used by an inquirer for just one of these meanings, references to documents relating to the other two meanings would also be retrieved, (a situation sometimes called a 'false coordination' or 'false drop'). This kind of system sometimes requires, therefore, additional words to indicate the roles played by ambiguous terms. (A precoordinate system using words is able to show these roles by the retention of the connecting words 'of', 'by', and so on, and also by the order of the words in the precoordinated index term).

## INDEX LANGUAGES: GENERAL AND SPECIAL

Some index languages are categorised as 'general', others as 'special'. The general systems are those which endeavour to encompass the whole universe of knowledge (that is to say all disciplines, fields, subjects or topics found in the existing literature). General index languages often have the virtue of being widely used (sometimes internationally), making searching easier for inquirers who need to consult a number of different collections in different places. Another advantage is that no matter what the subject of any document may be, it is likely that it can be represented by such a language, even if only by a broad term.

Special index languages are limited to a single discipline, field or group of related subjects, such as medicine, environmental studies, music, business studies, and architecture, building and construction. They frequently provide greater detail in their specification of complicated topics, and reflect more relationships between topics, than do general index languages, and are more likely to be applied to collections of material focused on a particular area of activity, such as the technical reports file of a chemical manufacturing company, a collection of photographs, plans and supporting documents in an architectural practice, a press cuttings file in the publicity department of a charitable organisation, or a local studies collection in a public library. Such languages may have no place for subjects outside their areas of activity — and since most collections do receive and incorporate some material from other than their immediate interest areas, this may be a slight disadvantage. The ability, however, of a well-constructed special index language to portray the detail of the subject field, to reflect the current perspectives and activities of the users of a collection, and to provide the flexibility and helpful order needed for their individual and perhaps idiosyncratic approaches, makes such a language invaluable in the context of a specialist collection of material.

## INDEX LANGUAGES: PUBLISHED AND 'HOME-MADE'

There are many index languages already in existence, a large number of them published and therefore available for purchase by an intending user. These are all, obviously, of the 'artificial' variety, since the natural kind is self-generating (from titles, or titles and texts, of the documents indexed). The published languages include precoordinate and postcoordinate, general and special types, and vary considerably in their aims, scope, structure, detail, symbol set (words, notation), areas of application and nature of users. Some are well known and widely used, others found only in a handful of specialist situations. Brief details of some follow on p. 77 – 89.

It may appear from the foregoing that, for every collection need, there must exist at least one suitable scheme. However, there are situations in which organisers still feel that no existing language provides exactly what is needed for their circumstances; this may be related, for example, to the peculiarity of the subject area (such as an unusual combination of topic interests), the special nature of the documents in the collection, or the information needs of the inquirers. Provided that the theoretical basis of the construction of index languages is understood, there is no reason why an individual organiser cannot successfully compile a language specifically catering for the needs of one single collection. It should be borne in mind also that some home-made systems eventually find application in a wider range of situations, and may then become worth publishing on a commercial basis. The disadvantages of being the sole user of a system are that it is less easy to exchange data with other organisations using other systems, and that inquirers using the system have to adapt to a different mode of searching from those which they employ for other collections.

Guidance on the construction of index languages is given in Chapter 5.

## INDEX LANGUAGES: DESIRABLE FEATURES

It can be seen from the preceding pages of this chapter that there are several ways in which index languages may be categorised: natural or artificial, precoordinate or postcoordinate, general or special, published or home-made. None of these types is intrinsically better than its partner; each has features which make it more, or less, appropriate for a particular situation. The selection of an index language must be made in the light of the features of the collection for which it is intended. There are, however, certain criteria which must be met by any index language, whatever its type and wherever it is to be used:

1) it must be capable of representing documents within the required area(s) of interest,

2) it must be able to provide the degree of detail, accuracy, and comprehensiveness that is appropriate for the situation,

3) it must be able to be kept up to date with developments in the subjects on which the collection is based, and with new terminology, and

4) its method of application must be clearly and adequately described, in order to ensure consistency in operation.

The degree of detail and extent of specification of complex topics which are needed will be related to the level of indexing required for the collection. For some situations 'summarisation' of the document contents will suffice — so that, for example, a document on matters involved in the packaging of oranges, lemons, limes and grapefruits could be represented by a term meaning 'packaging of citrus fruits'. Such a document may contain information on a number of topics, such as cost of packaging, suitable materials for packaging, mechanical handling and wrapping, fruit sizes, and supermarket requirements; in order for these topics to be individually highlighted, 'in-depth' indexing has to be applied — each of the topics being separately represented by the appropriate index term. The more detailed and specific the index language, the more satisfactorily it can represent such topics.

Further information on the choice of an index language is given in Chapter 9. Courses on the application of existing index languages, and the construction of own vocabularies, are staged from time to time by the schools of library and information studies, Aslib, the Library Association and other organisations.


## REVIEW OF SOME PUBLISHED INDEX LANGUAGES

**Languages using words.**  Some methods of indexing using words have already been described (KWIC and so on,  see page 61 – 63). Since they are methods which generate index terms directly from titles, or titles and texts, with little or no control over vocabulary, they do not result in published lists of terms for selection and use by other collection organisers in other situations, and therefore they are given no further attention here.  The languages to be treated in this section exist as formal lists of terms (often known as 'subject headings lists' or 'thesauri') which can be obtained and applied to a variety of situations.

There is at present no general list of subject headings compiled and published in the United Kingdom, although the vocabulary built up by the British National Bibliography (BNB), by application of the PRECIS method (see Chapter 5) and used in its printed and machine-readable (MARC) outputs since 1971 provides a comprehensive and detailed collection of headings and references for use in alphabetical files.

Perhaps the best-known general list used in the UK and the US is the Library of Congress *Subject headings* (LCsh) (1980) – a lengthy list, including index and entry vocabulary in precoordinate form. Arising, as it does, from practice in the Library of Congress in the US, it is both detailed and comprehensive, though (from the point of view of British application) biased towards the needs of US inquirers, employing US spelling and vocabulary (Sulfur, Railroads, for example) and providing very fully for the representation of concepts relating to US society, organisations, customs, law, education and government. It is, nevertheless, used successfully in the UK by some university libraries – sometimes with local modifications to spelling and vocabulary, in order to provide for easier searching in a British context.

Its format is easy to comprehend, the alphabetical listing consisting of the index terms in bold type, and entry terms in light type, with recommendations for the consideration of related terms. Its application is aided by references to guides such as Chan (1978), and it is perhaps most appropriate for summarisation indexing of book-type documents. Some index terms are long (containing six or seven words), but there may be frequent occasions in the indexing of a document in a specialised situation when no sufficiently specific term is available, and the indexer must settle for a broader term, or must index separately under two terms, each of which represents part of the theme, but which cannot be combined into a single term.

Use of the list is encouraged by the inclusion of its indexing terms in the catalogue entries which often now appear in commercially published books in the US and the UK, and in the computer-produced, and published, national bibliographical (MARC) records of the BNB and of the Library of Congress. Updating supplements are published between editions.

78

Similar to LCsh is *Sears list of subject headings* (1982), also of US origin; this general list is shorter and less detailed and is aimed for use in small and medium-sized general libraries. Recognition is given to the use of subject headings with non-book materials.

*Special lists*

A large number of special subject headings lists and thesauri have been published, covering a wide range of subjects. Many were originally constructed to meet the needs of particular collections in certain subject fields and have now reached a wider market. Their levels of detail, structures, strengths of theoretical bases and revision and maintenance procedures vary considerably; an individual list should therefore be carefully scrutinised before being adopted for use, in order to ascertain its suitability. Some of these lists are intended for use as precoordinate systems, others as postcoordinate. (The word 'thesauri' is sometimes reserved for the latter kind). A few examples of special lists are given below by way of illustration; there are many more. A collection organiser seeking to identify a suitable list for a particular subject field should consult the usual information sources for that subject field, and also *Library and information science abstracts (LISA); Aslib information; Library literature*, as well as Gilbert (1979 and supplements).

Several of the published special thesauri and subject headings lists are combined with classification schemes and may be used for alphabetical subject or systematic (classified − notational) indexing, and provide notation for shelf locations. Others are solely alphabetical lists of terms. Whatever the format, an alphabetical list is unlikely to be successful in application unless it has been worked out in relation to a hierarchy of class terms from the particular subject field (as will be seen from Chapter 5).

Some of the best-known, in their fields, and some of the more recently published lists are. Aitchison (1969) *Thesaurofacet* (a thesaurus and classication scheme) − engineering and related subjects; *Medical subject headings* (MeSH); *INSPEC thesaurus*

(1981) – physics, electrical engineering, electronics, computers and control; *Food Science and Technology Abstracts thesaurus* ([1981]); Wilmot (1981) *Classification/thesaurus for sport and physical recreation (and allied topics)*; Vernon and Lang (1979) *London classification of business studies: a classification and thesaurus . . . ;* Foskett (1974) *London education classification: a thesaurus/classification . . .; Construction industry thesaurus* (1976); *BSI ROOT thesaurus* (1981) – technology; Aitchison (1981) *Thesaurus on youth: an integrated classification and thesaurus for youth affairs and related topics; Greater London Council Research Library housing thesaurus* (1981).

These examples indicate the wide range of subjects for which thesauri and subject headings lists exist; the number is increasing steadily and many collection organisers will find a ready-made list which suits their purposes.

**Languages using notation.** Notational languages for information retrieval – which are largely for precoordinate use – are related to schemes of classification in which it is intended that the desired topics should be arranged in hierarchical (and therefore 'logical' and 'helpful') order. Two kinds of classification schemes are sometimes identified – enumerative on the one hand and faceted (or analytico-synthetic) on the other; it is more appropriate to view some schemes as being combinations of the enumerative and the faceted types. A purely enumerative scheme attempts to list all possible class terms, from the most simple (a single concept, such as 'bridges') to the more complicated (involving many concepts, such as 'design of prefabricated press-formed steel bridge components') and allocates a notational symbol to each. A faceted scheme, on the other hand, lists only single-concept classes, but provides for them to be combined (synthesised) with each other when needed to portray a more complicated class.

Enumerative schemes (which tend to be older in origin than faceted schemes) depend for their success on the identification

**80**

and listing (at the time of compilation) of all likely combinations of concepts — in terms of document contents. As time passes, these schemes may become outdated by their inability to provide coextensive notations for new, previously unknown, combinations, and therefore require frequent revision if they are to remain useful. Faceted schemes, permitting the synthesis of concepts whenever needed, are less likely to need frequent revision for this reason; if new concepts, as opposed to new combinations, appear in documents, then the faceted scheme is at an equal disadvantage with the enumerative variety.

Of the four major general classification schemes currently in use in the UK, one (*Bliss bibliographic classification*, 2nd ed.) is fully faceted, one is almost entirely enumerative (*Library of Congress classification*) and two (*Dewey decimal classification* 19th ed., and *Universal decimal classification*) combine enumerative and faceted features. Each of these schemes groups topics on the basis of recognising areas of knowledge ('disciplines') which form foci of study and within which literature occurs, such as agriculture, medicine, social sciences, and history; all except the *Library of Congress classification (LC)* identify and list these disciplines according to an overall perspective of the universe of knowledge — *LC* reflecting the groupings which have been found appropriate for the collections of literature in the Library of Congress and their users. The identity and sequence of disciplines in the *Dewey decimal classification (DDC)* and *Universal decimal classification (UDC)* are similar, but that of *Bliss (BC)* is quite different. The result of these different basic outlines is that sequences and placings of topics vary according to the scheme used. *DDC* and *UDC*, for example, include politics, economics, law and education in the main social sciences class, *LC* includes economics but not politics, law or education, in its social sciences class, though these subjects are all placed adjacent to each other in the scheme, and *BC* includes none of them in social sciences — education precedes social sciences in the scheme, but the other subjects are separated by several other classes. In addition, discipline-based classification schemes such as these separate the different aspects of a particular phenomenon (object, attribute, activity) according to the discipline within which it is treated in a document; for example, economic aspects of transport in one main class, engineering aspects in another, management aspects in another, literary allusions in another.

When selecting a scheme for a particular application, this grouping and separating of subjects which may be regarded as related must be taken into consideration, and the most appropriate scheme for the situation chosen.

*Bliss Bibliographic Classification*

*BC*, the first edition of which was published in the US, is now compiled and published in the UK and therefore reflects the practice and vocabulary of British libraries and other information collections. The second edition, which began publication in 1977, is only partially available as yet, though work continues towards its completion. The schedules published so far, each with its own index, are: Education (class J); Social welfare (class Q); Anthropology, human biology and health sciences (class H); Religion, the occult, morals and ethics (class P); Psychology and psychiatry (class I); another volume contains the Introduction and auxiliary schedules. Listing single-concept classes, on the whole, and providing for the synthesis of the notations in order to provide for detailed themes, it enables very specific and precise subject indication to be achieved. Detailed instructions are given in the Introduction and at the start of each separate schedule; these are essential reading for those intending to apply the scheme, and include useful theoretical background on the nature of and needs for bibliographic classification.

Alphabetical notation is used for concepts within the main classes (such as QGX G for 'unemployed persons') and numerical symbols introduce further notation for common concepts listed in the auxiliary schedules (8 for 'place', EGK for 'Oxfordshire), synthesised, the notation for 'unemployed persons in Oxfordshire' is QGX G8E GK. Other categories of common concept provided for in the auxiliary schedules include 'form of publication' (including non-book and non-print forms), 'persons', 'language', 'ethnic groups' and 'periods of time'; with these, it is possible to indicate, for example, that a document is in Russian, or that it is a survey, or that it deals with the subject in the 18th century, or that it is a set of slides. (After a time, much-used notations may be memorised, easing the process of 'translation' for both indexer and inquirer).

At present used in a comparatively small number of collections, and in those specialised fields so far covered by the schedules of the current edition, *BC* reflects a modern theory of bibliographic classification and up to date topic hierarchies, and its use seems likely to increase as more schedules become available. Revision and maintenance are organised by the Bliss Classification Association, which issues an annual bulletin of comment, clarification and amendment.

*Universal Decimal Classification*

*UDC* has found its widest area of use in the special library and information environments of the UK, Europe and the Soviet Union. Based originally on an early edition of *DDC*, it has developed along different lines and now has a number of significant and unique features. The detailed specification of topics in science and technology has always been one of its particular aims, and the increased output of literature in these disciplines has been reflected in the continued expansion of the scheme. Central responsibility for the scheme lies with the International Federation for Documentation (FID) in the Netherlands, with the British Standards Institution (BSI) being the organisation delegated to produce the English edition, which it does under the British Standard number BS 1000. Three levels of the English edition are at present available for use — the full edition, consisting of over 100 separate parts (dated between 1943 and the present time) most having their own indexes, the 3rd abridged edition, 1961, which contains about 10% of the topics specified in the full edition, and some special subject editions, which combine full specification for a particular subject area (such as pharmacy, class 615, and building and architecture, classes 69 to 72) with brief outlines of the other classes. A medium edition (comprising approximately 30% of the full schedules) is expected soon and should prove particularly useful, in terms of coverage and currency. This variety of edition provision means that an individual collection organiser can use either a special subject edition (if one is available for that subject), or the full edition part for the core subject and the abridged edition for the remainder, or the full edition thoughout, or the abridged edition on its own (though this is now over twenty years old, and therefore outdated in places).

The schedules enumerate more than 210,000 topics as direct subdivisions of classes, and many more can be synthesised by the use of features such as the colon (:), which can be employed to connect any number of topic notations from the main schedules, and the auxiliary schedules, which contain lists of common concepts (form of publication — including non-book forms, time, place, language, and so on) which can be added to main schedule notation for more detailed specification. The colon is a unique feature of *UDC* and can link topics from different classes as required by the indexer, for example (from the 2nd full English edition of class 628, public health engineering, water, illuminating engineering), 628.977.1 represents 'interior lighting for working purposes in factories, workshops, workrooms'; this can be linked with the notation from class 77, photography, for 'darkroom lighting', to give 628.977.1:771.24 'lighting of photographic darkrooms'. (In a multiple-entry file this notation can also be rotated, to give an entry under 771.24:628.977.1).

The notation is numerical and decimal, but with the addition of symbols (normally used for punctuation) like the colon and — to introduce concepts from the common auxiliary tables — the hyphen, the equals sign, parentheses, quotation marks and others. For example, 'water supply', '628.1', can be extended by the use

84

of common auxiliaries (667) 'Ghana' and "197" 'the 1970's', to give 628.1(667)"197", 'water supply in Ghana in the 1970's'. (In a multiple-entry file entries may also be made under (667)628.1"197" and "197"(667)628.1 — and other permutations if required). Considerable flexibility is possible, in terms of the order in which the notational elements may be combined, making the scheme suitable for idiosyncratic needs, but care must be exercised as a result, in order to ensure consistency of application and construction in relation to a particular collection.

*UDC* is available in many countries of the world, in several different languages; this may make it particularly appropriate for use in organisations having branches, subsidiaries or associates in more than one country. *Extensions and corrections to the UDC* gives details of changes in English, French and German. Detailed instructions for the use of the English edition are given in the abridged edition, and each part of the full edition gives brief guidance on the use of the scheme as a whole, with the schedules containing further instructions. Essential guides to the scheme are Robinson (1979) and *Guide to the Universal Decimal Classification* (1963). Revision of the English edition is coordinated by the British Standards Institution and amendments and new editions of parts are listed in *BSI news*.

## *Dewey Decimal Classification*

*DDC* is used by the majority of public libraries in the UK, and its notations are included in the centralised bibliographic data available from the BNB, as well as sometimes being printed inside commercially published documents, along with other cataloguing information. Some collection organisers wish to take advantage of this and make their systems compatible by using *DDC* for their own material, while others feel no need for this compatibility, their documents, users and information needs being individual. Currently in its 19th edition, *DDC* contains in three volumes the schedules for all classes, a detailed introduction and set of auxiliary tables and an alphabetical index to all subjects listed.

Published in the US, it employs US spelling and vocabulary, though recognition is given to some British usages, and the latest edition contains some revisions which remove some of the emphasis on US society and culture.

The basic outline of the scheme is similar to, but not identical with, *UDC*, in terms of the main classes and their sequence, and specification of topics is provided for by a combination of enumeration and synthesis, as in *UDC*, but using only numerical decimal notation. Synthesis in *DDC* is enabled by the additional tables of common concepts (including standard subdivisions for forms of publication, areas, languages, persons and others), from which notation may be taken as instructed, and by the combination of notations from different classes in the main schedules. In the latter case, no connecting symbol (like the colon in *UDC*) is used – the notations are directly merged; but the occasions on which it is permitted to do this are limited, instructions being given in the schedules at the places where synthesis may be carried out. For example, '331.2' represents 'salaries and wages' in class 330, 'economics'; in order to specify payment in regard to a particular industry or occupation, instructions are given to add the notation representing the particular activity. This can produce notation such as: 331.281378 (salaries/in specific industries and occupations/other than extractive, manufacturing, construction/ higher education) – 378 being the main schedule notation for 'higher education'; to this could then be added, from the tables of standard subdivisions and of areas, 0944 (place/France) for 'salaries in higher education in France'.

Though providing a comprehensive coverage of subjects (29,528 entries, plus synthesisable combinations), *DDC* does not give the level of detailed specification, for example in science and technology, that is to be found in *UDC*. It is frequently revised (approximately every seven years) – the Editorial Policy Committee including a British representative from the Library Association – and users can keep up to date with amendments and clarifications between editions by reference to *Dewey decimal classification*

86

*additions, notes and decisions* (free to purchasers of the 19th edition). It is a highly successful and much used scheme — collection organisers who select it can be sure that many of their inquirers will already be familiar with it from school, college, university or public library experience; differences in usage may still exist, due to the use of different editions, practice of broader or closer classification and so on, but the basic sequence and structure will be the same.

## *Library of Congress Classification*

*LC* — another US scheme — has been developed to supply the appropriate arrangement of documents in the Library of Congress, and has been much more concerned with the means of achieving helpful order on the shelves, than with the provision of a detailed information retrieval system. 'Helpful order' is defined, in this case, in terms of the needs of the users of the Library of Congress; the result, however, is a scheme which has found favour with some academic libraries in the UK, in that it also supplies a suitable arrangement for the users of those collections. The scheme is not based on a philosophical view of the universe of knowledge, but rather on the way in which the subjects of documents have appeared in the collections of the Library of Congress; 'disciplinary' areas are still recognised, such as agriculture, medicine, social sciences, technology, and fine arts, but the separate parts of the scheme have been said to be more like individual special classifications rather than integrated parts of a whole.

The scheme contains considerable detail for topics in classes such as D, E. and F, history and P, language and literature — with particular emphasis in regard to the US — so that individual events and named works of particular authors may have their own notations, but may be found less satisfactory in the science and technology areas, since it does not always present topics in a hierarchical order, but resorts to alphabetical sequences, and does not use synthesis to produce combined notations for complicated themes. In class V, naval science, for example, in 'Lifesaving apparatus, stations, etc.' are found VK 1473 – boats, lifeboats, VK 1475 – buoys, VK 1477 – life preservers, VK 1479 – rockets, and then at VK 1481, any other special apparatus is to be represented by symbols constructed from tables for alphabetical characters, giving VK 1481.F6 – *f*og bells, VK 1481.S2 – *s*afety anchorage, VK 1481.S4 – *s*hark protection, and so on. Such alphabetical sequences may not always be the most helpful, and there may be differences of opinion regarding the naming, and therefore the alphabetical representation, of particular classes.

The notation is mixed, using alphabetical capital letters for the main classes and their immediate subdivisions, then numbers (used as whole numbers, not as decimals); further extensions can be given, using symbols of the kind shown above, and also by the use of decimal numbers where the Library of Congress has found need for further subdivisions. Each of the separately issued parts (over 30 in all) contains its own index and is updated as it becomes necessary; some parts are now in their 6th or 7th editions, others only in the 2nd or 3rd. An index to *LC* has been compiled by Olson (1974). Between editions, users can keep up to date by reference to *LC classification – additions and changes*. The Library of Congress is responsible for maintenance and revision, which is carried out with particular regard to the needs of the Library of Congress stock and users; subjects which are not well represented in the Library will not be well represented in the classification. Because of the size and nature of the Library, however, coverage is comprehensive. *LC* notations, like *DDC*, are included on the centralised bibliographic MARC data supplied by *BNB* and the Library of Congress, sometimes printed in commercially published documents, and this is an encouragement towards wider use. Instructions in the scheme are few and brief; those intending to apply *LC* to their collections should consult Immroth (1980) for clarification and guidance.

*Special schemes*

As in the case of subject headings lists and thesauri, there are many special classification schemes in existence; some have already been named ((see page 79 – 80) as they combine both classification schedules and alphabetical lists. Others (again by way of illustration) include: *INSPEC classification. . .* (1981) – physics, electrotechnology, computers, control; Coates (1960) *British Catalogue of Music classification* Moulds (1980) *FIAF classification scheme for literature on film and television* Moys (1968) *A classification scheme for law books;* Ray-Jones and Clegg (1976) *CI/SfB construction indexing manual.* Organisers of collections seeking a suitable scheme should consult the sources given on page 79. In the event of no scheme appearing appropriate, the construction of an 'own' scheme may be indicated – guidance on this is given in Chapter 5.


## REFERENCES

Aitchison, Jean, Gomersall, Alan and Ireland, Ralph. (1969) *Thesaurofacet: a thesaurus and faceted classification for engineering and related subjects.* Whetstone, Leics.: English Electric Co.

Aitchison, Jean. (1981) *Thesaurus on youth: an integrated classification and thesaurus for youth affairs and related topics. . .* in association with Inese A. Smith and Susan Thompson. Leicester: National Youth Bureau.

*Aslib information* (Monthly). Aslib.

*Bliss bibliographic classification.* (1977–) 2nd ed. J. Mills and Vanda Broughton, with the assistance of Valerie Lang. Butterworths.

*Bliss classification bulletin.* (Annual). Bliss Classification Association.

*BSI news.* (Monthly) British Standards Institution.

*BSI ROOT thesaurus.* (1981). Hemel Hempstead: British Standards Insitution.

Chan, Lois May. (1978). *Library of Congress subject headings: principles and application.* Littleton, Colo.: Libraries Unlimited.

Coates, E J (1960). *British Catalogue of Music classification*, compiled for the Council of the British National Bibliography . . . Council of the British National Bibliography.

*Construction industry thesaurus.* (1976). 2nd ed. Compiled by the CIT Agency at the Polytechnic of the South Bank under the direction of Michael J Roberts. Department of the Environment, Property Services Agency.

*Dewey decimal classification and relative index.* (1979). Edition 19. Edited under the direction of Benjamin A Custer. Albany, N.Y.: Forest Press.

*Dewey decimal classification additions, notes and decisions.* (Occasional). Albany, N.Y.: Forest Press.

*Extensions and corrections to the UDC.* (Annual) The Hague: Federation Internationale de Documentation.

*Food Science and Technology Abstracts thesaurus.* (1981). 2nd ed. Reading. International Food Information Service.

Foskett, D J and Foskett, J (1974) *London education classification: a thesaurus/classification of British educational terms.* 2nd ed. University of London Institute of Education Library. (Education libraries bulletin, supplement 6).

Gilbert, Valerie. (1979). A list of thesauri and subject headings held in the Aslib Library. *Aslib Proceedings,* vol. 31, No. 6, June, p.264–274; and supplements in September and June each year following.

*Greater London Council Research Library housing thesaurus.* (1981). Prepared by Alan Gomersall. Greater London Council. (Research documents guide no. 13).

*Guide to the Universal Decimal Classification (UDC).* (1963). British Standards Institution. (BS. 1000C:1963).

Immroth, John Philip. (1980) *Immroth's guide to the Library of Congress classification.* 3rd ed. by L M Chan. Littleton, Colo.: Libraries Unlimited.

*INSPEC classification: a classification scheme for physics, electro-technology, computers and control.* (1981). Institution of Electrical Engineers.

*INSPEC thesaurus.* (1981). Institution of Electrical Engineers.

*Library and information science abstracts* (LISA). (Monthly) Library Association.

*Library literature.* (Bi-monthly). New York: H W Wilson.

*Library of Congress classification.* Washington, D. C.: Library of Congress.

*Library of Congress classification – additions and changes.* (Quarterly). Washington, D.C.: Library of Congress.

Library of Congress. (1980). *Subject headings.* 9th ed. Washington, D.C.: Library of Congress.

*Medical subject headings.* (Annual). Bethesda, Md.: National Library of Medicine.

Moulds, Michael. (1980). *FIAF classification scheme for literature on film and television*. Aslib.

Moys, Elizabeth. (1968). *A classification scheme for law books*. Butterworths. (2nd ed. due 1982).

Olson, Nancy B (1974). *Combined indexes to the Library of Congress classification schedules*. Washington, D.C.: Historical Documents Institute.

Ray-Jones, Alan and Clegg, David. (1976). *CI/SfB construction indexing manual*. RIBA Publications.

Robinson, Geoffrey. (1979). *UDC: a brief introduction*. The Hague: Federation Internationale de Documentation. (FID 574).

*Sears list of subject headings*. (1982). 12th ed. Ed. Barbara M Westby. New York: H W Wilson.

*Universal decimal classification: English full edition*. British Standards Institution. (B.S.1000).

*Universal decimal classification: abridged English edition*. (1961). 3rd. ed. British Standards Institution. (BS. 1000A:1961).

Vernon, K D C and Lang, Valerie. (1979). *The London classification of business studies: a classification and thesaurus for business libraries*. 2nd ed. revised by K G B Bakewell and David A Cotton. Aslib.

Wilmot, Carole E (1981). Classification/thesaurus for sport and physical recreation (and allied topics). Sports Council.

**FURTHER READING**

Items, 1, 5, 6, 9, 11, 12, 13, 18, 20, 22, 23, 24, 25, 30, 38, 39, 41, 43, 45, 46, 49, 51, 54, 59, 63, 65, 66 from section B, p.274 – .

# CHAPTER 5: CONSTRUCTING YOUR OWN SCHEME

In this chapter, the processes by which an index language is designed and constructed will be discussed. They will be discussed both in relation to the languages using notation and resulting in a systematic order, i.e. artificial (non-verbal) languages, and in relation to artificial verbal languages. Because the content (i.e. the subject) of a document is almost certainly its most important feature, the construction of languages will be discussed in relation to so called 'subject schemes'; but the principles are applicable to the construction of schemes related to other features (e.g. physical form or media), and indeed, features not primarily associated with content can be incorporated in what are basically subject schemes. (See Chapter 6, Non-content approaches).

Index language construction is based upon classificatory and linguistic logic, but since classification and the use of language are almost literally 'common sense', many efficient filing systems have been constructed without reference to formally identified theories or principles. The process of design and maintenance of systems will, however, be speeded up and the results are the more likely to be long-lasting if common-sense and experience are illuminated by knowledge of theories and principles.

Classification problems in the design of systems fall into the following categories:-

1. Discipline/phenomena problems

2. Multi-element subject problems

3. Specificity problems

4. Citation order problems

## DISCIPLINE/PHENOMENA PROBLEMS

Disciplines (referred to already in Chapter 4) are frameworks for 'looking at the world' and for interpreting reality. They carry their own theories, explanations and terminology, their subject matter being the 'phenomena' studied. Disciplines are characterised, not only by the phenomena they study, but by their methodology and by the questions they ask about phenomena; and certain concepts may be peculiar to particular disciplines. The natural sciences are concerned with the material universe, asking questions about cause and effect and doing so by means of objective observation and mainly inductive reasoning. Religion is concerned with supernatural phenomena, and is not concerned with 'proofs' in any absolute sense, as are the natural sciences. A particular phenomenon may appear in a different guise within different disciplines. For example, the phenomenon of 'having sexual relationships with the spouse of another' appears within the framework of morals as 'sin or not sin'. Within the framework of law (an expression of sociology), the 'sinfulness' is irrelevant and the phenomenon may or may not be 'criminal'.

Phenomena transcend disciplines, and may belong to different groupings or classes within the disciplines. For example, suppose the phenomena studied to be four groups of people known as Barians, Darians, Farians and Karians; they might be differently grouped as:

**94**

Fig. 5:1
*Phenomena within the framework of different disciplines*

*Religion*                        *Sociology*

Monotheist people          Matriarchal societies

    Barians                            Darians
    Darians                            Karians

Polytheist people            Patriarchal Societies

    Farians                            Barians
    Karians                            Farians

*Physiology*

Giants

    Darian people
    Karian people
    Farian people

Dwarfs

    Barian people

Problems may be solved by reference to one discipline, but are as likely to be solved by reference to more than one; from 'cross-disciplinary studies' may emerge a recognised area of studies which may eventually be accorded status as an independent discipline. 'Environmental studies' appears to be in an early stage of evolution as a discipline. A particular activity may depend upon a number of different disciplines, whether or not it eventually emerges as in itself a discipline. For example, teaching draws on both sociology and psychology, but whether 'pedagogy' is a discipline or not might still be open to argument. Medicine historically and actually has drawn on many areas of knowledge, and has probably achieved social recognition as a 'discipline' by reason of the amount of intellectual and practical work which supports the activity.

The content matter of documents include phenomena, disciplines, and areas or focuses of activity. An information retrieval system may have to deal simultaneously with items on the Barian people (all aspects) or food (all aspects); with items on anthropology, dietetics and physiology; and with items on running a hospital catering department and the manufacture of automobiles in Upper Baria. These items, although differently focused, are likely to have much material in common. In respect of searchers' enquiries, a 'phenomenon search' (for e.g. Barians, food, hospitals, automobiles) would, if the classification were discipline based, lead to a search through scattered classes.

The fact that three individual 'peoples' could belong to different groupings within different disciplines is illustrative of the facts that individuals belong to different classes dependent upon the attributes chosen to define the classes; and that certain concepts are peculiar to disciplines. For example the concept of 'sin' belongs to morals and to religion, and the concept of 'crime' belongs to law. An action which is a 'sin' within one frame of reference may not be a 'crime' according to the law.

## THE PROBLEM OF MULTI-ELEMENT CLASSES

Each of the classes listed in Fig. 5:1, were within the context of the respective disciplines 'single element classes'. However in the context of the discipline 'anthropology' the concepts 'monotheism' and 'matriarchy' are both relevant; and therefore, the Darians would belong not only to the classes 'monotheistic societies' and 'matriarchal societies' but to the class 'monotheistic, matriarchal societies'. As shown in Fig. 5:2, this is a two element class, all the members of which belong to two single element classes and the two element class is subordinate to and contained by two single element classes.

The subjects of much documentary information are likely to belong to multi-element classes, and the subjects, therefore, are

96

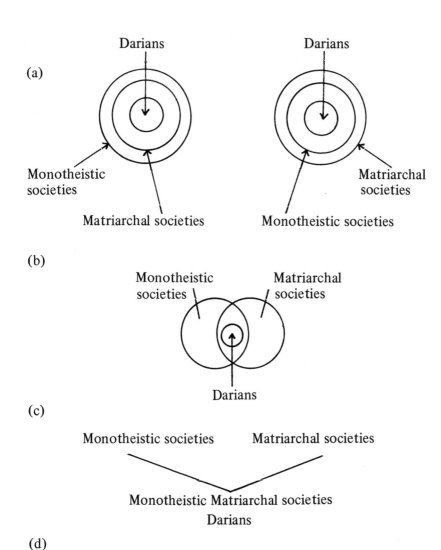

Fig. 5:2
*Multi-element classes (two elements)*

'multi-element subjects'. Whereas it is relatively easy to predict the existence of a single element subject, it is less easy to predict combinations. There are two reasons for this. The first is that the combinations are difficult to anticipate by reason of their number; and the second is that novelties are as frequently the result of new combinations of old elements as of the discovery of completely new elements.

Assume that there is a file of 'food-facts' the items in which deal with the following matters (amongst others):-

> High protein foods (defined by a nutritional element)
>
> Savoury foods (defined by a taste)
>
> Smoked foods (defined by a method of preparation).
>
> (The food 'kippers' belongs to all three of these)

These single elements are, however, capable of generating four more classes making a total of seven in all.-

> High protein foods
> Savoury foods
> Savoury high protein foods
> Smoked foods
> Smoked high protein foods
> Smoked savoury foods
> Smoked savoury high protein foods (kippers)

In terms of set theory a set of 'n' elements produces $2^n$ sub-sets. These sub-sets include the 'universal set' which includes all the elements, (smoked, savoury high protein foods), the one element sets (smoked foods, and savoury foods and high protein foods). and the sets of elements between one and 'n' in number. In set theory the sets also include the 'empty set' which has no members. Since the empty set is irrelevant in the present context, we can say that a set of 'n' single elements can potentially produce $(2^n - 1)$ classes or 'subjects'.

A modest list of ten elements is potentially productive of 1,023 classes. In practice the number of elements is likely to be much greater. (There are considerably more than ten ways of characterising food for example). However not all the elements will combine. Elements may be contradictory (protein and non-protein foods for example), and even if not contradictory may be unlikely to combine in the 'real world'. The subject 'knives for cutting soft boiled eggs' is unlikely to occur. However, there is no guarantee that even contradictory concepts will not co-occur in documentation as in 'A comparison of high and low protein foods for diabetics', and there is nothing which forbids authors writing on 'knives for cutting soft boiled eggs'.

Moreover it is not only at the conceptual level that the unexpected occurs. The combination of 'smoking' and 'cancer' may have been unexpected sixty years ago (when indeed tobacco was held to have beneficial effects); and the innumerable modern applications of petroleum and its by-products would have been considered fantastic at the beginning of the century. It is probably in the area of social policy and activity that the need for providing for the unexpected is most evident; for example 'tobacco and advertising', 'piracy and air travel' are recent novelties; as is 'road safety and seat belts and law'. the law is indeed extremely likely to produce new combinations, since law operates by fiat creating its own connections and its own realities.

## SPECIFICITY PROBLEMS

Classes can be divided and sub-divided, the purpose of arranging files according to a classificatory grouping, being — as already discussed in Chapter 2 — to reduce the necessary area of search. The specificity of the classes (the 'detail' of the classification) should depend in part on the number of items likely to belong to each class, since, as already discussed, 'searching the whole store' may not be an inconvenient proceeding if the store contains few items. If a file is likely to contain only twenty items on food, there may be little point in dividing these items into groups according to any criteria. However, if it is possible to make a useful distinction between one class and another, and if this distinction is represented in the documentation, there is a case for reflecting it in the filing system, even if the number of items does not appear to warrant such specificity. Collections grow in unexpected directions; the higher the specificity of the arrangement the better adapted it might be to growth.

## CITATION ORDER PROBLEMS

As discussed in Chapter 2, searchers are likely to use a classificatory procedure even when the search is for an individual item, and will serially reject items which do not possess the class characteristics required. For example both dietician and chef may be interested in the class characteristics 'nutritional elements' 'method of preparation' and 'taste', but whereas the dietician might look for the characteristics in that order, the chef might prefer the reverse order. It is possible that for the chef 'anything not suitable for a savoury course is of no use'. Given that the item is suitable for a savoury course, the other characteristics are of less importance: 'I would prefer a high protein to a low protein food, but will settle for the latter if necessary'. The order in which class characteristics are sought, (and conversely the order in which they are rejected), is, when reflected in a file arrangement, called the 'citation order'. (Citation orders are also applicable to non-content characteristics, and to the choice between content and non-content characteristics in searching (e.g. author/ subject or subject/author). This will be dealt with in Chapter 6.

There is a basic problem exemplified by the problem of providing for both the chef and the dietician, and of providing for any other citation order which might be required. The number of possible citation orders is the number of permutations of characteristics, which becomes the number of permutations of elements

**100**

produced by characteristics, (i.e. the characteristic 'nutrient elements' produces 'protein foods'). The number of permutations of 'n' elements is expressed as $n(n-1)(n-2) \ldots 1$. In the multi-element class 'smoked, savoury, high protein foods' there are three elements, and therefore $3 \times 2 \times 1$ ways of searching for it, i.e. of citing it. The number of possible permutations of 'n' elements is called factorial 'n', and is written as n! The number of ways of searching for 'smoked, savoury high protein foods costing less than £X.00' is $4 \times 3 \times 2 \times 1 = 24$.

The problem of the multi-element subject is firstly that of anticipating the combinations which are likely to occur, (provided 'smoked, savoury, high protein foods' can be easily found, the route taken in the search is irrelevant, and therefore the citation order may be irrelevant). However, although the search object may be a combination of elements, the search route is one of a number of permutations of elements and the search object is unlikely to be found if the permutations used are not provided for in the system.

## SOLUTIONS TO THE PROBLEMS

No filing system can please all the people all the time, unless it is of very limited scope in terms of kind of materials to be catered for, and unless the potential searchers are themselves a highly specialised group who are prepared to learn the system. These conditions are most likely to be present in the case of administrative documents or files associated with one highly specific problem, as for example fingerprint records, road accident records, records of genetic characteristics in a research file. In some of these cases it may be possible to devise a 'perfect' system. This is not to say that there are no problems to be solved, but that once the problems are solved the results are likely to please most of the users most of the time. In other cases decisions may have to be made as to which are the most likely use patterns, and, while providing for supposed 'majority' use provide compensatory devices for supposed minorities.

## Analysis of Classes

The problems may be exacerbated by the complexities of class relationships which may exist within document themes, and especially in the case of non-administrative documents. Some of these problems can be explained by reference to the concepts of logical division and of fundamental categories. Both these concepts are familiar to students of formal logic, and have been so since classical times. They have, however, been developed and given a practical application in documentary classification within the present century.

### Logical Division

Logical division is the process by which classes are divided into sub-classes by the addition of attributes (called 'differences'), to those already possessed by the class, and which differentiate members of a sub-class from members of another. For example, members of the class 'animals' possess attributes in common which differentiate them from other 'live' organic beings, and by which they are 'animals' and not 'plants'. Herbivorous animals are members of the class animals, but possess the additional attribute which differentiates them from other members of the class 'animals', i.e. from 'non-herbivorous animals'. Two sub-classes are created, the differences being respectively 'feeds mainly on plant substances' and 'does not feed mainly on plant substances'. The differences themselves belong to a class, which is called the 'principle' or 'characteristic' of division. Since 'non-herbivorous animals' includes 'carnivorous animals', we can say that 'animals' can be divided so as to produce the two sub-classes 'herbivorous' and 'carnivorous' animals according to the principle of division 'substances upon which animals feed'.

Principles of division constituting as they do a 'class', can themselves be sub-divided. Since 'plant substances' include 'fruit, 'leaves' and 'roots' (divided according to the part of the plant), herbivorous animals can further be subdivided into 'fruit, 'leaf'

**102**

and 'root' eating animals.

Logical division produces 'thing/kind' relationships, which are also called 'genus/species' relationships or 'generic' relationships. (NB. The terms 'genus and species' are here used in a logical sense and have no *necessary* relationships to the 'genera' and 'species' of zoological and botanical classification).

A leaf is a kind of plant substance. The leaf is not however a kind of plant. The relationship between leaves and plants is not a genus/species relationship but a thing/part relationship also called a partitive relationship.

Other examples of partitive relationships include spatial and time relationships (e.g. Europe/United Kingdom, eighteenth century/ 1796). These two relationships in common with the type exemplified by plant/leaf are essential partitive relationships which can be treated as generic relationships. (They might be called 'pseudo-generic' relationships). They differ from the relationship exemplified by 'motor cars/engines' in that in the latter case the 'parts' specified could be parts of other things. A leaf on the other hand cannot but be part of a plant, and 1796 cannot but be part of the eighteenth century.

A class may be divided by more than one principle of division, and if more than one principle of division is used at one time the result is likely to be 'cross classification'. For example, the question "Is this animal herbivorous or is it aquatic?" is unanswerable because the animal might be both. If the classification is to be used as the basis of a one-place filing system then the grouping must be made on the basis of one characteristic of division used at one time. For example, in Fig. 5:2d it is clearly shown that the two principles of division can be used in different orders, but that — within a linear one-place sequence — the class 'monotheistic-matriarchal societies' can appear in one place only.

Each step in division will produce at least two sub-classes (the

103

positive and negative classes, which respectively possess and do not possess the attribute), and may produce more. Each of the classes is a 'single element class' capable of being combined with other elements, as in 'monotheistic/patriarchal societies' or a 'comparison of matriarchal and patriarchal societies'.

Classes which are derived by the application of one principle of division are called 'simple classes'. Those derived by the application of more than one principle are called 'superimposed classes'. Thus if the class 'animals' is divided, the class 'herbivorous animals' is a simple class, as is the class 'leaf eating animals' ('leaf eating' being contained by 'herbivorous'). The class 'herbivorous aquatic animals' is superimposed. Fig. 5:2b shows 'superimposition' as an overlap between two classes; the overlap of the two circles representing 'societies which are both monotheistic and matriarchal'.

In a classification of 'things' as distinct from a classification of ideas, the problem of combinations is less acute. This is demonstrated in Fig. 5:3.

Fig. 5:3 is an example of an 'enumerative' classification, that is to say one in which an attempt is made to enumerate both single and multi-element classes. The class 'animals', as for a zoological classification, is divided successively by the characteristics of division 'physiological structure', 'habitat' and 'feeding habits'. It will be noted that:-

1. Every individual animal is accommodated because the division is rendered exhaustive by the inclusion of 'other' classes at each step of division.

2. There is only one place for each individual animal, since the classes are mutually exclusive. Only one characteristic of division has been used at each step, so that there is no division of animals into 'terrestrial' and 'herbivorous'.

104

Fig. 5:3   *A classification of animals*

## 1 – ANIMALS

| 2 Vertebrates | 23 Invertebrates | 44 Not Vertebrates or Invertebrates |
|---|---|---|
| 3 Terrestrial | 24 Terrestrial | 45 Terrestrial |
| 4   Omnivores | 25   Omnivores | 46   Omnivores |
| 5   Herbivores | 26   Herbivores | 47   Herbivores |
| 6   Carnivores | 27   Carnivores | 48   Carnivores |
| 7   Not 4, 5 or 6 | 28   Not 25, 26 or 27 | 49   Not 46, 47 or 48 |
| 8 Aquatic | 29 Aquatic | 50 Aquatic |
| 9   Omnivores | 30   Omnivores | 51   Omnivores |
| 10   Herbivores | 31   Herbivores | 52   Herbivores |
| 11   Carnivores | 32   Carnivores | 53   Carnivores |
| 12   Not 9, 10 or 11 | 33   Not 30, 31 or 32 | 54   Not 51, 52 or 53 |
| 13 Amphibious | 34 Amphibious | 55 Amphibious |
| 14   Omnivores | 35   Omnivores | 56   Omnivores |
| 15   Herbivores | 36   Herbivores | 57   Herbivores |
| 16   Carnivores | 37   Carnivores | 58   Carnivores |
| 17   Not 14, 15 or 16 | 38   Not 35, 36 or 37 | 59   Not 56, 57 or 58 |
| 18 Not 3, 8 or 13 (Terrestrial Aquatic or Amphibious) | 39 Not 24, 29 or 34 (Terrestrial Aquatic or Amphibious) | 60 Not 45, 50 or 55 (Terrestrial Aquatic or Amphibious) |
| 19   Omnivores | 40   Omnivores | 61   Omnivores |
| 20   Herbivores | 41   Herbivores | 62   Herbivores |
| 21   Carnivores | 42   Carnivores | 63   Carnivores |
| 22   Not 19, 20 or 21 | 43   Not 40, 41 or 42 | 64   Not 61, 62 or 63 |

3. All 'real' animals must be placed at the lowest
   level of the hierarchy, since in the material world
   there can be no animal which does not possess a
   physiological structure, a habitat and eating habits
   (even if these are 'negative', e.g., not amphibious).

If a classification scheme is a system of labels plus pigeon holes, then in this scheme every 'real' animal can be accommodated in a pigeon hole, although not every real animal can be exhaustively labelled. There is no means of labelling 'social' animals for example because this attribute has not been used in the classification.

In a world of ideas (and therefore the world of documentation), not only are some labels missing but so are a considerable number of pigeon holes. A pigeon hole for 'amphibious animals in general' is necessary because it is possible to think about such animals without reference to physiological structure or habitat. In the tables it is not possible to specify amphibious animals without also specifying physiological structure; nor is it possible to specify herbivorous animals in general nor herbivorous amphibious animals. In the tables three simple classes are provided for and sixty superimposed classes. Eight simple and twenty-four superimposed classes are unprovided for. The eleven simple elements constituting a set produces mathematically 2,047 sub-sets or potentially 2,047 classes. The number may be reduced in practice because of incompatibility of some of the set members, although there is no guarantee in documentation that these incompatibles will not appear together.

*Non-Generic Relationships*

Logical division accounts for the 'thing/kind' relationship. It does not appear to account for the kinds of relationship illustrated in Figure 5 : 4.

Fig. 5:4
*Non-generic relationships*
Zoology
Animals
Birds
Mating
Southern England
Digestive organs

Birds are kinds of animals, but mating is not a kind of bird, nor Southern England a kind of mating. Digestive organs are parts of birds, but do not have the pseudo-generic relationship since digestive organs are not exclusive to birds.

The process of logical division might be made to apply if it were postulated that the 'universe' being divided is not 'birds' but 'ideas about birds'. However a less tortuous and more convenient 'model' is that provided by the theory of 'fundamental categories'. As developed during this century in the context of documentary classification, it is proposed that within any area of knowledge (e.g. automobile engineering, agriculture, social welfare, architecture, metallurgy . . . ) there will occur groups of concepts of a highly generalised character which are mutually exclusive, and which, between them 'exhaust' or 'completely divide' the universe. Within any area of knowledge, a test of whether two concepts belong to the same or different categories is the answer to the question "Can they be kinds of the same thing?" Thus although 'digestive organs' and 'birds' can be brought together in thought and practice, they are not kinds of the same thing (nor indeed kinds of each other). In the context of philosophy and logic, Aristotle distinguished eight categories into which our experience of the world could be divided. These included 'place' (e.g. London), 'time' (e.g. 1982), 'action' (e.g. eating) and 'passion' (e.g. being eaten). Fundamental categories were 're-invented' in the twentieth century by the librarian S R Ranganathan, (1962) who applied them to the construction of documentary classification schemes, and who proposed categories very like those of

107

Aristotle, although as far as is known Ranganathan was not influenced by occidental classical philosophy. Ranganathan's model, an area of knowledge (about which there is documentation) must be accepted, and the fundamental categories are distinguished within this area. Ranganathan proposed the existence of five which he claimed would be manifested in most areas. These are: 'personality', 'matter', 'energy', 'space' and 'time'. The so called 'personality' category (with some affinity to Aristotle's 'substance' category), can best be defined as the 'focus' of an area of study. 'Matter' is the 'materials' or 'constituents' and 'energy' is 'activity'. 'Ferrous metals' would form part of the 'personality' category in a classification of metallurgy, but would become 'matter' in a classification of automobile engineering, for which the different kinds of automobile would form the personality category. Ranganathan's theories have had considerable influence and are indeed part of the 'general consciousness' of librarians and others concerned with information retrieval. Since his time other categories have been proposed by Vickery (1975) and others. A commonly proposed set is:- personality, parts, materials, actions, tools, agents, space and time. Within automobile manufacture the theme 'Women operators of presses for the extrusion of steel for engine parts in the manufacture of tanks at Dagenham during World War II' includes elements from each of these categories.

It must however be emphasised that no lists of categories are prescriptive, although lists may form useful guides in the construction of classification schemes and indexing languages. The concept of the personality category is an especially useful one, since it points to the identification of the most important classes, to 'what the subject is 'about'. For example, agriculture is 'about' crops, education 'about' pupils, metallurgy 'about' metals.

The categories manifested in Fig. 5:4 include members of a supposed 'personality' category (animals and birds), an 'activity' category (mating), a 'place' category (Southern England) and a 'parts' category (digestive organs).

108

Classes in one category which are divided by classes in another are called 'compound classes'. Thus, in Fig. 5:4, 'mating of birds' is a compound class.

In Ranganathan's terminology 'categories' become 'facets'. Thus 'the mating of birds' is a 'multi-faceted subject' or 'multi-faceted class'. A facet comprises all the classes belonging to one category. A sub-facet comprises all the classes within a category derived by the application of one principle of division. Thus Fig. 5:3 might represent the 'personality' facet of a zoology classification. The classes 'vertebrates', 'invertebrates' and 'other' represent the physiological structure sub-facet, and the classes 'herbivorous, carnivorous, omnivorous and other animals', the 'feeding habits' sub-facet.

It would be easy to define superimposed and compound classes as respectively 'classes with elements drawn from more than one sub-facet' and 'classes with elements drawn from more than one facet' (e.g. 'herbivorous vertebrates', and 'mating of herbivorous vertebrates'). These definitions are serviceable ones, but leave out of consideration a third kind of non-simple class. This is the kind in which a particular relationship between two elements is expressed, even although the elements in the 'external world' might be mutually exclusive. For example, 'vitamin C and vitamin B' are two mutually exclusive classes within (let us suppose) the same sub-facet of a dietetics classification. But the theme 'the influence of vitamin C on vitamin B' is not unlikely to occur. In dealing with the themes (classes) of documents, we must be able to deal with subjects drawn from the same or different sub-facets, and the same or different facets, brought together in this kind of relationship, in which the separate elements remain distinct. Examples might include 'the effects of education on social mobility', 'a comparison of English and French education systems,' 'the effects of atmospheric pollution on the incidence of lung disease'. Some of these relationships are subjective (in the eye of the beholder). For example, there is a difference between 'the influence of Chinese upon British pottery designers'

109

in which a 'real world' connection is proposed; and 'a comparison of Chinese and English pottery', in which this relationship is not necessarily proposed. For purposes of documentary classification however, the so called 'complex class' is a manifestation of the fact that at the intellectual (conceptual) level, any connection can be thought about and written about.

To the number of simple and superimposed classes must be added the potential number of complex classes; and although, as stated above, not all elements in a classification are necessarily compatible, the potential existence of complex classes reduces the number of absolute impossibilities: themes more fantastic than 'The influence of Aristotle on the manufacture of custard' can occur.

Buchanan (1976) provides a very useful glossary with clear examples of the various kinds of classes, to which students of classification — confused by the wide variety of terms and the lack of standardisation — should refer. Buchanan divides classes into 'simple' and 'composite'. The former include the 'simple/simple classes' and the 'simple/superimposed classes'; and the latter the 'compound classes' and the 'complex classes' (which are also called 'phase relationship' classes). In this chapter the classes have been referred to respectively as 'simple', 'superimposed', 'compound' and 'complex'. It is ironic, that information retrieval, which is concerned with the standardisation of vocabulary, should itself have a vocabulary which is not absolutely standardised, although there is a high measure of agreement as to concepts.

## PROCEDURES FOR CREATING AN INDEX LANGUAGE

Facet analysis is a powerful method of analysing the themes of documents as a basis for the creation of an index language, whatever type of index language is to be created. However, the analysis usually leads to the creation of a 'faceted scheme'. It is proposed that if the subjects of documents are analysed such that a list of single element classes is produced, the relationship

110

between these elements can relatively easily be seen. If a means is provided for joining these elements at need, then all multi-element subjects can be provided for. In a postcoordinate system the elements are joined by the searcher and in a precoordinate system they are joined by the indexer.

The steps to be taken are the following:-

(1)  Identify the facets and assign classes to them. (Fig. 5:5b)

(2)  Identify sub-facets and assign classes to them. (Fig. 5:5c)

(3)  Identify generic and pseudo-generic relationships within sub-facets. (Fig. 5:5d)

Further steps depend upon how the analysis is to be used, whether for a verbal or non-verbal system and whether for a precoordinate or postcoordinate system.

A useful starting point is the examination of themes of documents, although consultation with users and examination of other index languages might also be necessary. Fig. 5:5 is a 'worked example' based on 20 themes in education. (Notice that some non-content, i.e. non subject categories are included as they almost inevitably must be in all but the simplest schemes). Such categories as 'form of presentation' may have to be considered (e.g. 'encyclopaedias', 'dictionaries', and 'media' such as films).

Facet analysis is an easy procedure if the number of factors to be considered is limited, and if the subject matter is relatively 'concrete'. For example, records of educational performance of pupils may be classed by a number of different characteristics of the student, but these are easy to identify (indeed they will clearly be known by the workers concerned), and it will not be difficult to list classes under age, sex, type of school, examination performance etc. The creation of a 'lasting scheme' for a collec-

111

## Fig. 5:5a
*List of themes to be considered in an*
*analysis of facets for Education*

1. Encyclopaedia of education

2. Dictionary of terms used in education in London (An ILEA publication)

3. Audio-visual materials for the education of adults: techniques for their use

4. Education of females in Asia

5. History of education in Europe

6. Education of exceptional children in France

7. Education of exceptionally intelligent children in Europe

8. Education of educationally sub-normal children in France

9. Adult education in rural areas of India

10. Education in villages of India

11. Education in urban areas of the UK

12. Bibliography of advanced text-books for exceptionally intelligent children

13. [A copy of] a film about the education of adults in rural areas of India, using audio-visual media, including films

14. The education of accountants

15. The education of male nurses

16. History of education

17. History of rural education (education in rural areas)

18. History of rural education in India

19. History of education in India

20. Bibliography of the history of Indian education

Figure 5 : 5b

Facet analysis. Identification of facets. (Note that documentary forms appear twice, as the form and as the subject of the document.)

| *Forms of document* | *Place* | *Educational materials* | *Educands* | |
|---|---|---|---|---|
| Encyclopedias | London | A/V media | Adults | Accountants |
| Dictionaries | Asia | Advanced materials | Females | Males |
| Films | Europe | Text books | Children | Nurses |
| Bibliographs | Rural areas | Films | Exceptional | |
| | India | | Exceptionally | |
| *Points of view* | Villages | | Intelligent | |
| History | Urban areas | | Educationally | |
| | UK | | sub-normal | |
| | France | | | |

Figure 5 : 5c

Facet analysis. Identification of sub-facets.

| *Forms of document* | *Place* | *Educational materials* | *Educands* | |
|---|---|---|---|---|
| (by mode of presentation) | (by boundaries) | (by medium) | (by age) | (by level/need) |
| Encyclopaedias | London | A/V media | Adults | Exceptional |
| Dictionaries | Asia | Films | Children | Exceptionally |
| Bibliographies | India | (by level) | (by sex) | intelligent |
| (by medium) | Europe | Advanced | Females | Educationally |
| Films | France | (by mode of presentation) | Males | sub-normal |
| *Points of view* | UK | Text books | (by occupation) | |
| History | (by use) | | Accountants | |
| | Rural areas | | Nurses | |
| | Villages | | | |
| | Urban areas | | | |

Figure 5 : 5d

Facet analysis. Identification of hierarchies and pseudo-hierarchies within sub-facets. Re-arrangement of classes accordingly.
The hierarchies identified are as follows:-

*Place by boundaries*
Asia
  India
Europe
  France
  UK
    London

*Place by use*
Rural areas
  Villages
Urban areas

*Educational materials*
*(by medium)*
A/V materials
  Films

*Educands by level/need*
Exceptional
  Exceptionally intelligent
  Educationally sub-normal

114

tion or database related to a collection of non-administrative documents, including books, periodicals and other materials, may be more difficult. For instance the worked example shows that some concepts can appear in more than one category (in more than one role), i.e. 'films' as both the subject and the form of the document. The classes 'boys', 'girls', 'men' and 'women' did not appear in the list of themes, but would do so in the real situation. These are examples of 'pre-fabricated classes', of combinations of attributes which are so common as to have virtually 'fused' and to be given special names. But a decision must be made as to whether, for example, 'the education of women' is to be treated as the education of 'adult females' or be given a pigeon hole in its own right. The same will apply to 'teaching techniques in primary schools' — which is when analysed — 'techniques for the teaching of younger children at the elementary stage of education in schools'.

It is obvious that many more themes would have to be considered and many more facets and sub-facets identified for a 'fully worked out' classification scheme for education. For example facets for educational institutions, for 'agents' (e.g. teachers), would have to be provided. *The London education classification* (1974) and *The Bliss bibliographic classification* 2nd edition, Class J, provide examples of 'fully worked out' schemes.

### Facet analysis and systematic order

If the analysis is to be used to produce a 'classification scheme', i.e. a non-verbal system which produces a systematic order of class inclusion, then the following further steps must be taken:-

1. A decision must be made regarding the citation order of facets and sub-facets.

2. A decision must be made regarding the order in which facets and sub-facets are to be listed, (regarding schedule order).

3.　A decision must be made regarding the order in which classes within each sub-facet are to be listed.

4.　A notation must be applied.

## Citation Order

It is assumed that (as is most usual in non-verbal systems especially when used for the arrangement of documents) there will be one place and one place only for each class, in the operational system. This entails deciding whether the most likely use pattern will be for example 'everything to do with the education of females, divided into (for example) 'adult females' and 'child females', or whether the reverse citation order would be most useful. In the worked example, Fig. 5:6, there are one hundred and twenty possible citation orders of facets and (within the educational facet) twenty four possible citation orders of sub-facets.

The citation order determines whether, (for example) books on rural India file after books on India or after books on rural areas; and whether books on monotheistic matriarchal societies file after books on monotheistic societies or after books on matriarchal societies. It determines whether books in the class 'matriarchal societies' are to be scattered or collocated. In Fig.5:2 it is shown that the class 'monotheistic matriarchal societies' is included in two classes. In Fig. 5:2c this is shown as a family tree, the class having two 'parents'; and Fig. 5:2d shows that in one case material on monotheistic societies is scattered and in the other material on matriarchal societies is scattered.

## Schedule Order

The schedule order (as distinct from the citation order) is the order in which classes are listed. It determines whether for example books on India in general file before or after books on rural areas in general; and whether books on monotheistic

116

societies in general file before or after books on matriarchal societies in general. If the including classes are to precede included classes (if general is to precede particular in the scheme as a whole) books on rural areas and books on India should *both* precede books on rural areas of India; and books on monotheistic societies as well as those on matriarchal societies should *both* precede those on monotheistic matriarchal societies. It follows that schedule order should be the reverse of citation order.

Fig. 5:6 shows the results of using schedule order which is the reverse of citation order, and of using one which is the same.

Fig. 5:6
*Schedule and citation orders*

(a)

| | *Citation order*<br>*India — Rural areas* | *Citation order*<br>*Rural areas — India* |
|---|---|---|
| *Schedule/*<br>*citation orders*<br>*reversed* | Rural areas<br>India<br>    — Rural areas | India<br>Rural areas<br>    — India |
| *Schedule/*<br>*citation orders*<br>*the same* | India<br>    — Rural areas<br>Rural areas | Rural areas<br>    — India<br>India |

(b)

| | *Citation order*<br>*Subject — Form* | *Citation order*<br>*Place — Time* |
|---|---|---|
| *Schedule/*<br>*citation orders*<br>*reversed* | General dictionaries<br><br>Chemistry<br>    — Dictionaries | 17th century in<br>general<br>London<br>    — 17th century |
| *Schedule/*<br>*citation orders*<br>*the same* | Chemistry<br>    — Dictionaries<br>General dictionaries | London<br>    — 17th century<br>17th century in<br>general |

117

*Orders in Array*

There are logical and practical reasons why the class 'rural areas' of India' should follow the class India and the class 'rural areas'; and logical and practical reasons why the class 'mammals' should follow the class 'vertebrates'. As demonstrated there are also reasons why combinable classes should be listed in particular orders.

Classes in array however are not in theory combinable and there is no clear logic which will determine in every case the order of listing. An array of classes is a set of 'equal classes', which are mutually exclusive and equal in ranking. For example, although there is good reason for 'Bombay' to follow 'India' in a schedule of classes, no reason exists for India to follow or to precede Pakistan. In such cases the order can be arbitrarily determined or an alphabetical order of names can be used. There may be a 'canonical' or 'expected' order: perhaps India should precede Pakistan as having 'taken over' the name of the sub-continent; perhaps Oxford should precede Cambridge because this is the way English people usually do cite them (the Oxford and Cambridge Boat Race). If any logic does underly the order of classes in array it is the logic of the intermediate superordinate class, and the logic which decrees that what comes first should be cited first; primary education is listed before secondary education, 17th century before 18th century, and invertebrates before vertebrates (in an evolutionary order).

The logic of the intermediate class is that which shows that classes in array are not necessarily equal. Like any group of siblings 'a' may be more like 'b' than like 'c'; and 'b' belongs to two intermediate classes: that which includes 'a' and that which includes 'c'. In a classification of zoology 'amphibia' usually come between 'pisces' and 'aves' (between 'aquatic' and 'terrestrial animals'). There is more likelihood of a book being written about pisces and amphibia (about an intermediate class to which both belong) than about pisces and mammalia. The idea of an intermediate class is

118

more clearly shown within space and time continua: there is more likelihood of a book being written about the 17th and 18th centuries together than about the 17th and the 19th; and about Northumberland and Durham than about Durham and Surrey. It might be impossible to provide in anticipation for every possible gradation of classes (and indeed may not be necessary). The Universal Decimal Classification provides for the *insertion* of intermediate classes by the use of the oblique stroke so that books on pisces and amphibia would be given the class mark 597/598 (pisces/amphibia), a device which would be less conveniently used if the order in array did not follow an 'evolutionary principle' in this case and implicitly recognise the existence of an intermediate class. The ability of a scheme to accept new subjects is in part dependent upon the existence of logical array orders. This is shown in Fig. 5:7:

Fig. 5:7

*Orders in array*

Fig. 5:7a shows an array of countries in alphabetical order of their names. Fig. 5:7b shows the same list of countries in an order of spatial contiguity to which intermediate classes can be added.

| (5:7a) | 7 | Trade | (5:7b) | 7 | Trade |
|--------|-----|-----------|--------|-----|-----------|
| | | | | | .... 701 |
| | 71 | Belgium | | 71 | Belgium |
| | 72 | Denmark | | 72 | Holland |
| | 73 | Finland | | 73 | Luxembourg |
| | | | | | .... 737 |
| | 74 | Holland | | 74 | Denmark |
| | 75 | Luxembourg | | 75 | Finland |
| | 76 | Norway | | 76 | Norway |
| | 77 | Sweden | | 77 | Sweden |

In 5:7b the classes 701 'Low Countries' could be inserted between 7 and 71, and the class 737 'Scandinavia' might be inserted between 73 and 74. In UDC-type notation these classes would be designated 71/73 and 74/77 respectively.

**119**

## Precoordination and Postcoordination. Enumerative and Synthetic Systems

In a postcoordinate system the problem of citation order will not arise, since items will be indexed under *each* of the elements and the searcher can search for the required elements in any order. Most precoordinate systems are however, verbal systems (using words as index terms not in a systematic order) and if systematic order is to be used the choice in practice is between enumeration and synthesis, i.e. are all specifiable multi-element subjects to be listed in advance or are they to be synthesised by the indexer according to the rules of the scheme? In practice (and for reasons already discussed) enumeration in anticipation is impracticable and the scheme will almost certainly be a 'faceted' or 'analytico-synthetic scheme', i.e. the elements are enumerated with rules as to how they are to be combined. Fig. 5:8 shows an extract from an analytico-synthetic scheme and demonstrates how class marks can be combined. It is obvious from this example that a notation has been applied to the scheme.

## Notation

An ordinal notation will be required in order to 'mechanise the order' by providing a point of reference. (It would otherwise be necessary to refer to classes by their names and to state verbally their place in the arrangement). The notation must consist primarily of symbols which have a known ordinal value (i.e. of either letters or numbers or both). UDC and other classification schemes make use of non-ordinal symbols (e.g. colons, oblique strokes) in order to extend the range of the notation: to introduce in effect further series of digits. The ordinal value of these symbols must be specially learnt however. and this increases the complexities of the system for the user.

A pure notation is one in which only one series of digits is used.

A mixed notation is one in which more than one series is used. Mixtures can consist of:

1. Letters and numbers.

2. Different 'allographs' of the same symbols (upper- and lower- case letters, Roman and Arabic numerals).

3. As in the case of UDC ordinal digits 'multiplied' by the use of arbitrary signs (e.g. (43) "43" – 43 etc.).

4. Any combinations of the above.

Mixed notations have the disadvantage that the relationship between the series must be learnt: does (43) file before or after "43", B file before 2, and A file before a? Notation should preferably be sayable' and for this reason the significant use of different allographs is inconvenient ('AbBc = upper-case A, lower-case B, upper-case B, lower-case C').

The notation can be integral or fractional. An integral notation consists of whole numbers or their analogy; a fractional notation consists of fractions or their analogy. Integral notations are almost invariably based upon numbers; but it will be seen that alphabetical order of words is in effect a fraction notation. Fig. 5.8 shows a fraction and integral notation; and a mixed and pure notation.

121

## Fig. 5:8
### Notation structure

| (a) | *Fraction notations* | | (b) | *Integral notation* |
|---|---|---|---|---|
| 1 | A | | | 1 |
| 12 | AB | | | 2 |
| 126 | ABF | | | 12 |
| 2 | B | | | 24 |
| 24 | BD | | | 126 |

(all the above are pure notations)

| (c) | *Mixed notation* | (d) | *Mixed notation* |
|---|---|---|---|
| | A2 | | L 64 |
| | AB | | L 72 |
| | AB6 | | L 642 |
| | B3G | | LX 70 |
| | BC | | |

(Fraction notation)                          (Integral notation)

In (c) numbers file before letters, and the double series in effect runs 0 . . . . . 9 , A − Z. In (d) the two series are kept in separate blocks respectively at the beginning and end of class mark. This is not confusing to the user as is the system in (c).

The fraction notation is more 'hospitable' (as could be seen in Fig. 5:7), since an infinite series can be inserted between any two class marks. Between '1' and '2' as integers no numbers can be inserted. However, (also as demonstrated in Fig. 5:7) the insertion of new classes may destroy the 'hierarchical structure' of the notation. Any notation indicates relationships in so far as it can be assumed that two classes which are near each other may be related. (This is not the case with alphabetical order of words:

'cats' and 'catalogues' are not related). The notation may however be used to express relationships with more precision. A hierarchical notation is one which expresses relationships of class inclusion by the addition of digits at each step of a division (analogous to the addition of 'differences' in logical division). It follows that only fraction notations can be hierarchical. An expressive notation is one which is capable of indicating the category of concept represented. For example in UDC 'time' is always expressed by a number within quotation marks, and quotation marks always express 'time'. Expressive notations (and to a lesser extent hierarchical ones) have something in common with non-ordinal codes such as chemical formulae and other special communication codes which enable the users to construct messages unambiguously and make communication easy. But although notations must be totally unambiguous they need not be either expressive or hierarchical. However they *must* express order.

Fig. 5:9 shows examples of expressive and hierarchical notation. Note that a notation can be both expressive and hierarchical, but in the examples this is not so.

Fig. 5:9
*Expressive and hierarchical notation*

| Hierarchical (Non-expressive) | | Expressive (Non-hierarchical) | | |
|---|---|---|---|---|
| 9 | Law | 527 | Law | |
| 92 | Criminal | 6 | Criminal | |
| 921 | English | 6(4) | English | |
| 921.2 | 20th century | 6(4)'19' | 20th | century |
| 922 | Scottish | 6(82) | Scottish | |
| 922.2 | 20th century | 6(82)'19' | 20th | century |

For the hierarchical notation 'equal' classes have equal numbers of digits, and the lower classes in the hierarchy have the higher number of digits. This is not so in the case of the non-hierarchical notation. In the expressive notation the concepts of place and time are uniformly represented.

Fraction notations almost always have hierarchical elements; although the hierarchical structure is not always consistently maintained.

If pieces of notation are to be joined together *ad hoc* some mechanism for distinguishing between the individual class marks is necessary. Provided hierarchical qualities are not required the device known as 'retroactive notation' can be used. For this it is assumed that synthesis is always 'retroactive' (i.e. that earlier classes are added to later classes, or − in other words − that schedule order is the reverse of citation order). This is reflected notationally. In the schedules a class symbol cannot be 'divided' by a symbol earlier in the sequence than itself: B can be divided by B - Z; L by L - Z and Z only by Z. Fig. 5:10 is a demonstration.

Fig. 5:10<br>
Retroactive notation

| B | Europe | M | Education |
|---|---|---|---|
| BC | UK | MN | Primary |
| BCD | Great Britain | MNO | Infants |

'Primary education in Great Britain' is synthesised by direct addition of the class mark BCD to the class mark MN. There is no possibility that the class 'Primary education, MN' (as enumerated) will be subdivided by 'B'. 'Primary education in Great Britain' = MNBCD.

Retroactive notation is an effective way of achieving a pure notation without any obtrusive 'synthetic devices'. In effect it can be used with letter notations only, since the narrow base of a number notation would result in the 9th class or division being divisible only by 9. An additional disadvantage is that the citation order is fixed, there being no opportunity to change it without disrupting the whole notational system.

Retroactive notation is effectively used in the *Bliss bibliographic classification* 2nd ed. (mentioned in Chapter 4). The designers of simple 'home-made' schemes would however be well advised to use the simplest kind of synthetic device, i.e. a single 'punctuation mark' (e.g. colon or oblique stroke) to separate the component parts of class marks. This is not because other devices are not effective (they may be considerably more effective) but because they are considerably more difficult to devise. The example of a classification scheme given in Fig. 5:11 uses a pure letter notation (fractionally) and an oblique stroke to separate the component parts of a class mark. Although the citation order is 'retroactive', it can be changed in any particular operational system without disrupting the whole notational structure.

**The Index to the Classed File**

A file arranged in systematic order (a 'classed' file) will, unless the classes are very few, require an alphabetical index to the subjects listed. The alphabetical index serves the primary function of 'pointing' to the place in the file where particular subjects may be found (the file not being in self-evident order). The index usually performs a secondary function: that of bringing together concepts which have been separated by the operation of the classification scheme. Thus in the example the concept 'rural areas' is scattered since it appears in a facet which is low in the citation order. It can be said that the alphabetical index provides an alternative route or alternative citation order. For example the subject 'rural areas of India' can be approached by two routes, of which the systematic file provides only one: 'India – rural areas'.

There are two kinds of problem encountered in the construction of alphabetical subject indexes. The first is the problem of determining what (in verbal terms) the concept shall be called ('rural areas' 'countryside' : . . ) and providing alternative terms on the

## Fig. 5:11a
### *Extract from a supposed classification scheme for Education*

Citation order:     Z . . . . . . . . . A

| | | | |
|---|---|---|---|
| B | *FORMS (PRESENTATION)* | G | *EDUCATIONAL MATERIALS* |
| BC | Encyclopaedias | | *(PRESENTATION)* |
| BD | Dictionaries | GH | Text books |
| BE | Bibliographies | | |
| | | H | *EDUCATIONAL MEDIA* |
| C | *MEDIA* | HJ | A/V media |
| CD | A/V media | HJK | Films |
| CDE | Films | | |
| | | J | *EDUCATIONAL MATERIALS* |
| D | *POINTS OF VIEW* | | *(LEVEL)* |
| DE | History | JK | Elementary |
| | | JL | Advanced |
| E | *PLACE (USE)* | | |
| EF | Rural areas | K | *EDUCANDS (SEX)* |
| EFG | Villages | KL | Male |
| EG | Urban areas | KM | Female |
| | | | |
| F | *PLACE (BOUNDARIES)* | L | *EDUCANDS (AGE)* |
| FG | Asia | LM | Children |
| FGH | India | LN | Adults |
| FH | Europe | | |
| FHJ | UK | M | *EDUCANDS (ABILITY)* |
| FHJK | England | MN | Exceptional |
| FHJKL | London | MNO | Exceptionally intelligent |
| FHK | France | MNO | Educationally sub-normal |
| | | | |
| | | N | *EDUCANDS (OCCUPATION)* |
| | | NO | Accountants |
| | | NQ | Nurses |

Fig. 5:11b
*Themes classed by the scheme and arranged in filing order*

| | |
|---|---|
| BC | Encyclopaedia of education |
| DE | History of education |
| EF/DE | History of education in rural areas |
| FGH/DE | History of education in India |
| FGH/DE/BE | Bibliography of the history of education in India |
| FGH/EF/DE | History of rural education in India |
| FGH/EFG | Education in Indian villages |
| FH/DE | History of education in Europe |
| FHJ/EG | Education in urban areas of the UK |
| FHJKL/BD | Dictionary of education in London |
| KM/FG | Education of females in Asia |
| LN/FGH/EF | Education of adults in rural areas of India |
| LN/HJ | A/V materials for the education of adults |
| LN/HJ/FGH/EF/CDE | The use of A/V media including films for the education of adults in rural areas of India (This item is itself a film) |
| MN/LM/FHK | The education of exceptional children in France |
| MNO/LM/FHK | The education of exceptionally intelligent children in France |
| MNO/LM/JL/GH/BE | Bibliography of advanced textbooks for the education of exceptionally intelligent children |
| MNP/LM/FHK | Education of educationally sub-normal children in France |
| NO | Education of accountants |
| NQ/KL | Education of male nurses |

Note that in Fig. 5.11 the notation is fractional and that in effect the alphabetical order is a 'word-by-word' order, each unit separated by a stroke representing a word. It should also be noted that the citation order chosen is not necessarily uniformly useful. It might well be that – in respect of India, but not in respect of the UK, for example – the collocation of *all* materials on rural education would be more useful than the separation of adult and non-adult education.

verbal plane. This problem is common to all verbal systems, and will be dealt with later in the Chapter. The alphabetical subject index is in effect a translating dictionary which leads the searcher from the language he knows (a verbal language) to one he doesn't know (the notational language).

The second problem is that of structuring the index. Basically both problems can be referred to one general principle: given that the piece of notation is a term in an 'unknown language' representing a concept, the alphabetical subject index must provide routes to this 'unknown word', beginning with a word which is already known to the user. Structurally the index can take a number of forms. The forms dealt with here are the 'simple index', the 'chain index' and the 'PRECIS index'.

*The simple index*

The simple index is a list of·words representing the concepts in the scheme, with an indiscriminate indication of where they may be found. The searcher must look under *each* of the class marks given in order to find the particular aspect required, or use the index as a postcoordinate index, i.e. look for *each* of two or more concepts and match the entries. This is demonstrated in Fig. 5:12.

Fig. 5:12 *A simple subject index*

| *INDIA* | FGH/DE | *RURAL AREAS* | EF/DE |
| | FGH/DE/BE | | FGH/EF/DE |
| | FGH/EF/DE | | LN/FGH/EF |
| | FGH/EFG | | LN/HJ/FGH/EF/CDE |
| | LN/FGH/EF | | |
| | LN/HJ/FGH/EF/CDE | | |

The searcher looking for material on India must examine all the class marks in Column 1. If what is required is 'rural areas of India', Column 2 can be examined and the two lists compared.

128

The simple index is obviously inconvenient for use in a very large file, and particularly so for use as an index to a collection (on the shelves). It has fewer inconveniences and is certainly economical when used for a small file.

*Chain indexes*

In a so-called 'relative index' (invented by Melvil Dewey) each concept is placed in context of its superordinate class. A method of routinely generating relative indexes was developed by S R Ranganathan. This method is based on 'chain procedure' and results in a 'chain index'.

A chain is an ordered set of superordinate-subordinate classes. Thus from Fig. 5:11 we can see that the class 'education of adults in rural areas of India' is at the bottom of a chain:

|  |  |
|---|---|
| Adults | LN |
| India | LN/FGH |
| *Rural areas* | *LN/FGH/EF* |

An index entry for this class is made by reversing and verbalising the chain:

Rural areas:   India:   Adult education   LN/FGH/EF

Provision is made for searchers who might enter the system at other points, by making additional entries under each successive 'bottom link':

India:   Adult education   LN/FGH
Adult education   LN

It is assumed that, for example, the person 'entering the system' at 'India' (India – Rural areas – Adult education), will find the appropriate class mark for 'India – Adult education' then go downwards to the specific class mark required. It is further assumed

**129**

that an item dealing with 'adult education in rural areas of India' is relevant to an inquiry on 'adult education in India' and therefore an index entry under the superordinate subject is justified.

There is an obvious disadvantage to chain indexing: that only one index entry is 'coextensive' with the subject sought, and only one permutation is provided. The searcher looking for 'adult education in rural areas of India' who looks for it as 'Rural areas: India: Adult education' is the privileged user. There is a considerable advantage, however, in that (for example) once the class 'adult education in rural areas of India' has been indexed two other classes are also indexed. As the collection or file grows so less alphabetical indexing must be done.

*Permuted and cycled indexes*

The alternative to simple indexes and chain indexes is some form of permuted index, in which entries are made under all or some of the permutations of the terms present in the subject statement. Full permutation is likely to be expensive, and indeed if there are more than five elements to be permuted, may in practice be beyond the intellectual capacity of an indexer (computers would be required). Moreover, full permutation is likely to produce a number of ambiguous, or at any rate useless, elements. A number of devices have been suggested for reducing the number of permutations to an acceptable and useful level, and for selecting the best permutations. One such method is that of *cycling* (KWIC indexes — see Chapter 4 — are cycled indexes). In a cycled index each significant term is brought into the entry position, but all the terms retain their positions in relation to each other. However, cycling will produce meaningless entries if the primary 'string' of terms is not in a useful order. Fig. 5:13 gives, firstly, a selection of permutations of five elements (from a possible total of 120), all of which have an element of ambiguity, and are less than maximally useful. Fig. 5:14 gives the same elements permuted as for a cycled index. In the first case the original or primary 'string' is in a useful order, and in the second what is suggested as a non-useful order.

Fig. 5:13

*A permuted index*

Selection of *non-useful* permutations from a total of 120 possible permutations.

The subject is: *Recruitment* of *teachers* for *schools* in *rural areas* of *India*.
The supposed class mark is XYZ.

1. India: Recruitment: Rural areas: Teachers: Schools   XYZ
2. Schools: Recruitment: Rural areas: Teachers: India   XYZ
3. Recruitment: Rural areas: Teachers: India: Schools   XYZ
4. India: Recruitment: Schools: Rural areas: Teachers   XYZ

Fig. 5:14

*A cycled index*

(a) Subject as for Fig. 5:13.

Primary string: India: Rural areas: Schools: Teachers: Recruitment

1. India: Rural areas: Schools: Teachers: Recruitment   XYZ
2. Recruitment: India: Rural areas: Schools: Teachers   XYZ
3. Teachers: Recruitment: India: Rural areas: Schools   XYZ
4. Schools: Teachers: Recruitment: India: Rural areas   XYZ
5. Rural areas: Schools: Teachers: Recruitment: India   XYZ

(b) Subject as for Fig. 5:13

Primary string:
*India: Recruitment: Schools: Rural areas: Teachers*

1. India: Recruitment: Schools: Rural areas: Teachers   XYZ
2. Teachers: India: Recruitment: Schools: Rural areas   XYZ
3. Rural areas: Teachers: India: Recruitment: Schools   XYZ
4. Schools: Rural areas: Teachers: India: Recruitment   XYZ
5. Recruitment: Schools: Rural areas: Teachers: India   XYZ

131

It can be seen that if the primary 'string' of terms is in a useful order, as in Fig. 5:14(a), it is more likely to produce a set of useful entries than if, as in Fig. 5:14(b), the primary string is in a non-useful and illogical order. Even so the entries in Fig. 5:14(a) are not all maximally useful. For example although there is a linguistic logic in the entry: 'Recruitment: (India: Rural areas: Schools: Teachers)', the searcher is unlikely to perceive the logic, and would not expect to find 'Recruitment' followed by 'India'. The problem is one of linear order. In this entry 'Teachers' is separated from 'Recruitment' (although properly placed next to 'Schools'), and 'India' appears to have a direct relationship with 'Recruitment' (which it hasn't). 'Teachers' has a two-handed relationship with 'Schools' on the one hand and with 'Recruitment' on the other. This is shown in three out of the five entries and not shown in two.

*PRECIS Indexing*

A PRECIS index is essentially a cycled index. PRECIS indexing is a method of establishing a primary string of terms in an appropriate order (in PRECIS the primary string is called 'the string'), and of converting the linear order into a two-dimensional order such that whenever a two-handed relationship occurs it can be shown: 'Teachers' can hold hands with *both* 'Recruitment' and 'Schools'.

This last is achieved by the use of a two-line format. In a PRECIS index the problem of a two-handed relationship is dealt with as shown below:-

Teachers.    Schools

Recruitment

Recruitment. Teachers. Schools

Terms in the second line are successively moved into the first line. Fig. 5:15 shows a PRECIS string and the resultant entries.

132

Fig. 5.15
*PRECIS string and entries*

*The string:*

India

Rural areas

Schools

Teachers

Recruitment


India
>   Rural areas.  Schools.  Teachers.  Recruitment

Rural areas.  India
>   Schools.  Teachers.  Recruitment

Schools.  Rural areas.  India
>   Teachers.  Recruitment

Teachers.  Schools.  Rural areas.  India
>   Recruitment

Recruitment.  Teachers.  Schools.  Rural areas.  India


Obviously the efficacy of PRECIS depends upon the 'string'. In PRECIS indexing recognition is given to the fact that in any set of terms representing a theme, there are likely to be sub-sets of more closely related items. Thus, in the example, 'Recruitment' is more closely related to 'Teachers' than to 'Schools'. In the PRECIS system the principle underlying the ordering of the basic string is based on the general principle that the order should reflect closeness of relationships, and on the special principle that closeness of relationships is dependent upon context. The order of items in a PRECIS string is an order *not* of importance but of context dependency.

Thus it can be established that India includes the rural areas; that the schools are in the rural areas, and the teachers in the schools; and it is the teachers *not* the schools or 'India' which are recruited. The order of context dependence is thus the order given for the string in Fig. 5:15. Here it can also be seen that apart from the first and last terms in the string all terms have a two-handed relationship.

PRECIS indexing is a system for providing a grammar or syntax to index languages; and it has been suggested that the PRECIS grammar is a 'deep-structure grammar' which is applicable to indexing in any language. For example, the 'surface structure' of English permits both a 'passive' and 'active' construction to describe the same situation: 'teachers manage schools' and 'schools are managed by teachers'. In PRECIS indexing this active/passive distinction is made without reference to the surface form or structure of language. For example 'schools' becomes 'object of transitive action' and 'teachers' becomes 'agent of transitive action'.

Although by no means essential to the use of PRECIS the codes which are used by the British National Bibliography provide useful reminders of term relationships. Fig. 5:16 gives a list of the most important codes:-

Fig. 5:16 PRECIS codes

| | |
|---|---|
| 0 | Location |
| 1 | Key system. Objective of transitive action. Agent of intransitive action. |
| 2 | Action |
| 3 | Agent of transitive action |
| (p) | Part. (A 'p' coding can be 'interposed' at any point in the string). |
| 0 | India |
| (p) | Rural areas |
| 1 | Schools |
| (p) | Teachers |
| 2 | Recruitment |

(This coding will produce the results given in Fig. 5:15)

PRECIS is easily manipulatable by computer. The intellectual effort is that of creating the initial PRECIS string.

## Verbal Indexing Systems

PRECIS and chain indexing were developed primarily to provide alphabetical subject indexes to files arranged in systematic (classificatory) order. However both (but particularly PRECIS) can be used where the alphabetical system is employed independently. The alphabetical index to the systematic file is only one type of verbal indexing system; but in common with other verbal indexing systems it must be based not only on a structure but on a selection of terms to be used. This is equivalent to saying that it must have a vocabulary as well as a grammar. Only the grammar has been dealt with so far.

Verbal systems may be classed according to whether a natural or artificial language is used (see Chapter 4); according to whether they are used as subsidiaries to index a systematic file or are used independently for e.g. alphabetical subject catalogues; according to whether the index language used is enumerative or synthetic (that is to say according to whether it consists of a list of terms representing both single and multi-element subjects, equivalent to an enumerative classification; or whether in common with an analytico-synthetic classification, the language consists primarily of a list of 'simple terms' — the latter type commonly called a thesaurus).

An example of an enumerative listing is Library of Congress *Subject Headings*. Examples of thesauri include the *INSPEC thesaurus* and *Thesaurofacet* (see Chapter 4).

The British National Bibliography has built up a list of terms to be used in its 'PRECIS index'; and this would incorporate decisions as to whether — irrespective of the structuring of the entries — 'rural areas' is to be called 'countryside' or 'rural areas'

**135**

and whether or not there should be a 'see' reference from the non-preferred term.    Most thesauri are used for postcoordinate systems. When, as in the case of the British National Bibliography, they are to be used for precoordinate systems they must include a grammar: i.e. a set of rules regarding 'citation order'. As could be seen in the case of PRECIS these rules almost necessarily relate to basic principles and meaning, and are not easy to reduce to simple formulae such as is possible in the case of classification schemes, (e.g. citation order Z. . . . . A).

*Problems of vocabulary and syntax in Verbal Indexing Systems*

As already demonstrated in Chapter 4 natural language systems use terms derived from text or title and no attempt is made to relate these terms conceptually. The problems of using natural language are related to the following characteristics of language.

*Homonymy.*    The use of the same 'name' for different concepts. (A homograph is a homonym in respect of the written language. Thus 'reed' and 'read' are homographs.    Index languages are concerned primarily though not exclusively with homographs).

A 'true' homonym has a set of totally unrelated meanings (although etymologically there may be a remote connection). A 'quasi-homonym' has a set of related meanings usually as the result of a 'spread' from a central meaning.  The phenomenon of 'spread' is called polysemia.  Homonymy may occur at the word, the sub-word and the phrase level.  Fig. 5:17 shows different kinds of homonyms.

*Synonymy.*    The use of more than one term for the same concept. 'True' synonyms are terms which are interchangeable in every circumstance (or nearly every circumstance), the interchangeability being both stylistic, and semantic. True synonyms are of very rare occurrence.  In English the terms 'pail' and 'bucket' approach the condition of true synonymy;   nevertheless at the stylistic level we are more likely to say 'It's pouring buckets of

136

*Homonyms*

*'True' homonyms*

    Fine (Money) — Fine (Grand)

    Spell (a word) — Spell (Period of time)

    Sound (Acoustic) — Sound (Passage of water) — Sound (Healthy)

        At sub-word level:-

            Man*hood*  Hood (Headgear)

*Quasi-homonyms*

    Breast (Physiology) — Breast (Chimney) — Breast (Coalface)

    Party (Convivial gathering) — Party (Political)

        At sub-word level:-

            *Un*do  and *Un*tie as distinct from *Un*feminine and
            *Un*seemly

*Phrasal homonyms*

    Usually quasi-homonyms and often derived from metaphor:

    Light fingers (Thieving fingers) — Light fingers (delicate fingers)

    Derived informally and meaning made clear by context:

    English literature (British English literature) — English Literature
    (Literature in the English language)

water (rain)' than to say 'it's pouring pails of water'. The most common kinds of 'true synonyms' are the spelling synonyms, e.g. as between British and American spelling (labour — labor; centre — center). Different regional varieties of a language otherwise provide instances of near-synonyms: terms which can sometimes though not always be used interchangeably (e.g. as between

American and English: tube/subway; flat/apartment; public school/private school). Other examples of near-synonyms include alternative technical and popular terms, as for example: $H_2O$/ water. (Note that even 'technically' it is not usual to drink $H_2O$ and the term 'water' as distinct from $H_2O$ is a homonym for urine and for a stream).

*Morphology and syntax.* A particular form of synonymy is that by which different forms of words express basically the same idea; and that by which different forms of phrases express the same idea. Morphology relates to the forms of words; syntax to the forms of phrases and sentences. For example, the two phrases 'tigers eat meat' and 'the tiger eats meat' would in most contexts be regarded as expressing *exactly* the same idea. 'Tigers' and 'tiger' 'eat' and 'eats' are in this case morphological synonyms. The two phrases are 'syntactic synonyms'. In general language such synonymy is very common. In many cases the synonymy is not absolute. there may be slight variants of meaning and certainly significant variants in style. Such variants are irrelevant in index languages, for which —without the help of context — the difference between 'the singing of the dolphin' and 'the song of the dolphin' and 'the dolphin singing' must necessarily be blurred and therefore ignored.

However, although in the examples given the variants would express — for purposes of indexing — basically the same idea, the converse can occur. The morphological difference between 'water' and 'waters' is vital to the meaning of the term 'water from the tap' and 'by the waters of Babylon'.

In all languages the relationships between words is made clear by one or more of the following devices.-

1. Word order: Philosophy of history — History of philosophy.

**138**

2. The use of 'function' words (also called 'relational' or 'non-content' words): Trains *from* Blackpool *to* Brighton; Philosophy *in* history — Philosophy *of* history.

3. Morphological variations (inflections): 'the government of France' can become 'France's government'.


In English word order and function words are more important than inflections. (Despite the confusion of word forms 'me love he' would probably be taken to mean that 'me' is the loving one; word order taking precedence over word forms in the conveyance of meaning).

*Context dependence.*   The ambiguities of language can often be resolved by context, which may be the context of situation or the linguistic context (context of words) or both.   For example, a prospective bride entering a 'bridal shop' and asking for a 'train' is (by the context of situation) assumed to be asking for a type of garment;   but in case this is not clear she might ask for a 'satin train' or a 'lace train', so that by the context of words it is apparent that 'trains' as means of transport are not under discussion.   The term 'express' (in common with the term 'train') is a homonym with several distinct, and several less distinct, meanings. In one usage it has the generalised meaning of 'fast' or 'non-stop', which will be made explicit in the combination 'express train'. However, the precise meaning of 'I will go by express' and 'I will send it by express' depends upon the context of situation.

*Classificatory relationships.*   Linguistic symbols are 'arbitrary' in the sense that there is no necessary relationship of likeness between the symbol (e.g. 'the word') and the thing it represents. The same 'object' can be represented by different words in different languages, each society operating according to an unconscious consensus about 'how things shall be called'.   There are strict rules in all languages as to how units of meaning shall be put together to form more complex symbolic representations, and indeed the rule about 'how things shall be called' are equally strict. For example, English speakers are in a sense not 'allowed' to call a song a *chanson*' nor to express the continued action of singing by placing the particle 'ing' *before* the word 'sing'. All English speakers will usually place the adjective before the noun, to say for example 'parliamentary privilege' rather than 'privilege parliamentary'. However, even at the synthetic level the meanings may be arbitrary. In the case of the term 'parliamentary privilege' the English speaker will probably know the arbitrarily assigned meanings of the terms 'parliament', 'parliamentary' and 'privilege', but there is an additional arbitrary meaning to be learnt: 'parliamentary privilege' has a highly specialised meaning which is not absolutely deducible from the meanings of its component parts. In language the 'whole' is not always equivalent to the sum of the parts.

Moreover, words — considered as units of meaning — do not reliably carry information about the nature of the concept they represent nor about its class relationships. In a formulaic language such as that of chemistry, and in index languages consisting of expressive and hierarchical notations, deductions can be made about the category of concepts represented and about their relationship. For example, in 'UDC language' it can fairly certainly be deduced that '621' (whatever it means) is a subdivision of '62' (whatever that means); and that certainly any numeral within quotation marks relates to time. These kinds of deduction cannot be made reliably in naturally developed languages: there is nothing in the word 'cub' to indicate that it is a kind of young animal, nor in the word 'house' to indicate that it is a building. Attempts to create totally logical and 'expressive' language have succeeded only in so far as the language has had limited application, and has lacked the subtlety and flexibility of naturally acquired languages (index languages are an example).

Two further characteristics of language which must be considered in the creation of index languages are firstly the fact that in naturally acquired languages the focal concept (the concept about which a statement is made), does not necessarily occupy the prime position in an utterance. In 'history of England', for example, the focal concept 'England' is last in the string of words. Secondly, the degree of 'semantic complexity' represented by a single structural unit in language varies from unit to unit; as does conversely the complexity of the structure needed to express particular concepts. For example, the word 'meat' is a structural unit in language which represents 'food derived from the flesh of animals'. No such convenient portmanteau word exists for 'food containing a high level of protein'; nor indeed for food derived from animals to include not only flesh, but bones, blood, milk and eggs'.

*The need for index languages based on natural language*

However, index languages based on natural language are essential to all but the most rudimentary information retrieval system, whether they are used in the main file or (as already discussed) as the 'translating dictionary' or index to the main file. As already mentioned in Chapter 1 all normal human beings learn to speak the 'natural language' of their society; and this natural language is a principal means of 'interpreting the world'. It is the only means of approaching an information retrieval system, the searcher consciously or unconsciously formulating the search question in terms of the 'natural language'. The 'natural language' file may or may not be based on a 'natural index language'. The natural index language derives its terms from text or title, with minimum modification. In other verbal index languages an attempt is made to remove some of the inconsistencies of language and make it more suitable for the purposes of indexing; and an index language which uses words but uses them according to rules peculiar to the index language itself is an 'artificial index language'.

141

## Necessary characteristics of an index language

An index language is a language of order, of signposts, and of labels. It must determine the relative position of things in a store (of items on a list); it must 'point' the searcher from where he stands (from what he understands) to where he wants to go (to what he wants to find out); and must ensure that the items are recognisable. In effect, the index language is a language of 'headings'. Headings must be brief, and must be comprehensible in a context-free environment, (and of course index languages must also have an ordinal value).

The index language need not be capable of expressing subtle differentiations, and indeed no context-free language would be capable of doing so. It should, however, be free of ambiguities. Hence, although the difference between 'education' and 'training' may be a real difference and important as in 'training of librarians' and 'education of librarians', the difference may be evident only within a whole text, and indeed usage may idiosyncratically vary between author and author. In such a case an index language may treat 'education' and training' as synonymous , or may create a compound general term 'education and training'. The removal of some of the refinements of language, while it leads to less precision in language, may paradoxically lead to greater accuracy, since there is considerably less likelihood of 'disagreement' as to definitions and instances of particular concepts.

## Vocabulary control in verbal index languages

The 'normalisation' or 'standardisation' of language for purposes of indexing takes its extreme form in the notational systems already described. At another extreme the so-called 'natural index languages' are subject only to the selection of key terms or content words from text or title; the idiosyncracies of language are accepted, the compensation being simplicity of input, and the possibility that terms chosen are those likely to be used by the searcher, since they occur in the literature with which she may be

142

familiar. The requirement of comprehensibility is usually met. However, no help is given to the user who chooses the 'wrong' term, and no help in leading her to related classes.

In controlled verbal languages content words are used as index terms, but these are not necessarily drawn from text or title. Homonyms are explained, and usually one of a set of synonyms is chosen as a 'preferred term' or 'descriptor' under which items are indexed. References are made from the other terms:-

|  | (Theatres (Surgery) |
| Homonyms | ( |
|  | (Theatres (Drama) |

|  | (Playwrights |
| Synonyms | ( |
|  | ( *see* Dramatists |

Given that an index language is not intended to and indeed cannot reproduce the subtleties of the general natural language the problem of 'synonym control' is that of deciding which terms are to be regarded formally as synonyms, and which of these are to be preferred terms, (the term under which items are to be indexed). Sets of terms which would not be regarded as synonymous in the general language include those which have a large area of overlapping meaning (further education/higher education) those which lie along a continuum (heat/cold); technical/popular terms (ornithology/bird watching) and sets of derivative forms (harvests/harvesting). In choosing the preferred term it is usual to choose the broader term if such a term can be distinguished, e.g. 'ornithology' rather than 'bird watching'.

The 'syntax' of a verbal index language has been exemplified in the grammar of PRECIS, in which a number of different terms are brought together to form what is in effect a sentence. Whether or not a grammar is necessary may depend upon whether there is a single 'word' to represent a semantically complex subject. For example, if there were no single word to represent 'meat' then the concept would be represented by more than one word and a decision as to syntax would be necessary. 'Meat' might be express-ed by the pair of words 'flesh food' which could be changed syntactically to 'food, flesh' or 'food from flesh'. There is, as it happens, no single word in English for 'animal-derived foods' in general, so that in this case a decision as to syntax must be made.

Thing/kind relationships are usually expressed in English by adjective and noun in that order; and in indexing it is common to invert the order. The majority of syntactical problems do not arise from the thing/kind relationship, however, but from inter-facet relationships exemplified by the theme damage to agricul-ture by floods'. The PRECIS-type syntax would produce the following entries, and in this case one entry has been chosen as the preferred entry:-

AGRICULTURE

Damage by floods

DAMAGE. AGRICULTURE

By floods

*see* AGRICULTURE

Damage by floods

FLOODS

Damage to agriculture

*see*

AGRICULTURE

Damage by floods

In a postcoordinate system syntax becomes almost irrelevant since, without destroying the simplicity of the system, syntax cannot be introduced. The disadvantages of this include accept-ance of the fact that, for instance, materials on the philosophy of history will be retrieved in response to a request for information on the history of philosophy.

A thesaurus is a list of verbal terms, usually in alphabetical order, usually representing simple classes and with indications as to the relationships between the classes. If the thesaurus is to be used for a precoordinate system instructions as to how the terms are to be combined must be included (there must be rules of syntax). If it is to be used in a postcoordinate system these rules are not necessary. For postcoordinate systems the thesaurus is itself used by the searcher, who consults it before searching the file. In precoordinate systems instructions as to use are usually incorporated in the main file. Fig. 5:18 gives an extract from a supposed thesaurus showing how it would be used in a postcoordinate and a precoordinate system.

*Conventions in thesaurus construction*

Thesauri are used by indexers compiling precoordinate systems and by both indexers and searchers in the case of postcoordinate systems. In thesauri used by searchers and indexers for postcoordinate systems certain conventions are usually employed, as follows.

i)  References are made between broader and narrower terms, using the BT/NT abbreviations; and between terms not generically related, using the related term' instruction (abbreviated to 'RT'):

> Root vegetables
> > NT Carrots
>
> Carrots
> > BT Root vegetables
>
> Harvesting
> > RT Combine harvesters
>
> Combine harvesters
> > RT Harvesting

ii) Synonyms are indicated by means of the 'USE' and 'UF' references:

> Fall (Season)
> USE: AUTUMN
> AUTUMN
> UF: Fall

'Scope notes' are provided under any term which is given a special meaning or might otherwise be misinterpreted by indexer or searcher; the abbreviation 'SN' is used:

> PRIMARY EDUCATION
> SN Education of pupils up to 11 years of age.

iii) In simple thesauri the generic relationships are displayed as one-step-up and one-step-down:

> UNITED KINGDOM
> NT GREAT BRITAIN
> GREAT BRITAIN
> BT UNITED KINGDOM
> NT ENGLAND
> ENGLAND
> BT GREAT BRITAIN
> NT LONDON
> LONDON
> BT ENGLAND

Other forms of display are possible.

*Classificatory problems in the construction of a thesaurus*

The classificatory problems in the construction of a thesaurus are almost identical to those associated with the construction of a faceted classification (of which a thesaurus is the verbal equivalent). The generic relationships to be indicated are those exemplified in Fig. 5:5. However, schedule and array orders are irrelevant, as is the problem of citation order if the thesaurus is to be used for a postcoordinate system. The thesaurus, however, permits the display of non-generic relationships, and these are not necessarily shown up in the analysis of facets.

Nevertheless certain commonly occurring relationships can be looked for. These include: the discipline/phenomenon relationship (sociology/society; political science/politics); the action/agent relationship (education/teachers); the action/tool relationship (harvesting/combine harvesters); as well as the thing/part relationship when this is not treated as generic (automobiles/internal combustion engines). The preliminary analysis into facets and sub-facets, followed by identification of generic relationships within sub-facets, will however show up in a high proportion of the relationships to be displayed. (It should be mentioned, however, that not all thesaurus designers use facet analysis explicitly as a basis for construction, although ultimately any grouping of terms becomes virtually an exercise in facet analysis).

Fig. 5:18

*Extract from a thesaurus for use in postcoordinate and precoordinate systems*

(a) *Postcoordinate systems*

CARROTS
    BT ROOT VEGETABLES    *(Broader term:* Root vegetables)
FERTILISING
    UF: Fertilisation    (*Used for*: 'Fertilising' is the preferred term)
Fertilisation
    USE: FERTILISING    (*See*: Fertilising)
PLANTING
ROOT VEGETABLES
    NT: CARROTS    (*Narrower term*: Carrots)

The searcher looking for 'Fertilisation of the soil' looks first in the thesaurus to find that 'Fertilisation' is not the preferred term, therefore looks as directed under the preferred term 'Fertilising'. The searcher looking for 'planting of root vegetables' consults the thesaurus and finds both terms are permitted. The searcher looks under both and compares results. Further information can be got by looking also under 'Carrots'.

147

(b) *Precoordinate systems*

CARROTS    xx    ROOT VEGETABLES (Make a *see also* reference from 'Root vegetables')

FERTILISING
     x  Fertilisation     (Make a *see* reference from 'Fertilisation')
Fertilisation
    *see*  FERTILISING
PLANTING
ROOT VEGETABLES
    *see also*     CARROTS

The *see* and *see also* references are incorporated in the file. (It is customary, though not necessarily to be recommended, for 'upward' references not to be supplied, e.g. as in the example a reference will be made from 'Root vegetables' to 'Carrots' but not *vice versa*).

The citation order is assumed to be the PRECIS-type order of context, which in this case will be the order 'thing – action on thing' (or 'object of transitive action – action'). The search is for 'Planting of root vegetables' and for 'Fertilising the soil'. Assuming there to be information in the file on these subjects it will be entered as follows:-

CARROTS – Planting
FERTILISING
Fertilisation *see* FERTILISING
PLANTING – Carrots  *see* CARROTS – Planting
PLANTING – Root vegetables  *see* ROOT VEGETABLES – Planting
ROOT VEGETABLES *see also* CARROTS
ROOT VEGETABLES – Planting

*Language problems in the construction of thesauri*

The language problems in the construction of thesauri are principally those of creating the vocabulary items. The problems of syntax become important only after the vocabulary has been created, and then only if the thesaurus is to be used for a precoordinate system. The principal linguistic problems are the following:

(a) Establishing sets of synonymous terms, and deciding which term of the set is to be regarded as the preferred term (descriptor) under which items will be indexed and which will form part of the auxiliary 'entry vocabulary' from which references will be made. (This is in part a matter of establishing classificatory relationships. To what extent and for what purposes are 'tangerines' and 'oranges' to be considered 'the same'?).

(b) Establishing synonymy of word forms — the morphological problem. (To what extent and for what purposes is 'education' the same as 'educating'?). A general principle in thesaurus-making is that different word forms are to be regarded as synonymous, unless (as in the case of 'water' and 'waters' referred to above) divergent word forms represent a basic divergence in meaning. The choice of the appropriate form is subject to suggested rules. For example, choose the infinitive rather than the finite forms of the verb ('running' rather than 'run'), for count nouns choose the plural form; for mass nouns use the singular. (A count noun is a 'how many?' type noun; a mass noun is a 'how much?' type noun. How *many* dishes? How *much* butter?).

(c) Morphology shades into syntax in the case of concepts (regarded as 'unitary concepts') which are expressed by more than one word. The stages by

**149**

which a multi-word phrase becomes a single word
are exemplified by the following:

Black clothes
Black cab
Black letter
Blackmail

The clothes are undoubtedly 'black'; the cabs less
indubitably so, although at present London's 'black
cabs' (taxicabs which ply for hire) are still in their
majority black in colour. 'Black letter' type is undoubtedly black but the term represents more than
simply the colour. 'Blackmail' is a word with a meaning in its own right, and one which has 'forgotten its
ancestry' being totally disassociated in present usage
from either of its component parts.

For 'Black clothes' and 'Black cabs' (particularly the
former) there is a case for inverting the phrase, to
bring the focal term into prominence. For 'Black
letter' and 'Blackmail' the component parts cannot
be separated, and indeed *together* form the focus.

## A thesaurus for Education

In Fig. 5:19 the classes displayed in Fig. 5:5 have been arranged in
alphabetical order, and the appropriate relational instructions
have been provided. Appropriate terms have been selected for the
concepts, and additional entry terms provided. Scope notes are
provided where necessary. Notice that synonyms for 'urban areas'
include 'towns', 'cities' and 'conurbations'. This is because these
terms are not always distinctively used in the literature, and any
attempt to distinguish them within an index language would result
in decreased rather than increased precision. 'Urban areas' is
chosen as the most comprehensive term (the broadest term).

150

*Thesaurus on Education*
*based on analysis in Fig. 5:5 (Cf: faceted classification in Fig. 5:11a)*

ACCOUNTANTS
    SN  As educands
    BT  EDUCANDS

ADULTS
    SN  As educands
    BT  Educands

ADVANCED EDUCATIONAL MATERIALS
    SN  For works *about* materials
    RT  EDUCATIONAL MATERIALS

ASIA
    NT  INDIA

AUDIO-VISUAL MATERIALS
    SN  For works *about* A/V materials in education.
    Use  AUDIO-VISUALS for materials in file in this form
    NT  FILMS

AUDIO-VISUALS
    SN  For materials in file having this form.
    Use AUDIO-VISUAL MATERIALS for works *about* A/V
        materials in education
    NT  FILMS (form)

BIBLIOGRAPHIES
    SN  Use for materials in file having this form

CHILDREN
    SN  As educands

Cities
    USE:  URBAN AREAS
Conurbations
    USE:  URBAN AREAS

DICTIONARIES
SN Use for materials in file having this form

EDUCANDS
NT: ACCOUNTANTS
ADULTS
CHILDREN
EXCEPTIONAL EDUCANDS
FEMALES
MALES
NURSES

EDUCATIONAL MATERIALS
NT: ADVANCED EDUCATIONAL MATERIALS
AUDIO-VISUAL MATERIALS
ELEMENTARY EDUCATIONAL MATERIALS
TEXT-BOOKS

EDUCATIONALLY SUB-NORMAL EDUCANDS
BT EXCEPTIONAL EDUCANDS

ELEMENTARY EDUCATIONAL MATERIALS
BT EDUCATIONAL MATERIALS

ENCYCLOPAEDIAS
SN Use for materials in file having this form

ENGLAND
BT UNITED KINGDOM

EUROPE
NT FRANCE
UNITED KINGDOM

EXCEPTIONAL EDUCANDS
BT EDUCANDS
NT EDUCATIONAL SUB–NORMAL EDUCANDS
EXCEPTIONALLY INTELLIGENT EDUCANDS

EXCEPTIONALLY INTELLIGENT EDUCANDS
    BT  EXCEPTIONAL EDUCANDS

FEMALES
    SN  As educands
    BT  Educands

FILMS
    SN  For works *about* films in education
         For materials in file having this form use *FILMS (Form)*
    BT  AUDIO-VISUAL MATERIALS

FILMS (FORM)
    SN  For materials in file having this form
    BT  AUDIO-VISUALS

FRANCE
    BT  EUROPE

HISTORY

INDIA
    BT  ASIA

LONDON
    BT  ENGLAND

MEN
    SN  As educands
    BT  EDUCANDS

NURSES
    SN  As educands

RURAL AREAS
    NT  VILLAGES
    RT  URBAN AREAS

TEXT-BOOKS
> SN  For works *about* text-books in education
> BT  EDUCATIONAL MATERIALS

Towns
> USE  URBAN AREAS

UNITED KINGDOM
> BT  EUROPE
> NT  ENGLAND

URBAN AREAS
> UF  Cities
>     Conurbations
>     Towns

VILLAGES
> BT  RURAL AREAS
> RT  URBAN AREAS

Although the thesaurus demonstrated is of a kind primarily designed for use by indexers and searchers in postcoordinate systems, very slight adaptations to its format make it suitable for use in precoordinate systems, as has been demonstrated.

## Verbal and Non-Verbal Systems

Verbal and non-verbal systems have the same basic problems: classificatory relationships must be established (if not within the system itself then by the user); and although the notational system appears to be 'language-free' it must nevertheless be approached through the medium of language. The principal advantage of the non-verbal systems is that they collocate related classes (although as demonstrated they also separate related classes). The principal advantage of the verbal systems are that

154

they provide a direct entry into the system (although as has been demonstrated the entry is not always direct, if the searcher chooses the 'wrong' term in the first place). An additional advantage of verbal languages is that, since position in the file does not depend upon relationships of concepts, new concepts can be included (provided they can be named) without reference to any other existing concept. Thus a newly discovered disease (provided it can be named) can be indexed irrespective of its supposed cause or any other relationship which is yet to be discovered. Isolated phenomena which are not 'assigned' to any area of discourse can be placed. For example, the phenomenon of 'sponsoring' (sponsored walks; slim-ins, swims etc.) need not be regarded as a sociological activity, as a sport, or as a charitable activity; and indeed is quite likely to be looked for under its common name.

The broad 'browsing' approach provided by files systematically arranged does, however, provide distinct advantages for the searcher who is not quite sure what he wants and who in any case does not know what to call it.

## REFERENCES

Buchanan, B (1976) *A glossary of indexing terms.* Bingley.

*Bliss Bibliographic Classification.* (1977–) 2nd ed. J Mills and Vanda Broughton, with the assistance of Valerie Lang. Butterworths. Class J: Education.

Foskett, D J and Foskett, J (1974) *London education classification: a thesaurus/classification of British educational terms.* 2nd ed. University of London Institute of Education Library. (Education libraries bulletin, supplement 6).

Ranganathan, S R (1962) *Elements of library classification....* 3rd ed. Bombay. Asia Publishing House.

Vickery, B C (1975)  *Classification and indexing in science.* 3rd ed. Butterworths.

## FURTHER READING

Items 1, 2, 4, 11, 13, 15, 18, 22, 24, 26, 36, 39, 41, 55, 59, 62 and 64 from section B of further reading on p. 274 et seq.

# CHAPTER 6: NON-CONTENT APPROACHES

Any feature of a document may be the object of a search, whether as the 'real' object or the tag by which the real object may be identified. For example the colour of a binding may be used as a recognition tag, as might the authorship or the publisher of a document; although it is unlikely that the former (the binding) will feature also as a 'real object'. Any feature may be used at various stages of the search. For example at the final stages of a search the number of pages of a book may affect choice, but it is unlikely to do so until other features have been considered (e.g. subject and authorship). This feature will have such low priority as not to affect arrangement. Thus pagination may be noted in the description but not appear as a 'heading'. On the other hand the dimensions of a film (as distinct from the pages in a book) may affect choice at an early stage, since on this feature depends the choice of apparatus to project the film.

Almost certainly document content and document authorship are the most frequently sought features, with document title as a recognition feature. Almost certainly content is the most difficult to deal with since content represents thoughts which are volatile, variable and (collectively) wide ranging. This chapter deals with title and author approaches. However, firstly other approaches will be considered.

These approaches are related to features which in practice are the most frequently used primary objects of search. The features are associated with the accessibility of the information contained in

157

the documents, at the intellectual, symbolic, sensory and techno-logical levels.

However important or relevant the content of a document may be it will be useless if the searcher is unable to understand it, unable to interpret the symbols used (e.g. musical notation, foreign language), unable to see (in the case of visual documents), or hear (in the case of audio documents), and unable (for example) to play a gramophone record for lack of a gramophone.    A visually handicapped person must *first* reject visual documents in favour of audio or tactile ones (irrespective of other features of the document).    But this fact is concealed by the fact that such choice is frequently provided for file content rather than file arrangement;   or by such broad general divisions between files that the divisions are not seen as belonging to the same file.

Similarly, a German speaker is invited to choose between German libraries and English libraries, or broad sections of a library, the musically 'non-literate' between scores and sound recordings, and the user of sound records, between discs and tapes. In terms of intellectual availability, books written for five-year-olds and those written for post-graduates — albeit on the same 'subject' — are seen as being radically different as to content;   and users are invited to choose between children's libraries and adult libraries.

Closely associated with both 'content' and 'accessibility' is the feature of 'time':   the period or date in which the work was created.

The following features will be dealt with:-

> Bias  (For whom is the work intended?
> Intellectual accessibility)
>
> Symbolic systems and language
>
> Sensory system (audio — or visual documents)

Technology
Time
Titles
Authors
Other features

## BIAS

The term 'bias' is used non-pejoratively to indicate an intended 'usership'. The distinction between a book written for five-year-olds and one written for post-graduates is sufficiently distinct to make a broad general division both desirable and feasible. However, the difference between third-year and post-graduate text-books is not so marked and the readership is probably inter-changeable, whatever the intentions of the author. All documents are biased to a greater or lesser extent. There is a distinction between bias which is explicit (a stated intention of the author), and that which is implicit. Some indeed may be deliberately concealed (as is the case with some advertising literature). The interchangeability of some biased materials, and the subjectivity of judgements regarding bias provide reasons for not making bias a major feature in arrangement, except when the bias is clear and unambiguous as in the case of children's literature.

A distinction can be made between bias which exists in the document and that which exists in a collection or file content. For example, the stock of a children's library may include materials which are not written specifically for children, but which are considered suitable for them; and bibliographies and 'lists of recommended reading' may use bias as a major feature both in selection and arrangement. In both these cases the opinions of the organisers or compilers can be allowed to obtrude, since — especially in the case of bibliographies — what is being provided is not only information but advice.

**159**

## SYMBOLIC SYSTEMS AND LANGUAGES

In the case of 'literature' the language of a document is in effect part of its content, since 'literature' is an art form which uses language as its medium. In other cases, language may or not be a matter of indifference to the user, depending upon whether the language is understood, or can be made available by translation.

In some libraries it may be appropriate to make a primary division of stock according to language, with the result that a searcher looking for items on a particular subject may have to look in a number of separate language sequences. In other libraries or collections it might be assumed that the subject interest is paramount, and that if the users cannot understand a particular item, it will be translated. In some cases, of course, the users can be assumed to understand the languages represented; and in others the individual items may be written in an international 'subject' language. Diagrams, charts and mathematical notation tend to be international, as indeed do art reproduction books which often have the minimum of 'legend'. An extreme case of language being irrelevant to the arrangement of files is that of files of administrative correspondence, most of which is likely to be in a 'favoured' or predominating language, and which — if it is worth keeping at all — *must* be made available by translation to users who cannot understand it.

The same principles apply to the arrangement of items using different kinds of non-linguistic code. Maps, diagrams, charts, tables, chemical and mathematical notation are usually subordinate to the subject, and comprehensible to subject users, who may, however, prefer — once the subject matter is identified — presentation in one form or another. Music is a special case in that many persons who are interested in music are non-literate (musically); and there are moreover, different kinds of musical notation (musical symbolisation). For a singer who can read both tonic sol-fa and staff notation, the distinction between the two becomes a matter of indifference or final choice. The totally non-literate person must begin by rejecting both in favour of sound recordings.

## SENSORY SYSTEMS

Closely associated with the symbolic system is the sensory system used for documentation. The non-literate musician must begin by rejecting written music in favour of sound recorded music, and any form of sensory deprivation on the part of the user imposes a primary choice irrespective of other features sought. In many collections all audio-materials are kept separately from visual materials on the assumption that it is in respect of this characteristic that a primary choice will be made. However, in other collections (especially learning resource centres) it is assumed that the user is primarily interested in a subject, and as far as is physically possible, all material on the subject is kept together (e.g. print materials, audio-visual materials, and maps, models, posters, etc.). However, whether or not a primary choice can be made at this level, may depend upon the technological factor. A teacher presenting a lesson on 16th-century London may wish to choose between all material relevant to the subject, but may be unable to do so through lack of technological resources.

## TECHNOLOGY

For many modern forms of document, access is through special apparatus and this is so of all audio-documents, and of many visual documents. The apparatus includes gramophone records, tape recorders, film projectors, slide projectors and computer terminals. The teacher in a well endowed school may be able to choose between the best method of presenting a subject irrespective of the apparatus required, and the technological factor becomes, relatively speaking, a minor one in respect of the arrangement of files. For most users — whether institutional or individual — the technological factor is a major one, however. The analogy with the language factor is obvious. If the user does not 'possess' German or a gramophone, and, if these cannot be made available then the primary rejection must be of German texts and gramophone records respectively, and the collection organised accordingly.

## TIME

By 'time' is meant the time of 'creation', which is not necessarily the same as the time to which the document refers, nor indeed, the same as the time of publication.

However, it is obvious that a book written in 1882 will be materially different as to content from one written in 1982; and that the content will be biased in favour of an 1882 readership. The relationship between time and content is most clearly seen in the case of History: a guide book to London written in 1882 will today be treated as source material for historical studies, and may, indeed, be treated as if it were itself a historical study, and in libraries may be classed with histories of London in the 19th century. Arrangement of items in a file by 'date of creation' will primarily be a response to the questions of the type 'What was being said or written about London in 1882?' rather than questions about London in 1882; but often, as in this particular example, the two types of question are the same. The sameness is the most obvious in the case of periodicals, which may have a function of reporting as well as commenting on news and therefore are source materials for information about both attitudes and events during certain periods.

The individual numbers of periodicals are usually arranged in chronological order under each title; and this arrangement not only provides the answer to the questions about specific periods or dates, but may also illustrate developments and changes over a period. For the same reason some non-periodical documents may be arranged chronologically; for example, research reports within a relatively narrow subject area; and administrative correspondence under subjects or 'jobs'. A chronological arrangement specifically provides the answer to questions of the type 'What is

162

the *latest* information or news', and answering this type of question is specifically the role of newspapers, 'current bibliographies' and 'current awareness' services. A current awareness service is one which provides information to users as the information becomes available, or as events happen; a current bibliography is a bibliography which publishes lists of documents as they are published (i.e. the bibliography is itself a periodical). Current bibliographies and newspapers are obviously types of current awareness service, although the term is usually restricted to lists of documents issued by an 'information service'. Anybody using a current bibliography such as the *British National Bibliography* must *first* approach the search with the question 'What was published last week, last quarter or last year'; and then search the author, title or subject files within each chronological division.

Because chronological arrangement is developmental arrangement, it may be a useful arrangement for 'instructional bibliographies' which do more than simply list items but have the purpose of illustrating a theme. For example, a bibliography of works about Darwin, if arranged chronologically, might usefully illustrate changing attitudes to his theories; and a bibliography of works published by a political party, arranged chronologically, would illustrate the development of its philosophies.

However, the greater part of the stock of most public, academic and other libraries, is arranged irrespective of date; and even office files are arranged primarily by subject or 'job'. This is because collections are already heavily biased in favour of certain periods – usually the modern one. For example, although a library may include works *by* 18th- and 19th-century novelists, works about these novelists are likely to be modern works; and non-current administrative documents are usually discarded or removed to secondary files.

## ACCESS POINTS AND DESCRIPTIONS

The features so far discussed are such as might affect choice. Whether or not they are the subject of high or low priority choice depends upon user or collection or file; and it should be noted that even when they are the subject of high priority choice, this choice may be provided for by the contents rather than the arrangement of the file or collection. However, even low priority features may be vital at the service end. For example, the difference between Finnish and Swedish may be a matter of indifference to the ultimate user of a text, if either language can be translated; but the difference affects the choice of translator; as the difference between a 35 mm and a 8 mm film will affect the choice of projector. Such vital information should appear in the representations file as part of the description. The technical description of a book is less important than that of a document for which special apparatus is required; and in so far as description of content is concerned, this is more important in the case of foreign language materials and of 'technologically inaccessible' materials than of those materials which are comprehensible and directly accessible.

Features which appear in the description but do not affect arrangement are the low priority search features. In the case of computer-held files the distinction between 'arrangement' features (which might also be called 'search features', 'access features' or 'search term features') are almost irrelevant. In a computer-held file any piece of recorded information can become an access point. Thus although it may be economically infeasible to distinguish between English and Japanese texts in a manual file, in a computer-held file it will be possible for the searcher at the primary level to request items on 'microelectronics in *English*' or 'microelectronics not in *Japanese*'.

## TITLES AND AUTHORS

Although the features so far discussed are important ones, they

**164**

are not (as already stated) the most frequently sought, once the contents of a collection or a file have been established. The most frequently sought features are content, author and title, and it is usual in most files to provide a direct approach to each. Content approaches are provided for by an alphabetical ordering of subject names or by a systematic ordering of subjects under a notation (as already discussed in Chapters 4 and 5). Author and title approaches are provided for by an alphabetical ordering of authors' names and or titles respectively. The order in which these features are sought varies from user to user; and in most libraries the following orders are provided for in the catalogue:-

(1)   Content – author – title

(2)   Author – title

(3)   Title

The order content–title is sometimes provided for in bibliographies, though not usually in library catalogues. The order content–author–title is the one commonly used for the arrangement of documents on shelves.

In Fig. 6:1 the alternative 'citation orders' are illustrated. Note that for shelving of documents the subject approach would almost certainly be through a systematic rather than an alphabetical order.

Fig. 6:2 shows an integrated alphabetical file in which author, title and subject entries are presented in one alphabetical sequence. (This is an example of 'dictionary order' or of a 'dictionary catalogue').

Fig. 6:1 *Content/author/title: citation orders*

1 (a) *Content – author – title arrangement*

GIRAFFES

Brown, James
African paradise / by James Brown
The book of the giraffe / by James Brown

Smith, Gerald
Amazing adventure / by Gerald Smith and James Brown

ZEBRAS

Adamson, David
Zebras in my path / by David Adamson

1 (b) *Content – title arrangement*

GIRAFFES

African paradise / by James Brown
Amazing adventure / by Gerald Smith and James Brown
The book of the giraffe / by James Brown

ZEBRAS

Zebras in my path / by David Adamson

1 (c) *Author – title arrangement*

Adamson, David
Zebras in my path / by David Adamson

Brown, James
African paradise / by James Brown
Amazing adventure / by Gerald Smith and James Brown
The book of the giraffe / by James Brown

Smith, Gerald
Amazing adventure / by Gerald Smith and James Brown

1 (d) *Title arrangement*

African paradise / by David Adamson
Amazing adventure / by Gerald Smith and James Brown
The book of the giraffe / by James Brown
Zebras in my path / by David Adamson

Fig. 6:2  *Dictionary order*

Adamson, David
    Zebras in my path / by David Adamson

African paradise / by James Brown

Amazing adventure / by Gerald Smith and James Brown

The book of the giraffe / by James Brown

Brown, James
    African paradise / by James Brown
    Amazing adventure / by Gerald Smith and James Brown
    The book of the giraffe / by James Brown

GIRAFFES

    Brown, James
        African paradise / by James Brown
        The book of the giraffe / by James Brown

    Smith, Gerald
        Amazing adventure / by Gerald Smith and James Brown

Smith, Gerald
    Amazing adventure / by Gerald Smith and James Brown

ZEBRAS

    Adamson, David
        Zebras in my path / by David Adamson

Zebras in my path / by David Adamson


**Titles**


Individual works or documents — as any other individuals — are identified by a combination of class features.  In the case of documents the class features include the subject or content of the work and the author. Although the author is an individual and not a class, authorship of documents is itself a class characteristic of the documents; for instance in Figs. 6:1 and 6:2 'Brown', 'Smith' and 'Adamson' are respectively characteristics of works which have been, or might be, written by these authors. Similarly, individual persons are identified by combinations of class characteristics (e.g. sex, age, appearance, nationality). Proper names are labels for individuals, (people, places, institutions . . . ). Documents have proper names when a work receives a unique code such as a Standard Specification number; but the most commonly used kind of proper name is the document title. In Figs. 6:1 and 6:2 'Zebras' and 'Giraffes' are class terms when used to indicate content, but are part of the proper name of the work in 'Zebras in my path' and 'The book of the giraffe'.

Proper names are 'terms of variable reference'. That is to say they are terms which refer to individuals and not to classes, but may be used to refer to more than one individual. 'Mary Smith' represents an individual not a class of individuals, but it may be the name or label of more than one individual. The title 'History of England' may refer to one or more individual works, and as a unique identifier, may have the same value as the personal name 'David Davies' might have in Wales. On the other hand the title 'Twelfth Night or what you will' is probably sufficient to identify the work without further information that it was written by Shakespeare.

Although proper names do not represent classes, they may be oblique indicators of classes. This is because kinds of proper names tend to be reserved for kinds of individuals, and because the proper names may be made up of a number of class terms. For example, 'Mary' is likely to be the name of a female human being in an English-speaking society, and 'The British Medical Association' is likely to be British and associated with medicine. On the other hand 'Mary' might be the name of a ship or of a cat, and 'The British Medical Association' the fanciful title of a pop group. Similarly the titles of works may be indicative or

**168**

non-indicative of content, and, if the latter, may be absolutely deceptive. For example 'The child's history of England' is likely to be about the history of England, and written for children, but could be a satirical television commentary on nuclear proliferation. Totally fanciful titles ('The waste land', 'Bleak House') which give no indication (deceptive or otherwise) of content are not confined to fanciful works.

Titles or words in titles can, as discussed in Chapter 4, be used to provide a subject approach, but obviously cannot be used for this purpose if the titles are non-indicative. In this chapter the title approach proper will be discussed: i.e. the use of the title itself as a search term and not as a source of search terms. If the title is memorable and fanciful it provides a useful and much-used approach. In most systems title entries would be provided for titles such as 'The waste land', 'Bleak House' and 'Old Possum's book of practical cats'; as well as for the titles 'African paradise' and 'Amazing adventure' from Figs. 6:1 and 6:2.

However, if the title is simply indicative of content, and not especially useful as an identifier, it is common to reduce the number of entries by omitting the title entry. Thus an entry might not be made under 'Book of the giraffe' in Figs.6:1 and 6:2. It is assumed in this case that the searcher can look under the subject entry for 'Giraffes'. However, as many librarians know, this assumption is not always correct! Many users have difficulty in translating remembered titles into search terms chosen by the indexer, and persist in looking for 'History of England' under 'History of England' rather than 'England: History', and for 'Book of the giraffe' under 'Book'. This is due in part to lack of experience, and in part perhaps to a well-founded distrust of indexing systems, which for very good technical reasons, do not always precisely match the questions of the enquirer. 'Zebras in my path' is an example of a semi-fanciful title; one can well imagine that the content of this work might be seen by indexers to relate to zebras, animal welfare, zoos, wildlife conservation, and be indexed accordingly.

There is a case for making title entries for every work in order to reduce possible areas of 'disagreement' between searcher and indexer. An additional reason for doing so is that it reduces the number of decisions to be made by the indexer; and for the user it creates a more 'reliable' system. For example 'Zebras in my path' is a case where the indexer — given freedom to decide — might, or might not, decide to make an entry, and a searcher would be left in doubt as to whether or not he had 'looked in the right place'. Computer-held files — provided the program allows — automatically provide the title approach.

Titles assume greater importance when for any reason a work is considered to be 'authorless', since in these cases the title rather than the combination author/title becomes the major identifying feature. Periodicals (as distinct from articles in periodicals) are conventionally considered to be authorless, since the 'author' (usually the editor), can change without changing the character of the periodical, and may indeed be unknown to the reader. Periodicals are usually filed under title, and in representation files under title and under subject/title.

*Problems of providing the Title Approach*

The problems of providing for the title approach fall into two categories:- firstly titles are misremembered, and secondly works may have more than one title.

Titles frequently consist of multi-word phrases of which the non-content or function words are confused by the user. Retrieval may be affected by inaccurate recall of a minor word  For example if the hymn 'I will tell the wondrous story' is misremembered as 'We will tell the wondrous story' the item may not be found. The trivial mistake of confusing a definite and indefinite article may frustrate a search. For example, in letter-by-letter filing 'Painting a house' files before 'Paintings of Turner' and 'Painting the house' files after. The case for word-by-word filing includes the fact that since words represent meaningful concepts

170

(and meaning is what is recalled), distortion of concept order is less likely to occur than if letter-by-letter filing is used. On the other hand, word-by-word filing entails the making of arbitrary rules regarding acronyms, initials and apostrophes which may not agree with the rules imagined by the searcher.

Remembering key words rather than the whole title is the more likely to occur when key words are typographically emphasised on the title page. For example, 'Magazine of GARDENING TODAY' is likely to be remembered as 'GARDENING TODAY', and 'The personal history of DAVID COPPERFIELD' as 'DAVID COPPERFIELD'.

A partial solution to the problem is provided by the old method of bringing the key word or phrase to the front position, e.g.

GARDENING TODAY, Magazine of

This solution is especially useful when only one approach and only one entry is provided. The method has obvious affinities with the KWIC and KWOC systems described in Chapter 4. In that chapter the systems were suggested as a means of providing for the subject approach. They might be considered extravagant (one entry per key word), when the subject approach is otherwise provided for.

There is indeed a case for using the unadapted title 'as found' as the basis for arrangement by title (if author and subject approaches are otherwise provided for), since this method does provide for the user who remembers the title 'as found', and (as already discussed) does not easily 'translate' titles into index terms. In a representation file references can be made from keywords to the title, and general reference can be made between standard and frequently confused words, e.g.

GARDENING TODAY
*see*       Magazine of gardening today

MAGAZINE OF . . .
*see also*  Bulletin of . . . Journal of . . .
Transactions of . . .

These devices are most frequently used in the case of periodicals for which (as already stated) title entries may be of primary importance, and for which standard words are most frequently used. There is no reason why it should not be used in other cases, e.g.

Autobiography of . . . . .
*see also*  Biography of . . . Life of . . .

Works may have more than one title for one or more of the following reasons:-

(1)    Particularly in the case of periodicals, titles may change. 'The Manchester Guardian' becomes 'The Guardian'.

(2)    The same work may be issued in different editions (different publications) under different titles.

      (a)    Without changing the work.

           'The personal history of David Copperfield' becomes 'David Copperfield'; and the same version of St Mark's Gospel may be called either 'Gospel according to St Mark' or 'St Mark's Gospel'.

      (b)    The work as represented by different titles is in some way varied:

           Essentially the same 'Bible' is titled 'The Good News Bible', 'The Basic Bible' or 'The Holy Bible'.

172

The title may be translated: The Holy
Bible, 'La Santa Biblia'.

(c)   Works may have more than one title in
a single publication. A bi-lingual dictionary is likely to have two facing title pages,
one in each language, for example 'Spanish-
English Dictionary' — 'Diccionaria español-
inglés'. (This is an example of 'parallel title').

Notice that there is a distinction between works having more
than one title, the different titles manifested in different publications or documentary units, and publications which have more
than one title (i.e. two or more titles in one documentary unit).

The usual solution to (c) is to choose one title and to make
reference from the other, both titles being mentioned in the
description. (In the example Fig. 6:3, the choice of the English
title is based on a 'favoured language' principle: in Spain the
favoured language would be Spanish). In some cases there is no
principle for guidance, and the preferred title is usually the one
mentioned on the right-hand title page or first on the title page.

Fig. 6:3 *Alternative titles*

Cameron, James

> Spanish-English school dictionary = Diccionario escolar
> español - inglés / by James Cameron.

Diccionario escolar español-inglés

> *see*    Spanish-English school dictionary

Spanish-English school dictionary

> Spanish-English school dictionary = Diccionario escolar
> español - inglés / by James Cameron. 1982

Note: the '=' in the description is a conventional sign to indicate parallel
titles.

For (a) and (b) it is necessary to decide whether the arrangement of documents or representations is to be under the title of the publication with (in the representation file) references between titles (Fig. 6:4) or under one title, a preferred or so called 'uniform' title, with references from the non-preferred title (Fig. 6:5). In the case of periodicals the decision must be made as to whether the original or changed title is to be used as the uniform title. For periodicals there is a case for using the title as found, with references between the various titles, since early issues of periodicals are likely eventually to be discarded, and because changes in title tend to represent a change in identity (e.g. 'The Sun' bears very little relationship to its so-called predecessors).

Fig. 6:4 *Arrangement under title of publication*

David Copperfield
> David Copperfield / by Charles Dickens  [Rest of description]
> *see also* The personal history of David Copperfield.

Dickens, Charles
> David Copperfield / by Charles Dickens [Rest of description]
> *see also*  Dickens, Charles, The personal history of David Copperfield

Dickens, Charles
> The personal history of David Copperfield. [Rest of description]
> *see also*  Dickens, Charles. David Copperfield.

The personal history of David Copperfield
> The personal history of David Copperfield / by Charles Dickens
> [Rest of description]
> *see also*  David Copperfield / by Charles Dickens

Gardening today
> Weekly. [Rest of description]
> *see also*  under former title 'Magazine of gardening today'

Magazine of gardening today
> Weekly. [Rest of description]
> *see also*  under changed title 'Gardening today'

Fig. 6:5 *Arrangement under uniform title*

David Copperfield
David Copperfield / by Charles Dickens [Rest of description]

[David Copperfield] *
The personal history of David Copperfield / by Charles Dickens
[Rest of description]

Dickens, Charles
David Copperfield / by Charles Dickens [Rest of description]

Dickens, Charles
[David Copperfield] * The personal history of David Copperfield / by
Charles Dickens [Rest of description]

Dickens, Charles
The personal history of David Copperfield.
*see* Dickens, Charles. David Copperfield

The personal history of David Copperfield
*see* David Copperfield

Magazine of gardening today
*see under new title* 'Gardening today'

Gardening today
Weekly. [Rest of description]

*Square brackets indicate that title does not appear in publication.

## Authors

Authors are important for purposes of identification of works
('History of England by *Trevelyan*'), but may frequently be
the real objects of search. Authors may be a guarantee of quality
and authority; and in many cases provide an important indication
of type which may be difficult to provide otherwise. (For
example, an Agatha Christie type detective story is easy to recognise but difficult to define). Pseudo-authorship labels are

**175**

frequently given to works from a variety of hands in order to establish a type identity, this being a common journalistic device. ('Columns' are written by different journalists writing under· a single pseudonym). Authorship directly affects content, in that the content of a message has different values and different implications according to the 'sender' of the message. Administrative and legal documents provide obvious examples of this: the statement 'All vehicles should be fitted with safety belts' is in effect a different statement according to whether it is made by a judge, by the legislature, or by the local representative of a safety organisation.

One of the problems of providing for the author approach is that of determining 'who is the author'. It should, however, be emphasised that it is not the task of the indexer, nor the function of an information retrieval system, to examine bibliographic and historical evidence regarding authorship. The determination of whether 'Hamlet' was written by Shakespeare or by the Earl of Oxford is the task of a historical bibliographer and literary critic. While the general consensus attributes this work to Shakespeare, and while the work appears under his name, Shakespeare is the author for purposes of information retrieval.


*The problems of providing for the author approach*

The problems of providing for the author approach are analogous to those associated with titles. Firstly, the decision must be made as to whether or not in a formal sense the work has an author, and if so which person or organisation (in a formal sense) is to be considered the author, and who the principal author.

Secondly, a decision must be made as what the author shall be called, and whether if an author writes under more than one name which shall be used. Thirdly, decisions must be made as to how the authors' names shall be presented in the headings, i.e. as search terms).

**176**

*Who is the author?*

Authorship may be known or unknown; and if the former, may be declared in the document or undeclared. Anonymous works are works of undeclared authorship, whether or not the author is known or unknown. Anonymous works are of three kinds:-

1. Authorship is unknown. E.g. 'Beowulf'.
   In an author *or* title file, such works are
   entered under title.

2. Authorship is undeclared but is commonly
   known. E.g. 'Elizabeth and her German garden'.
   In such cases it is usual to arrange documents
   and representations under the author's name.

3. Authorship is undeclared and although known
   is not common knowledge. Practice may vary,
   It is equally usual to reveal and not to reveal
   the identity of the author.

Authors may write under more than one name. These different names may represent different official identities or be used to represent different kinds of work. For example, a prime minister of the United Kingdom may write an autobiography under a personal name or issue a policy statement under the title 'Prime Minister'. In such a case it can be assumed that the identities are different, and the items are arranged respectively under the two different names. An author may write romantic novels under one name and detective stories under another. In this case although the identity is the same, it would probably be unkind to both author and reader to arrange all items under one name. The different names are intended to be type labels. On the other hand, for the benefit of persons interested in the entire collection of an author's works, a connection should be made between works written under different names (if the connection is known). It must be emphasised, however, that practice varies in these respects and rules for cataloguing under author will propose different solutions to the problems.

Works of multiple authorship (which have more than one author) or for which there is a conflict between the organisation as author and the persons as authors (the persons who inevitably must create the work) are dealt with below, (problems of 'multiple authorship' and 'corporate versus personal authorship').

As already stated it is not the function of the indexer to conduct research as to the authorship of works, and indeed, for certain purposes the rules as to 'who is the author' are purely conventional. For example (paradoxically) works which have very many authors (works of diffuse authorship) are often conventionally considered to be authorless; as are periodicals taken as a whole. Typical of cataloguing rules which adhere to a convention rather than what might be considered the 'truth' are those which propose that 'ghost writers' are secondary authors, and that the principal author is the person 'ghosted'.

*What shall the author be called?*

A pseudonymous work is one which is produced under a name which is not the so-called 'real' name of the author. (The 'real name' would presumably be one which in the UK would appear in a baptismal or voters' register). The question of what shall the author be called is obviously closely related to the question of who is the author and the ways of dealing with pseudonymous works are the same in principle as those relating to anonymous works.

The 'real name' may be unknown and indeed, the pseudonym may not be recognised as such. If the 'real name' is known and is common knowledge, it is usual to enter under the real name provided that this name has been used in publication. For example, 'Jane Eyre by Currer Bell' is arranged under the name 'Charlotte Brontë', since the 'real name' of Currer Bell is known

178

and later editions of her work have Charlotte Brontë as the declared author. On the other hand although 'George Eliot' and 'George Orwell' are known to be pseudonyms of Mary Anne Evans and Eric Blair respectively, their novels are arranged under the pseudonyms since the 'real names' were not used for publishing. The special case of authors writing under more than one name is dealt with above.

It may be that authors produce work under more than one name because the 'real name' itself changes. Women change their name on marriage; commoners are given titles of nobility; and organisations change their names for various reasons. Quintin Hogg becomes Viscount Hailsham, becomes again Quintin Hogg, and advances once more into the nobility as Lord Hailsham. There is no doubt in this case that these changes do not affect the identity of the person. In the case of organisations the changes of names may represent changes of function and identity. The Board of Education becomes the Ministry of Education, which eventually becomes the Department of Education and Science. Is the 'DES' simply a different name for the 'BoE'. Or do the names refer to different organisations?

In the case of persons it is customary to use the name which has been used for publication or used most frequently for publication, with references between the various names if more than one name has been used. In the case of organisations it is probably most convenient to use the name 'as found' and if necessary to make references between the names. Especially in the case of government publications successive re-alignments of function would make any other course impossibly difficult. It would entail for example detailed research into the successors of the United Kingdom's Department of Scientific and Industrial Research. This particular case provides an example of series of publications which were taken over by a successor department and in such a case 'see also' references become all the more necessary.

**179**

Once the authors' identities and names have been established .it remains to decide how the latter shall be represented in the file. Most authors have complex names consisting of multi-word phrases, and in some cases these names may be seen as consisting of alternative names. For example, most persons in English-speaking communities will have names at least as complex as 'George Smith'. The present Queen's full name could be said to be 'Elizabeth Alexandra Mary Windsor, Elizabeth II Queen of the United Kingdom.

There are some problems associated with the representation of authors' names, for example the natural language order of a name is not necessarily the search order. For English language names the natural order is forename, surname; the search order is nearly always the reverse, George Smith becoming Smith, George. The problem of institutional names is analogous to that of personal names and analogous to the problems in citing titles. Initial words are often not key words, and the former are often highly generalised and inter-changeable in memory: 'Department' and 'Ministry' are confused, as are 'Institute' and 'Institution'.

Again, names of authors may be phrases and they may include, or consist of, 'compound words' which are of two kinds: the surname with prefix (Du Maurier) and the 'compound surname' (Wedgwood Benn). Documents are arranged under one or other of the parts and references made from the other form.

Solutions to these problems vary from language to language and from country to country. Codes of rules (intended for broadly based collections) must necessarily take cognisance of the naming practices in different languages. Solutions to these problems as provided by codes of rules, include the use of forenames as entry terms for monarchs, saints, popes and for persons within language communities where surnames are not used. (This includes mediaeval European societies as well as some modern societies).

**180**

They include the surname, forename citation order for most modern Western authors; and 'direct entry' (i.e. under initial words) for institutional names, with possible references from key words.

## Problems of multiple authorship

The problem of 'who is the author?' is exacerbated when there is more than one author, since in this case entries should be made under each author in the representation file (although, as mentioned above, if there are very many authors the work may be formally considered to be 'authorless'). Authors of a work may have the same or different functions; for example as in the case of this book two authors collaborate in performing the same function, but in other cases one author may be the writer, the other an illustrator, and the third an editor. In some circumstances it may be necessary to establish a principal author (for example for filing documents on the shelves under author, or for filing under subject as in Fig. 6:2). Notice that 'Amazing adventure' has two authors and there are author entries under each. The author arrangement under subject, however, is under the first author only. A general principle is that 'originators' take precedence over 're-workers' (e.g. translators, editors, adaptors) and that where the originator is unknown (e.g. as in the case of 'Beowulf') the work is treated as anonymous – i.e. is filed under title – even although there may be a known 're-worker'. A second principle is that the indications given on the title page should be accepted, for example the statement that a work is 'by John Smith with the assistance of Mary Jones' is a statement that John Smith is the principal author. The indications may be typographical rather than verbal. Where no indication is given the convention is that the author given first on the page is treated as the principal author.

## Corporate versus personal authors

It may be that a work is of corporate authorship (institutional authorship) and that no personal author is declared. In many cases, however, the names of personal authors are given in works which are obviously 'sponsored' and represent the opinion of an organisation. For example the members of a research team may be mentioned although the research report is essentially the work of the organisation which employs them. The problem in these cases is to determine which of the authors is to be considered the principal author. A principle proposed is that where the authors have acted as mouthpieces of an institution or as employees of the institution, the institution should be regarded as the principal author. This is a difficult principle to follow. In practice the 'research' required to make the appropriate decision in doubtful cases would be beyond the means of a routine indexer. Most workers in a library and information department do however have an intuitive recognition of the 'author' which their users are most likely to remember.

## Author/ Title Cataloguing Rules

In almost any situation a set of rules for entry under author and title is a useful adjunct to the cataloguing procedure (to the procedure of making bibliographic listings). For subject entries it may be possible to anticipate the terms which may be used as index terms and to create a scheme or list of such terms. For author and title entries this is not possible, because here what are dealt with are proper names (of persons, organisations or documents), there being no basic 'logic' and no basic restrictions as to what individuals may be called. The code of rules (the procedural code) takes the place of the classification scheme or thesaurus.

The *Anglo-American Cataloguing Rules* (mentioned in Chapter 3) provides rules for author and title entry as well as for description.

182

These rules are used both by the Library of Congress and the British Library, internally, and for their centralised cataloguing services. It is impossible to make rules which will fit every type of information organisation; and the *AACR* is perhaps biased in favour of the large and academic library. What it does do is provide fairly comprehensive listing of *bibliographic* or *documentary* situations. Even if it is not possible to accept in every case the proposed solution to problems, the listing of these problems (together with examples) is in itself a valuable service. An understanding of principles helps the interpretation and adaptation of rules; and in the case of the *AACR*, the rules themselves help to illuminate the principles.

## OTHER FEATURES

Other features which might be used as search features include the publisher's name, the series name and artificial codes used for administrative and identification purposes.

In computer-held files publishers' names can be used for searching; in manual files they are usually given low priority on the grounds that few searchers will ask specifically for works by a publisher until (for example) authors or subjects have been established. This is not however true of all publishers, and in many cases the distinction between corporate author and publisher is difficult to sustain, as is the distinction between publishers' names and series names: a 'Mills and Boon' novel is a more distinctive class label than either 'Romantic novel' or the name of a particular Mills and Boon author. If publishers are used as search terms the rules determining entry in a catalogue will be similar to those governing author entry.

A series is a group of publications, usually from one publisher, having something in common. Some series have a specific subject or type of content in common; and there is no doubt that in these cases the series may become a primary search term. For example the 'Teach yourself' or 'Made simple' series have an attraction of their own — even before the users have decided what it is they want to learn. Series carry some guarantee of a uniform standard and may be an important identification feature; in some cases over-riding that of authorship. Series titles and series editors are used as access points following the same rules as for author/title entries; except that within some operational systems there may be more discretion for the indexer to make, or not to make, entries.

Entries will probably not be made when the content characteristic of the series is highly generalised, and the common characteristics are uniform bindings and format rather than content. The 'Everyman' and 'Worlds Classic' series are of this kind; being mainly a means of publishing 'good quality' literature in attractive format. In such cases although the series is noted in the description there is a case for not making an entry in a file.

Many works are coded for purposes of unique and unambiguous identification. Standard specifications, patent specifications, special series of government publications and series of research reports are examples. It is important, for instance, if a product is to be manufactured according to a particular specification, that the standard should be unambiguously specified. The code numbers must be given in descriptions, and usually are available as search terms. In many cases a list of publications under code numbers is available from the publishers (e.g. the British Patent Office or the British Standards Institution): and the code number is not given as an entry point in local representation files. The documents themselves are however frequently arranged by code number, and this arrangement usually provides a useful chronological order.

The International Standard Book Number is a number now given to most published books in the United Kingdom and in other countries. It usually appears on the back of the title page and it specifies country of publication, publisher, and particular edition. This coding system is a book trade device intended primarily to facilitate ordering and distribution procedures. It is not usually familiar to the ultimate user who indeed has no means of decoding the number. It is now often specified in descriptions however, and (apart from its administrative uses in libraries) it can be used to access computer files provided that the ISBN number is known (from a book trade or other bibliography).

## SUMMARY

All features of documents may be used as access points. In manual files it may be necessary to restrict the number of access points for economic reasons; and especially in the case of files of original documents (as distinct from representations) it may be necessary to select a unique access point. It may be easier to make copies of administrative documents for filing at each access point, than to obtain copies of published non-administrative documents, but considerations of space, and the problems of maintaining the file (of 'filing' and 'unfiling') may make such a course undesirable.

The features used as access points may not be used as primary access points (i.e. they may affect arrangement only after other and more important features have been used) and where only a limited number of access points is possible it is important to determine the 'citation order', (e.g. to determine whether the order 'Subject divided by author divided by title' is more useful or less useful than the order 'Subject divided by title'). Some highly important features can be ignored or given low priority within particular files because they are already implicit in the file content (e.g. children's as distinct from adult literature) or sound recordings as distinct from visual documents. Finally there are features which, although important in determining choice, become so only after all other features have been dealt with. Such features must be récorded in descriptions. Most features can, however, be used as search terms in computer-held files (provided of course they are recorded).

The importance of the various features varies from collection to collection and from database to database.

## FURTHER READING

Items 6, 7, 31, 32 and 35 from section B of further reading on p. 274 − 277.

# CHAPTER 7:  PHYSICAL FORMS OF FILE


A range of 'output' forms is now available, and collection organisers should ensure that they are aware of all of them and their particular features in relation to the needs of an individual collection. The factors influencing the choice of physical form are detailed in Chapter 9 (Design, organisation and evaluation); it suffices to say here that each form performs better with regard to some criteria than to others. The present chapter seeks to identify the existing forms and the features which may be desired in an information retrieval context, bearing in mind the wide variations in available resources which are apparent when comparing information environments, from the one-person operation with basic stationery to the large multi-personnel organisation with several computers, and multiple-user access on different sites, using terminals and visual display units. It must be emphasised that, despite the increasing use of computer-held files (encouraged by reductions in size and comparative cost), many information collection organisers continue to make use of the earlier forms of file (typed cards in cabinets, for instance) and achieve entirely satisfactory results from them, in relation to particular working contexts.

## OUTPUTS

The simplest form of record of the contents of a collection is the *stock*, or *accessions, register*, this is merely a file (perhaps in book form) of entries in order of receipt, with each item being entered against the 'next running number in the register − the

187

number sometimes incorporating the year of acquisition (1716/82, for example). This serves as an identification record, showing what was received and when, and may include an indication of location (shelf-mark, departmental symbol or other code), but is of little use in retrieving, say, documents by a particular author or on a particular subject — unless one is prepared to search the entire register.

Instead of a fixed chronological order of this kind, it is possible to enter the descriptions of the items in a loose-leaf file, ensuring that each one is inserted in its correct place — say, alphabetically by author, to give an author sequence. This provides help for inquirers searching by name of author (assuming that each document has an identifiable and 'agreed' author), but not for those searching by subject, title, series or any other element — these inquirers, once again, have no alternative but to search the whole file.

Clearly, what is needed for efficient retrieval is a file in which these various approaches may all be followed up with equal or near equal ease. *Sheaf and card files* have long provided this facility and are common today. The sheaf variety consists of paper sheets (of which various sizes are available), each containing the (written, typed or printed) description of a document and fastened into a binder. More than one copy of a description can be produced, either by carbon paper, or by additional writing or typing, or by reproduction from a master of some kind; the appropriate heading (author, title and so on) may then be added at the top of the sheet or the relevant element in the description underlined, providing a 'filing element', and the sheets inserted in their appropriate places in the sequence or sequences — depending on the type of file (dictionary, systematic and so on). The binders in which the sheets are held may be housed on shelves, or in specially-made units.

The card file has been perhaps the most familiar form for some years; over time the methods of reproducing the copies have

**188**

changed and increased in number, and many new collection organisers turn to this form as their first stock record — perhaps later turning to a more 'technologically complex' form. A variety of sizes of card is available, and they may be housed in metal, wooden or plastic drawers, boxes or cabinets — some incorporating mechanisms for retaining the cards in place. Production methods for the copies are similar to those for sheaf files.

Some collections (of periodicals, for example) can be very adequately recorded using the *visible index* type of file. There is a variety of these, a typical one consisting of metal frames suspended against a wall, or on a rotating stand, in which are placed (in alphabetical order) strips of card bearing the titles of periodicals, the holdings of each title in the collection and the location (shelf or class-mark or other code). Entries are brief —usually only one line (strip) per title — and may be written or typed, the strips being supplied in sheets, enabling insertion into a typewriter.

Catalogues in *microform* are becoming common. Originally produced by microphotography of cards, slips or strips in existing files, they are now frequently generated by computer from data input directly to the computer store, without the necessity to supply copy first for the camera. Microform includes microfiche (film sheet), film strip in cassettes, film strip on open reels and in jackets, and some rarer kinds; the forms most commonly found in use for catalogues are microfiche and cassette film. The images cannot be read with the naked eye (reading equipment is required), but the title line (fiche) and the leading frame (film) are normally in eye-readable characters in order to aid identification and searching. Microfiche can be stored in envelopes in a box or drawer, or in slots on a stand, film in boxes in a drawer or cabinet.

Another form of card file found more often in specialised information environments is that composed of *optical coincidence cards* (sometimes known as feature, body-punched or peek-a-boo cards). They are available in a variety of sizes, the cards being overprinted with grids of small numbered squares; each card represents an index term, with which it is labelled, and the accession numbers of all documents to which that index term is allocated are punched on the card, through the appropriate numbered squares. Ancillary equipment required includes a light source over which to place the appropriate cards in order to identify those related to a particular index term (unless holding up to available light near a window is feasible), a punching tool and (unless the documents themselves are filed in accession number order) a separate file (cards, slips or other form) of document descriptions filed in accession number sequence, in order to provide further information to inquirers once the accession numbers have been retrieved.

A simpler form of 'coincidence-type' file can be constructed from basic stationery, using cards (one for each index term) ruled or printed in columns numbered from 0 to 9; accession numbers of relevant documents are entered in the appropriate column for the last digit of the number (1614 in column 4, for example). Cards for two or more terms can then be compared with the naked eye (without the need for any other equipment) to discover which accession numbers are held in common by the cards.

The application of *computers* to information retrieval operations has led to a variety of output forms. *Printout* on a paper roll or stack can be produced on a printer linked to the computer, cut or folded and fastened into binders; *cards* may also be generated, and *microform* (known as COM — Computer Output Microform). The desired layout, style, headings and sequence are produced by instructions given to the computer. Once data has been input to the computer store, it is possible for a variety of outputs (cards, paper, microform) to be produced from the same set of data, according to the needs of the organisation, and used for different purposes. These forms are usually produced off-line (not in direct connection with the central processor) and supplied some time after the input of the data. If no hard copy outputs are required, however, an *on-line* catalogue can provide the most up to date and the most immediate access. In this form, the data, once consigned to the computer store, are immediately available

**190**

for searching.  The retrieved entries are displayed on a visual display unit (VDU) from which inquirers can copy and take notes; it is possible in some cases to order a hard-copy print (produced off-line) of those retrieved entries of interest in relation to a particular inquiry.  Some files have facilities for multiple access, with several terminals.

## DESIRABLE FEATURES OF CATALOGUE FORMS

It is not possible to list all the features which each and every catalogue must have, since some possible requirements are in opposition to each other and others are not desirable in all circumstances.  The following list is therefore intended to act as a prompt to enable organisers to identify those which are important in their situations, and therefore to select the most appropriate form (in association with the information given in Chapter 9).  For that reason also the order in which the factors are dealt with should *not* be taken as an order of priority – this can only be established in relation to a particular set of circumstances.

### Amount of Information per Entry

The amount of information included in the description for a document is the subject of a policy decision, as indicated in Chapter 3, but it is of course important that the required detail is able to be presented to the inquirer as a whole unit, not split up into parts.  The various forms of file differ in the amount of space available for the presentation of an entry.  Sheaf sheets and cards – even the smaller (125 x 75 mm, 5 x 3 in.) size of the latter – can incorporate very full written, typed or printed descriptions, only occasionally requiring to run on to another sheet or card.  Visible indexes of the strip-type are limited in capacity to what can be presented on a single strip, perhaps running on to a second for a longer entry.  The use of colour in sheaf, card and strip files can add to the information given, either by the use of tinted papers and cards or by coloured stickers, to differentiate

191

between kinds of document – white cards for monographs, gold for conference proceedings, blue for periodicals, or red dots for audio materials, green for microforms, for example; this can be helpful to inquirers seeking a particular form. Microforms can give as much or as little information as is required. Computer-generated hard-copy forms, like printout, similarly may contain full entries or brief ones – a familiar form in some environments is the printout of single-line entries consisting of minimal identifying information, with a location symbol. The optical coincidence type of file provides, at first sight, only the accession number of relevant documents – the amount of further information available depends on the nature of the supplementary file, if there is one. In on-line files the amount of information available per entry can be considerable, but the amount presented to the inquirer on the VDU is limited by the screen frame – in most cases this is adequate for a detailed description, but if there is in addition a lengthy abstract or annotation or the whole text of the document, the complete unit may not be visible at one time.

## Number of Entries Visible at one Sight

Searching a file is speeded by the presentation of several entries at a time, allowing the eye to run quickly through the sequence. Not all catalogue forms permit this; sheaf and card files present only one entry at a time, for example. Book-form, microform, printout and visible strip files allow the perusal of a page, frame or column of entries at one showing, while on-line files can show more than one entry – depending on the amount of information given in the entries (it is usually possible to choose either several brief entries or a full single entry).

## Number of Simultaneous Users

In environments where inquirers appreciate the value of the catalogue, there is likely to be a need for more than one person to use the file at one time – and this is augmented by consultation by staff. The ideal situation is for each user to have her own copy of the file, but this is not always feasible (see *Reproducibility* p. 196 ). Given the existence of a single copy, some forms are more amenable to multiple use than others. Sheaf files consisting of several binders may be consulted by as many users as there are binders, though a single binder cannot be used by more than one person at a time; since the binders are removable from their housing, they can be taken away to a desk and consulted in comfort. Card files can, in theory, be consulted by as many users as there are drawers in the cabinet, though the nearer the required drawers are to each other (and the larger the users), the more difficult it becomes. Visible index files can usually be scanned with ease by a group of people, depending on the means of display and the spacing between the frames. Book-form and printout are limited to one user per volume, and optical coincidence files can be used by more than one only if additional light sources are provided and the users do not wish to search by the same index terms. Microforms similarly are limited in use by the number of reading machines available; if more than one, and users do not wish to consult the same parts of the file, multiple use may be possible. On-line files may have one or several terminals through which users may access the data; multiple-access systems allow several people to interrogate (search) the file simultaneously (or apparently so), from different terminals — perhaps on different sites.

Failure to make sufficient provision for the desired level of use may result in inquirers giving up in their attempts to use the file, and referring their inquiries to the staff, or taking their business elsewhere, or leaving with their information needs unfulfilled.

## Legibility

The highest degree of legibility can be achieved by the use of print on paper, employing the full range of type-sizes and styles available to the printer, with ample spacing and good layout. This is not, however, often a possibility for catalogue production; the collection organiser must therefore endeavour to produce the highest quality file possible within the constraints placed on her. The information should be presented in clear characters, using whatever variations in size, style and layout are available. Sheaf, card and strip files can utilise the facilities of the normal type-writer — upper and lower-case (capital and small) characters, underlining, variable spacing and so on; computer-generated paper forms are dependent on the character set(s) provided by the printing component used — which in some cases may be upper-case only. Microform legibility is dependent upon the character set or original copy from which it is reproduced, also upon the spacing and layout of the entries adjacent to each other, and the colour and type of film; entries may be arranged in columns — one above the other — or in rows — side by side, and may be posi-tive (dark on light) or negative (light on dark). On-line systems presenting information on VDUs may use upper and lower-case or upper-case only, with the data appearing light against a dark screen, and readable from a few feet away.

Legibility is, of course, also related to the amount of information presented at one time, the speed of consultation, and the amount and detail of the information desired to be retrieved (as well as the visual acuity of the inquirer).

## Ease of Handling, Speed of Retrieval

The easiest of all forms to handle, scan, find and keep one's place in is the book; it can be laid on a flat or inclined surface for consultation, carried to the shelves for reference and so on. This form, however, has a number of disadvantages, as will be seen, and most catalogues, as a result, take other forms. The sheaf type is perhaps the nearest to the book form in that the binders may be removed for consultation, the 'pages' turned and marked in the same way, but only one entry is visible at a time, and fewer entries are available in the same amount of space. Cards in boxes or drawers may be fixed in position, and therefore not always removable — in large free-standing units the user has to stand while consulting and taking notes from the file; place-markers

194

may be provided, which the user can move about within the file as needed, but continuous consultation of such a file can be tiring. Visible index frames may not need to be handled at all, merely looked at – in which case they should be hung at an appropriate level for comfort; some types of these are housed horizontally in a cabinet and pulled out for reference – situated on a desk, this can be a convenient arrangement. Optical coincidence cards, often housed in open-topped containers, can be quite easily selected and placed over or against the light source; cards must be replaced in their correct alphabetical (or other) sequence. Microforms are very light in weight, easy to insert into the necessary reading equipment (except in some early models); finding the exact place seems easier on microfiche than microfilm (though some film equipment incorporates finding mechanisms, which aid retrieval). Computer printout can be similar to book form, but the (unreduced) copy makes for large, and in some cases, floppy volumes, which are less easy to handle – though a large amount of information per page is presented when opened, enabling quick scanning. Any catalogue employing a computerised system requires that the operators familiarise themselves with the mechanical methods for instructing the computer to find information and obtain copies in the required form; a set of instructions has to be followed and certain procedures memorised for speedy access. Once competence has been achieved, retrieval can be very fast.

The question of 'portability' of files has two aspects; on the one hand, it is very convenient if the file, or part of it, can be consulted wherever the user requires it; on the other, organisers may be concerned that files may disappear or become disarranged, a particular problem if there is only one copy and it cannot easily be replaced. For forms such as microform and optical coincidence cards, there is little additional value in their portability, unless several pieces of equipment are distributed for their use. Speed of retrieval is dependent not only on the form, but on the nature of the search, the amount of information to be sifted and so on: it should be noted that – given enough light to see by – sheaf, card and strip files have immediate and uninterrupted access, while those forms (such as microform, and computer files) which are dependent on a power supply and sustained technical performance for their use, are slightly more vulnerable to interruptions in availability of the records.

It is observed that some inquirers are reluctant to pursue their inquiry if the operation of mechanical equipment is necessitated; the familiar, full-size, print file is likely to be more readily used. The introduction of a form requiring such equipment, therefore, must normally be carried out with appropriate notice to users, guidance and instruction, so that there is no falling-off in user numbers or in user satisfaction.

**Need for, and Ease of, Guiding**

Except in the case of very small, single sequence files, there is a need for indication of the various parts, the beginnings of sub-sequences and so on, in order that inquirers may proceed quickly to the appropriate place. Sheaf and card files may be guided externally by labels on binders and drawers, and internally by protruding tabs, and guide cards; internal guides should appear at frequent intervals. Microforms, printout, and on-line book forms require headings to be included in the data when input, so that they appear in the appropriate places on the final product. In any file, when it becomes apparent that a sequence has developed — because of additions — further guiding should be considered.

**Reproducibility**

In some situations it is necessary (or at least desirable) to have available more than just a single copy of the catalogue, so that several inquirers may have access to the complete file at one time — those inquirers sometimes being on different sites. Sheaf and card entries can be produced in multiple copies at the outset, all of equivalent quality; if required to be dispatched to other locations, though, these forms can be costly, due to their bulk. An existing sheaf, card or strip file can be laid out in frames and

196

photocopied or microphotographed, thus reducing the total size and therefore weight; it is possible to bind the photocopied pages, making a book - form catalogue. Multiple optical coincidence files can only be supplied by the production of duplicate sets of punched cards. Microform is now cheap to reproduce and, being light (and in the case of microfiche, flat and thin), is inexpensive and easy to distribute; it is only useful, however, when the recipients possess the appropriate reading equipment. Computer-generated printout can be reproduced, either by multiple print-ings (a slow process) or by photocopying and perhaps reducing the original. As already mentioned, on-line systems can be pro-vided with multiple access through a number of separate terminals — but it is also possible to produce duplicate files on tape for distribution. A valuable facility of computer-held files is that they can be produced in whatever physical form, and in whatever sequence(s) the situation requires.

If not merely distribution to members, staff or other limited group of recipients is required, but rather full commercial publication, book form is the most suitable; this situation may arise in an information collection specialising in a particular subject area — the catalogue then effectively becoming a bibliography of that subject, and extending its use beyond that of a record of one collection. For a certain clientele, microform may be suitable (and is cheaper to dispatch), but is likely to be acceptable to a smaller number of potential purchasers.

## Compatibility with other Files

Many collection organisers are free to make decisions about the appropriate form of file without taking into account factors external to their own collections. Others are more constrained because they are part of a larger organisation, because they wish to buy in catalogue data from commercial suppliers for some of their material, or because they have agreed to cooperate with other collection organisers in pooling their cataloguing input, perhaps with a view to producing a union catalogue (showing locations for documents in whichever collection they belong to).

In these latter cases, the need for compatibility may restrict the organiser's choice, in that card output may not be available, or microfiche but not film, for example, If the 'bought-in' data relates to one specific kind of document only (specifications or trade literature or periodicals, for instance), then a separate cat-alogue in the form available may be maintained, other material being represented in the main file — though it is usually more beneficial to file the entries for all kinds of documents together.

## Capacity

The majority of file forms are unlimited in their ability to incor-porate additional entries, all that is necessary being to add extra drawers, cabinets, binders, containers, reading equipment and so on, as long as space allows. The optical coincidence file is restric-ted by the capacity of the card, since each square on the card represents a document accession number, if it contains only 2000 squares, then once 2000 documents have been indexed, a new file must be started ( a new series of 2000 or whatever size is thought appropriate). This means that separate searches are involved (of the two files) when information is needed; it is important, therefore, to select at the outset a card size which permits the indexing of an ample number of documents. In some cases, a yearly file is required, therefore a card size which allows a single year's input to be recorded is satisfactory and a new file is opened for the next year. One of the features of computer-held files is their capacity to hold large amounts of data, but the actual amount will be determined by the size of the store, ancil-lary facilities, how much information is to be processed at the same time and so on. As time passes it is likely that additional facilities may become available, or that an opportunity to upgrade and expand the system may occur. Whatever the form of file, consideration must be given initially to:-

a) the amount of data to be filed immediately and

b) the expected rate of input.

## Size and Space Requirements

The amount of space taken up by a file depends not only on its form, but on how many documents are represented in it, how many entries there are for each document and how much information is given in each entry. Sheaf and card files are rather greedy for space, card cabinets because room has to be allowed for drawers to be pulled out their full length – and they may also incorporate pull-out shelves for note-taking. Visible strip index files suspended on walls can take up much space, but are situated in a place which is unlikely to be used for anything else. Microforms can reduce enormously the amount of space needed for a file, even when room for the necessary reading equipment is allowed, Printout tends to be large and bulky, needing flat surfaces on which to rest for easy consultation. The size of an on-line system depends on the type, the number of terminals and other peripheral equipment; the tendency now is towards smaller, more stream-lined, equipment. Optical coincidence file size depends on the number of cards, the size of the cards and their containers, and the type of light source used.

## Security

Sometimes the contents of files are required to be kept restricted to a limited number of inquirers. Multiple copies are unlikely, therefore, to be produced and the single file may be either locked into a room or cupboard or kept in the staff area of the accommodation, or secured in some other way. On-line files can be protected by a system of passwords and identity codes – only those inquirers possessing knowledge of the password and an approved user identity being able to call up files from the store;

files of this kind also need protection from:-

a) unauthorised additions and other alterations and

b) inadvertent deletion of entries or files, as a result of an incorrect command or the discarding of a supplementary store.

Card, sheaf and strip files have a certain amount of protection, in that they are retained in drawers with rods, in binders or frames, but entries can be removed and interfered with; microforms similarly can be abused.


### Ease of Maintenance, Staff Use and Amendment

Catalogues are usually not static in terms of their contents, but need to be kept up to date with the day by day changes in the collection — new documents, additional copies, changed locations and so on. Up-to-dateness is aided if such changes, once recorded, can be rapidly incorporated into the file. The on-line file is potentially the most up-to-date form, since data, once input to the store, are immediately available for searching and printing out; bought-in data supplied on magnetic tape may be incorporated automatically. Other forms (cards, slips, strips, microforms) depend heavily on the speed of reproduction and on staff availability and experience. The book form of catalogue is the least useful in this respect, since it cannot be updated by the insertion of new entries, but only by the issue of supplements or completely revised editions — day by day updating is therefore impossible. Amendment and withdrawal of existing entries and addition of new entries is quick and simple with sheaf, card and strip files (once the entries have been reproduced); microforms are updated by the issue of supplementary films or fiches, or by revised editions.

No file, whatever its level of technological sophistication, is updated without sufficient staff resources being available to feed

**200**

the data into the file in the appropriate manner, and it is essential that, as well as being convenient for the non-staff inquirer, the form of file should be agreeable to those members of the information staff who work with it. Filing, or making amendment to, large numbers of cards, slips or strips can be a tedious process and if carried for too long a period of time, becomes prone to error, prolonged sessions using microform readers (particularly if the equipment is ill-designed) may tire the eyes and produce mental fatigue, and there is currently a debate about the possible harmful effects on operators of continuously using terminals with VDUs.

## Length of Life

Most files are expected to be required for a length of time measured in years; many still in existence started life decades ago and retain some of their original handwritten or typed entries. Card files seem to withstand considerable handling, when properly housed, and forms like microfilm and fiche last well — again if appropriately protected from harmful influences. In some cases it is the equipment required for reading microforms which needs repair or replacement rather than the files themselves — particularly if users are inexpert or careless operators. On-line systems may be supplied with regular service and maintenance contracts, and opportunities for replacements when needed.

Whatever the form selected, it should be borne in mind that it is as inefficient to establish an expensive, long-lasting file for a temporary purpose, as it is to set up one which begins to show signs of stress after two years, when it is required to last for fifteen.

## Cost

It is neither possible nor advisable to quote exact or estimated costs here, as so much depends on the individual circumstances. The factors to be taken into account include: cost of first purchase of equipment; cost of associated stationery; area of space required; special environmental conditions to be arranged (heat, light, humidity and so on); staff requirements to set the system in operation; reproduction costs; dispatch costs (if multiple copies are to be distributed); rate of input; staff and time needs for amendment and updating. There may be no need for the collection organiser considering the setting up of a file to budget for large sums at first (or at all); the particular virtue of the card and sheaf types of file, for a new small collection, is that they incur a very small financial outlay in starting the record – a few packets of cards or packs of paper and a box, drawer, or binder, which can stand unobtrusively on a staff desk.

## PREPARATION OF INPUT

With each of the forms dealt with above, the data have to be prepared in some way from the documents, for their addition to the file. In small information units, the same person may be involved in all stages of the work, in larger departments the tasks may be divided between staff (see Chapter 9). Whatever the situation, when entries are prepared on site (rather than being bought in) a description must be produced for each document, with an indication of the elements or terms by which it should be accessible in the file. A large number of methods exist for the preparation and reproduction of catalogue data, and much depends on the number of staff, their particular skills, the amount of data to be processed and the facilities readily available. In small units, as indicated above, the cataloguer may himself produce the final copies, in others the typist (already familiar with the requirements of the catalogue and with the features of documents) may be given the documents with an indication of the main entry heading and a list of other index terms, and then produce the records direct; or the cataloguer may dictate the details on a tape cassette (requring the typist to be familiarised with the required layout and style, and the 'dictator' to be skilled in matters of clear speaking and indicating spacing, spelling, punctuation and capitalisation, in cases of doubt). Alternatively, the data may be handwritten on a plain slip and given to a typist for multiple or single

202

reproduction (that is, for the production either of all needed copies, or of a master for reproduction by another process — stencil duplication, spirit duplication, photocopying, dyeline copying, for example); or the data may be entered on a work-sheet, with each part of the description written or printed in a particular (named or numbered) position on a grid, and then be given to a keyboard operator for entry into the computer file (either directly, or through the medium of punched cards, or tape).

The accuracy of entries should be checked before reproduction, since errors in catalogues can have serious effects on filing and retrieval; in the case of multiple typings, every copy of the entry requires checking.

## COMPARISONS AND SURVEYS

Reports of comparisons and surveys of different forms of file appear from time to time in information studies literature. These can be useful in providing results acquired through observation and experience of usage under particular circumstances, though caution must be exercised in applying the results without question to any information environment. A survey of use and attitudes in a university library, for example, does not necessarily have relevance to the information collection in a neighbourhood law centre or an engineering standards department.

## FURTHER READING

Items 6, 7, 8, 20 and 42 from section B of further reading on p. 274 − 278.

# CHAPTER 8: SEARCHING

Librarians and other information workers probably spend more time searching other people's files than they do in operating and maintaining their own; and this is almost certainly true of persons who are not information workers. Other people's files may include 'other people's' libraries, reference books, catalogues, bibliographies and other databases. Schools of librarianship and information science have devoted some time to the techniques of searching (to the techniques of 'finding out'), as have librarians of academic institutions in their 'user training' programmes. However, much of this instruction has concentrated on choosing the right file; upon choosing the right source of information rather than in using the particular file once it has been selected. The advent of computer-held files has, however, necessitated more formal instruction on how to use particular files, partly because the inefficient use of on-line search facilities is itself expensive, and partly because inefficient use may totally frustrate the search. Computers respond to the 'correct' instructions correctly formulated. Instructions with 'vague edges' are permissible and indeed may be efficient in a manual search but not in a computer search. Moreover, computers offer very much enlarged possibilities in terms of search approaches; and indeed very much enlarged databases. If advantage is to be taken of these facilities, systematic searching becomes necessary.

The principles and procedures identified for instruction and training in computer searching are essentially no different from those used in manual searching; the difference is that they are more frequently made explicit.

## STARTING THE SEARCH

For any search (whether in a manual or computerised file) the following steps are taken, or should be taken.

1. Selection of the file (the collection or the database including catalogue, bibliography, reference work . . )

2. Finding out how the file is organised; and finding out about its defects and idosyncracies.

3. Selecting search terms, and if necessary changing the search strategy, broadening and narrowing the search according to the results.

The procedures are likely to differ in detail according to whether the file is a precoordinate or a postcoordinate file; and according to whether it uses natural or artificial language. However, in all cases the user (in all probability without knowing it) will be using Boolean logic to pursue the search.

### Selection of the file

As already discussed (Chapter 6) the primary search features may be provided for in file content rather than in file arrangement. At an extreme it is no use looking for works on test-tube babies in a bibliography of books for five year olds; and no use looking for works on offshore drilling for oil in bibliographies with a time span finishing in 1910. For computer searching (and to a lesser extent in manual searching) the smaller the file searched the quicker and more economical the search will be. Therefore, although a file may cover literature from 1910–1982, it might be more economical (and much simpler) to look for 'offshore drilling' in a file covering the years 1970–1982.

206

## The Characteristics of the File

In the case of many databases, including computerised and manual bibliographies and catalogues, and in the case of many libraries open to the public, instructions as to use are provided. But this is not so of all databases and collections. New staff approaching an office filing system and users of many reference books (including directories) are often not adequately instructed. Obviously the user should establish whether the file is arranged in systematic or alphabetical order, and under which kinds of term entries are made. Failure to find what is required may be due however to a number of almost hidden factors:

1. The item is not in the file. (To what extent can the searcher assume that failure to find an item is an indication that the item does not exist either (a) in the file or (b) elsewhere? The former situation relates to file arrangement, the latter to file content).

2. The search terms used by the searcher may not match those in the file. They may be too general or too specific; or the searcher may have failed to note whether a natural or artificial index language is used. In an index to quotations, the quotations 'Let me not to the marriage of true minds admit impediments' and 'Thou shalt not covet thy neighbour's wife' will be separated if the indexing is by keyword; may be brought together if the indexing is by concept (controlled vocabulary); or indeed may be separated on the grounds that the first quotation has nothing to do with marriage. The searcher may be frustrated in a search for a particular quotation (keyword known) or for quotations about a particular subject unless he first ascertains which system is used, and indeed, notes the idiosyncracies of the indexing.

3. The searcher may not understand the arrangement. For example, the filing order in the Universal Decimal Classification; or whether in an alphabetical order the word-by-word or letter-by-letter system is in use.

4. The searcher comes to the file with the wrong information, for example as to spelling of a proper name; and the file gives no assistance.

5. The searcher uses the wrong feature as a search term, and may be unaware that, for instance, no entries are made under indicative titles or under secondary authors. For example, the assumption might be that the book 'Railways of the world' is not represented in the file, although it is there represented under author and subject.

## Selecting the Search Terms (1): Browsing and Precise Object Searches

If the searcher knows precisely what is required and knows what to call it the search is usually (though not invariably) a 'precise object search' for which a file in indicative (alphabetical) order is usually more useful than one in systematic order. If, on the other hand, the searcher is seeking inspiration or 'does not know what he wants until he sees it' the search is a browsing search, for which systematic orders are usually more useful, since the searcher can arrive within a 'broad field' and wander around more conveniently than if the related sections are widely separated as is the case with alphabetical orders.

Irrespective of the aims of the search, however, precise object searches and browsing searches may be imposed upon the searcher either by the deficiencies of the file or by the user's own ignorance. For example, a map user may be looking for a *precise* location but not know its name or how the name is spelt. In such a case the searcher must 'browse' in the map itself, rather than go direct to the name in the alphabetical subject index. On the other hand, even if the searcher knows precisely and accurately the name of the location required, he will not be able to use this knowledge if the map is not provided with an index. Most maps and atlases, but not all reference or other 'fact' books, are provided with indexes; and not all indexes are efficient. In such cases 'browsing' through contents lists, and examining running titles, or even scanning the text for 'key words' may be the only way of reaching the 'precise object' sought. (Very few novels are provided with indexes – perhaps properly not so. However, English readers of 'War and peace' must often have wished the custom of providing indexes were more common).

The searcher may not know precisely the *name* of the thing sought (as in the example of the map reader), or the concept may be difficult to define (because, for instance, of its newness or its 'blurred edges'). In both these cases browsing in a systematically arranged file may be the only way of reaching the desired object.

An alternative device is to find an item which is known to fulfil the requirements, but which has in addition characteristics for which the name is known. The searcher can then note how the item has been dealt with in respect of the particular sought characteristic. For instance a few years ago a searcher might have had some difficulty in beginning a search for information on 'children who are injured by their parents in a non-accidental but non-criminal way; the cause of the parents' behaviour being attributable to social factors'. There is considerable literature on this subject, and the searcher today would have little difficulty in starting a search under 'battered babies' or 'non-accidental injuries'. However until a concept is established and named (by society in general or by the searcher), the searcher could begin by looking up (for example) under *author* 'Golightly and

**209**

McAdam. The child in the socially deprived home: physical and psychological risks', which the searcher has read and knows to be about the required subject. The searcher can then note that the item is also indexed under 'Non-accidental injuries' (etc.), or is at a particular place on the shelves of the library; and presumably other works on the same subject will be similarly treated. This device is used intuitively by many searchers and forms part of the formal instructions in many computer search manuals. Essentially the same device is used in so called 'citation indexes'. In such indexes items may be listed under author or title, and under each item are noted other items in which the first listed item is quoted or cited. There is at least a chance that any articles which quote Golightly and McAdam will deal with the same subject.

## Selecting the Search Terms (2):
### Recall and Precision

The terms recall and precision were referred to in Chapter 4 and are further discussed in Chapter 9. Basically recall and precision ratios are means of evaluating a system. Recall is the ratio of relevant documents retrieved in relation to the number of relevant documents in the system; and precision the number of relevant documents retrieved in relation to the total number of documents (irrelevant or relevant) retrieved. Thus it might be that in order to retrieve *everything* in the system which relates to straw as a building material (100% recall) it might be necessary to retrieve a large mass of material which is not relevant (e.g. information on straw dollies, fire risks when using straw, reeds as a building material). If, of two hundred documents retrieved 100 are on straw as a building material, then the precision ratio is 50%. If this 50% includes all the available items on straw as a building material then the recall ratio is 100%. The ability of the system to provide high levels of recall and precision is affected by the design of the system itself. But the searchers can themselves decide in respect of any search whether high recall or high precision is required. For example a searcher wishing for total recall might search under 'building materials in general', under 'straw as a building material' and under 'reeds as a building material'. The searcher wishing for high precision would confine the search to the terms representing 'straw as a building material'.

High recall will usually be required in the following circumstances:-

1. The database or collection is small, therefore everything even slightly relevant becomes important.

2. The information sought is critical (e.g. a list of *all* the persons who have escaped from a high-security prison).

3. It is necessary to prove the 'universal negative', e.g. that there is NO information on the subject, or indeed, that NO prisoners have escaped. In order to prove this (and indeed it usually cannot be proved absolutely) it is necessary to be sure that if the information *were* available it would be found.

4. The searcher is not quite sure what is required and wishes to be presented with the widest possible choice.

High precision is usually required in the following circumstances:-

1. The database or collection is very large, is likely to contain much repetitive information and there is therefore a good statistical chance that a low recall result will produce all the useful information; conversely that a high recall will produce an unmanageable amount of irrelevant information.

2. Speed at service point is essential. The user has no time to separate the relevant from the irrelevant, after the material has been retrieved from the system.

3. The conditions requiring high recall (2, 3, and 4) do not apply.

**Selecting the Search Terms (3):**
**The Shortest Route**

The shortest route to the information required is likely to be one which begins at a point about which the searcher is absolutely sure; which leads to the smallest possible group of items compatible with the aims of the search; and to the point at which there is likely to be least disagreement between searcher and system. For instance if the searcher is looking for the book by 'Golightly and McAdam' on 'non-accidental injuries', and knows the names of the authors, is not quite sure of the title, and is totally vague about the name of the subject, then obviously the shortest route is via the names of the authors. On the other hand if the title is known beyond any doubt this might be the shortest route since the title is likely to be in a 'group of one' (unlike the subject and probably unlike the authors). There is most likelihood of disagreement between searcher and system in the case of the subject.

Other methods of working to produce economical and effective results include the following:-

1. For multi-element subjects choose the element which seems to have the narrowest scope as the primary search term. This is most likely to reflect the arrangement within the system. For example in a general collection or database a book on 'education and libraries' is most likely to be placed with other books on libraries, as the 'narrower subject'.

In a postcoordinate system where the item would
be indexed under both elements without sub-division
(for the searcher to match at the search stage) there
would be the further advantage (probably) that the
narrower element would produce such few items
that further matching would be unnecessary. For
example a search for 'the effect of nuclear fall-out
on camomile daisies' might (in a general file) produce such few items on camomile daisies that the
few which dealt with nuclear fall-out could easily
be distinguished by examining the whole result.
Consideration should be given however to the overall subject of the file. One devoted exclusively to
librarianship would have 'education' as the minority
subject; and one devoted to botany or horticulture
would include relatively little on nuclear fall-out,
and the 'minority' subjects would be the narrower.

2. 'Taken for granted' elements might be ignored in
the indexing. For example in a database concerned
with botany, the term 'botany' might be reserved
for those items which deal with botany in general;
there might be no references from this term to the
main branches of botany, and items dealing with
botany in the curriculum of secondary schools
would be indexed only under headings representing
'curriculum in secondary schools'.

## Selecting the Search Terms (4):
## Minimum Input: Maximum Output

A filing system should lead the searcher from what she knows to
what she doesn't know. In the discussion on browsing and precise
object searches there was a suggestion that not all systems do this
with absolute efficiency; and, indeed it is virtually impossible
for other than the most circumscribed and 'localised' system to

anticipate everything that a searcher might not know. (For example the surname 'Cholmondeley' might be spelt in half a dozen different ways by potential users; and in this, as in other cases it is not possible to provide for all possible errors). The deficiencies of a system may however be compensated for to a limited extent by the skills of the searcher, who may 'work the system' in order to produce the required results and to produce them economically, using her own knowledge as a starting point and using it maximally.

The examples so far given have included:

1. Using knowledge of author and title as the entry key when the subject is elusive.

2. Browsing over a wide area which is known to contain the required subject.

Basically both these methods consist of using known class characteristics, however generalised and diffuse these characteristics may be.

The same method essentially is that of using known parts of the symbols employed in the system. If the searcher is not sure how to spell 'cataloguing' she can still search under 'catal' and this will not only lead (though not by shortest route) to 'cataloguing' it will also lead to 'catalogues', 'cataloguers' and 'catalogue', (which may be what is required). This device is a common enough one in manual searches, and is formalised in computer searches under the term 'truncating'. The example is an instance of 'right-hand truncating', expressed in a computer instruction by some such device as 'catal:'. In computer searching left-hand and internal truncation is possible, as for example '+natal' for 'prenatal', 'perinatal' and 'postnatal' and 'encyclop+dia' for 'encyclopaedia' and 'encyclopedia'. Right- and left-hand truncation are most useful in broadening the search in respect of concepts. Internal truncation is most useful for dealing with

214

variations in spelling. (Computers do not usually tolerate variations in spelling, so that a request for 'Encyclopaedia of art' might be frustrated if the alternative spelling were used in the instruction, unless the internal truncation device were used).

## Selecting the Search Terms (5):
### The Use of Boolean Operators

Boolean search logic is based on the symbolic logic of the mathematician George Boole (1815–1864). Most searchers use it whether efficiently or inefficiently and whether consciously or unconsciously; and in effect it provides a model for describing what happens intellectually during a search. The logic is made explicit in computer searching, and indeed in manual postcoordinate systems.

The three 'logical operators' used are exemplified in Fig.8:1. A logical product (Fig. 8:1(a)) is a class which lies at the intersection of two or more classes, and thus any superimposed, compound or complex class is a logical product. However the term is used in searching to indicate any item in a file which has two or more sought features or two or more labels. A logical difference (Fig. 8:1(b)) is a class the members of which exclude the members of another class, or a set of items which have a common label but which exclude features which have another specified label. A logical sum (Fig. 8:1(c)) consists of all the members of two or more classes including those which belong to more than one of the classes. Products, differences and sums are expressed respectively by the three logical operators 'AND', 'NOT' and 'OR', as demonstrated in Fig. 8:1.

215

## Fig. 8:1(a)

*Logical products: classes which lie at the intersection of two or more classes*

A search for.

Straw as a building material:

Straw AND Building materials.

Items which exhibit *both* these features.

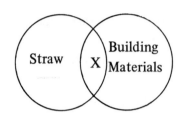

A search for:

Building materials. Items issued by the Building Research Station:

Building materials AND Building Research Station.

Items which exhibit *both* these features.

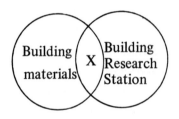

A search for:

Building materials. Items issued during 1982:

Building materials AND 1982.

Items which exhibit *both* these features.

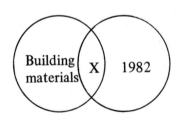

Items dealing with straw as a building material issued by the Building Research Station during 1982.

Straw AND Building materials AND Building Research Station AND 1982.

**216**

*Logical differences: classes the membership of which excludes
members of one or more other classes.*

A search for:

Building materials other than
straw:

Building materials NOT Straw,

Items which exhibit the first but
not the second feature.

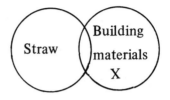

A search for:

Building materials NOT issued by
the Building Research Station:

Building materials NOT Building
Research Station

Items which exhibit the first but
not the second of these features.

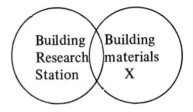

A search for:

Building materials. Items issued
before 1982. (Search taking place
in 1982):

Building materials NOT 1982.

Items which exhibit the first but
not the second of these features.

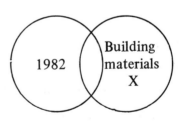

Items dealing with building materials other than straw and issued
prior to 1982 by organisations other than the Building Research
Station: Building materials NOT Straw NOT Building Research
Station NOT 1982.

## Fig. 8: 1(c)

*Logical sums: classes the membership of which consists of the membership of two or more classes including the overlap.*

A search for:

Building materials in general
and straw in general:

Building materials OR Straw.

Items which exhibit one or both
of these features.

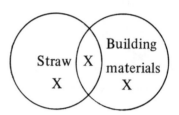

A search for:

Building materials in general and
for publications of the Building
Station:

Building materials OR Building
Research Station.

Items which exhibit one or both of
these features.

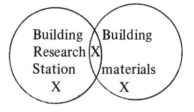

A search for

Building materials in general
and items issued in 1982:

Building materials OR 1982.

Items which exhibit one or both
of these features.

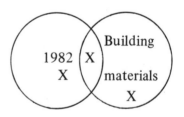

Items which deal with building materials or straw or which were issued by the Building Research Station or issued during 1982 or combine any two or more of these features:
Building materials OR Straw OR Building Research Station OR 1982.

218

*Combination of logical operators 'AND', 'OR' and 'NOT'.*

Search:

Straw as a building
material. Items issued
in 1982 excluding items issued
by the Building Research Station.

(Straw AND Building materials AND 1982) NOT Building
Research Station.


Search:

Straw as a building
material with the
exception of items
issued in 1982 by
the Building Research Station:

(Straw AND Building materials) NOT (Building Research Station
AND    1982).


Search:

Straw as a building material.
Items issued by the Building
Research Station at any period,
and items issued by other organisations
in 1982:

(Straw AND Building materials) AND (Building Research Station
OR 1982).

Fig. 8:2 shows two schedules of classes, respectively in systematic and in alphabetical order, and both precoordinate.

Fig. 8:2

*Precoordinate files in systematic and alphabetical orders*

| Systematic order | | Index |
|---|---|---|
| 7 | Building materials | Building materials 7 |
| 72 | Straw | Building materials: Roofs 82 |
| 8 | Roofs | Building materials: Walls 9 |
| 82 | Materials | Roofs 8 |
| 822 | Straw | Straw: Building materials 72 |
| 9 | Walls | Straw: Building materials: Roofs 822 |
| 92 | Materials | Straw: Building materials: Walls 922 |
| 922 | Straw | Walls 92 |

*Alphabetical file*

Building materials. *see also* Straw: Building materials
Building materials: Roofs
Building materials: Walls
Roofs. *see also* Building materials: Roofs
         Straw: Building materials: Roofs
Straw: Building materials
Straw: Building materials: Roofs
Straw. Building materials. Walls
Walls. *see also* Building materials: Walls
         Straw: Building materials: Walls.

Because these are precoordinate files certain of the logical products are already established. The searcher who is looking for 'Straw as a building material for roofs' does not need (in terms of the system) to establish a logical product, since this class is already established under a single research term. However a search for all material on straw as a building material would entail searching for a logical sum, e.g. 72 OR 822 OR 922, and the equivalent verbal terms in the alphabetical file.

Fig. 8:3 demonstrates the structure of a postcoordinate file.

Fig. 8:3
*Postcoordinate manual file*

*A book index*

| Building materials | Pages | 63 | 78 | 92 |
| Roofs | Pages | 91 | 92 | |
| Straw | Pages | 62 | 63 | 92 |
| Walls | Pages | 62 | 92 | |

*A card file*

*Numerical list of items*

Building materials

63  78  92

Roofs

91  92

Straw

62  63  92

Walls

62  92

62   Straw-reinforced walls
63   Straw as a building material
78   Building materials handbook
91   Roofs
92   Materials for roofs and walls.
                                    straw

# ADAPTING THE SEARCH STRATEGY

An initial search attempt may be unsatisfactory for one or more of the following reasons.-

1. Too much information is obtained.

2. Too little information is obtained.

3. The information is not relevant or appropriate.

The embarrassment of obtaining too much information is most likely to occur in the case of computer searches of large databases; and obviously there need be no embarrassment if it can be accepted that from the document retrieved (or list of documents retrieved) an appropriate number can be selected at random, (e.g. in computer searches 'the first twenty'). However, it is quite likely that with a very high recall of materials there will be a high proportion of 'repetitive materials' (e.g. complete retrieval of information on a campaign against vivisection is likely to include a high proportion of documents which report exactly the same information); and it is also likely that the assumption that all material retrieved is equally relevant is erroneous. The searcher will probably scan the 'whole store or collection' to choose by unanticipated and 'luxury' criteria, e.g. 'not in Japanese' or 'after 1982' or 'with pictures'. On the other hand the arrangement itself might provide this facility. (A computer file usually does so). For Fig. 8:2 for example, the search could be restricted to 'Straw for walls' or 'Straw in general'.

In documents a general treatment may be more relevant to an inquiry than a specific treatment: to the searcher who wants general information on 'straw' the documents dealing with 'dehydration of straw for use as material for roofs in wet climates' may be highly irrelevant. A disadvantage of the postcoordinate system (Fig. 8:3) is that the distinction between general and

222

particular is difficult to make without destroying the essential simplicity of the system. (Postcoordinate systems, are most appropriate when the majority of the inquiries are of the 'dehydration of straw . . . ' type).

If the search results are not delimited by arbitrary criteria then essentially the searcher will use either the 'AND' logic or the complementary 'NOT' logic. For example for Fig. 8:2 the searcher might decide to concentrate on 'Straw for building materials (in general)' (Class 72), which is in effect represented by the instruction 'Straw AND Building materials NOT (Roofs OR Walls): or might decide to limit the search to 'Straw for walls' (to class 922) — this is in effect represented by the instruction 'Straw AND Walls'. The same results would be obtained using the postcoordinate system (Fig. 8:3) although in this case it would be more difficult to know what to exclude or what to add. Using 'AND' (i.e. adding to the conditions which must be complied with), will tend to reduce the number of items recalled and make them more relevant. The same result is obtained by using 'NOT', since this is equivalent to searching for a negative characteristic. For example 'Straw AND Walls' is replaced by 'Straw AND (NOT Roofs)'. Effectively the same results can be obtained by using either the 'AND' or the 'NOT' operator. For example if the file includes materials on electronics in French, Spanish, German and English, the searcher who wishes for material only in English either chooses the English texts or excludes the French, Spanish and German texts. In a manual search the difference between the two techniques may be almost unnoticeable. In a computer search the most economical method should be chosen, and the instruction made accordingly. The two instructions are:

Electronics AND English

Electronics NOT (French OR Spanish OR German)

Since the 'NOT' instruction results in more work for the computer, the 'AND' instruction is more economical; and, if what is required is texts in English, this instruction is also more appropriate.

Obtaining insufficient information may be due as much to file content as to file arrangement and search strategy. However an attempt to obtain more information from the file usually entails sacrificing some precision. The search may be for 'Straw walls' but will be extended to include a search for 'Straw in general' and 'Walls in general'. In effect the 'AND' instruction is replaced by an 'OR' instruction. For Fig. 8.2 if the original search had been for class 922 (Straw for walls), the search would be adapted to become '922 OR 72'. For Fig. 8:3 no item fulfils the conditions for an inquiry on 'Straw as a building material for walls'. A change from 'AND' to 'OR' will produce four items. Since any of these terms singly might produce much irrelevant material, combinations of two might be. used: for example 'Building materials AND Straw' (two items) and 'Straw AND Walls' (two items). This result would be produced by a strategy represented by:

(Building materials AND Straw) OR (Straw AND Walls).

The strategies used when the information retrieved is too much or too little are equally appropriate when the information is irrelevant; although in this case an examination should be made as to whether the terms are in the first place appropriate. For example a searcher who wishes for information on growing beans might make the mistake (if using a discipline-based classification scheme), of looking in the botany class; and finding, indeed, much information relating to leguminous plants none of which is relevant to his needs.

Thesauri, classification schemes, and subject headings lists should be consulted if there is difficulty in finding appropriate terms. More especially in postcoordinate systems and computerised systems where instructions as to use (e.g. references) are not necessarily included in the main file. In a manual postcoordinate

224

system based on a thesaurus, and in many computerised systems it is at least desirable first to consult the thesaurus before using the system itself.


## NATURAL AND ARTIFICIAL LANGUAGES


The situations so far discussed have related mainly to systems in which artificial (controlled) languages are used. There are many small-scale files which use natural language, and many computer-based files have a natural language facility. Although the logic for searching in natural-language files is basically the same as that used for controlled-language files, it may differ in detail principally through greater use of the 'OR' logic. A paper on 'straw as a building material' might be called 'Some observations on organic plant materials for structural parts, with particular reference to cereal by-products'. Whereas this paper might be retrieved in a controlled-language file by using the strategy 'Straw AND Building materials'; searching in natural-language file might entail using the following:-

(Straw OR Plants OR Cereals OR Organic matter) AND
Building materials.

This example demonstrates that the difficulty is not simply one of identifying possible synonyms, since none of the terms within brackets are synonyms or near-synonyms.

The use of natural language may involve the searcher in the following procedures:-

1. Identification of classificatory relationships, where classes and sub-classes are to be treated as synonyms (e.g. cereal by-products = straw).

2. Identification of classificatory relationships, in

225

order to broaden or narrow the search (e.g. cereal by-products include straw; and higher education is related to universities).

3. Identification of synonyms and near-synonyms (e.g. railways/trains; tubes/underground railways).

4. Identification of spelling variants (a type of synonymy) (e.g. labor and labour).

5. Identification of word form variants. (e.g. dog and dogs; catalogue and cataloguing).

6. Distinguishing between homonyms (e.g. tubes (railways) and tubes (pipes)).

Spelling and word form difficulties are often solved intuitively by searchers when using manual systems, provided the variant spellings are identical initially. The device of left-hand truncation is available in both manual and computer searches. Right-hand truncation and internal truncation is available only in computer searches. Truncation is a powerful means of overcoming spelling and word form difficulties.

In most manual searches 'homonyms' can be distinguished only 'on sight'. In computerised systems and in manual postcoordinate systems it may be possible to distinguish between homonyms by combining. 'Tubes AND Transport' is unlikely to produce information about pipes.

Fig. 8:4 gives examples of term coordination for natural language systems. For many manual systems the coordination is performed intuitively by the searcher, although experienced searchers will recognise the process when it is formalised for computer searches. In the examples it is assumed that the search is a computer search and that the instructions are being typed at a terminal.

226

Fig. 8:4

*Term coordination. Natural index languages*

*A search for: Problems of recataloguing university libraries*

(University OR Universities) AND (Cataloguing OR Recataloguing

OR Cataloging OR Recataloging) AND (Library OR Libraries)

With truncation this becomes:-

Universit: AND +Catalog: AND Librar

The search is to be broadened to become:-

(Universit: OR Academic) AND +Catal: AND Librar:


*A search for information on: Forster Education Act*

(Primary OR Elementary OR Compulsory OR Forster OR 187: ) AND
Education.


(Note that in an international database or collection it might be necessary
further to specify (Great Britain OR England OR United Kingdom).


## SEARCHING A COMPUTERISED DATABASE


The computer can be 'programmed' and therefore 'instructed'
to provide access to any recorded feature of a document or any
characteristic of a piece of information. It can 'find' authors,
titles, subjects or any other features; and can recognise
connections between different items, e.g. between *'cataloging'*
and *'catalyst'* at the superficial level; and between *'catalogues'*
and *'bibliographies'* at the conceptual level.

227

An on-line search of a computer database parallels manual searches; and indeed experienced manual searchers will recognise that many of the procedures are explicit manifestations of what is done implicitly and intuitively in manual searching. In computer searching however, it is necessary to use the 'language' the computer 'understands' (this is the 'command language'), and to use it precisely. Moreover procedures which can be 'fudged' in a manual search must be precisely designed in a computer search if the purposes of the search are not to be frustrated, or the search is not to become impossibly expensive. (Note, however, that developments in computers are making computer searching less expensive, and indeed, at the logical level it may be that the relatively rigid relationship between instruction and output may be relaxed.)

At present, unfortunately, it is usually necessary to obey fairly strict protocol, as to whether (for example) an instruction to find items on 'straw as a building material' is to be prefaced by the word 'Find' or 'Search' or by no word at all. Command languages (again unfortunately) are not standardised, so that although the experienced on-line searcher can adapt quickly from one to another there is nevertheless a necessity to devote some time to the learning of what are relatively trivial matters.

It is further necessary to learn what facilities are available. A bibliographic database will consist of records which use the descriptions as discussed in Chapter 3 and the index terms. Which parts of these records are available for searching?

In a manual file it is likely that a standardised form of the author's name, the title as a whole, and various terms representing the content will be available. In a computerised file it is likely that any word in the title, and part of the author's name, and a variety of terms representing the content will be available; as well as date of publication, publisher's name and place of publication and ISBN number. Fig. 8:5 shows a bibliographic record, and indicates which features are likely to be available for searching

228

Fig. 8:5
*Bibliographic searching.*
*Manual and computer-held files.  Access points.*

*The bibliographic record*

Jones, Mordecai.                                                    BDXY
         Straw in the attic:  the use of straw as an insulating material
for domestic buildings. 2nd ed. edited by Valerie Cranmer-Freud. London
and Norwich, Yellow Fields Trust and the Straw Development Council, 1982.
363p. illus. (Making the most of what we've got series).
ISBN 55326.
(A contribution to the Energy Conservation Campaign 1982)

A manual file arranged in systematic order of subjects with separate author/
title sequence would probably provide direct and indirect access as follows:-

*Direct*
    Author
         Jones, Mordecai
         Cranmer-Freud, Valerie
    Title
         Straw in the attic . . .
    Series
         Making the most of what we've got.
    Subject
         BDXY

*Indirect*
Freud, Valerie Cranmer -
Straw: Insulating materials     BDXY
Insulating materials (Straw)    BDXY
Buildings: Insulation. Straw.   BDXY

A computerised file would provide direct access to all the above with in
addition access to:-

Yellow Fields Trust
Straw Development Council
Mordecai Jones (as distinct from Jones, Mordecai)
Energy conservation
Conservation
ISBN    55326
1982.        (and to any other characters or series of characters).

**229**

in respectively manual and computerised files.

Using a computer on-line means accessing a computer and conducting a 'conversation' with it. The computer may be owned or in some way hired by the user organisation. In such a case it may be likely that the database or databank used and which is held by the computer is itself a database or databank designed for the purposes of the organisation, (e.g. equivalent to a library catalogue, or to personnel or sales records held in manual files). On the other hand it may be that the organisation has acquired an external database, and this is equivalent to a library acquiring externally produced bibliographies.

The databases accessed may on the other hand be held by computers 'owned' by external organisations, and access to them, usually on the basis of a subscription and use-time charge, is equivalent to accessing a library. The so-called 'database providers' do not necessarily create the databases they provide, but rather they make them available, usually on a commercial basis. Well-known database providers include the British Library Automated Information Service through which the British Library's own databases can be accessed, as well as a number of others (including the 'Medline' database of the US's National Library of Medicine). Other well-known providers include Lockheed (Palo Alto, California), and the Systems Development Corporation (Santa Monica, California). An attempt at international cooperation in the provision of databases has been made by the Commission of the European Communities under the title of 'Euronet Diane'.

One of the self-imposed tasks of Euronet is that of standardising the command languages. Whether a command to search is indicated by the word 'Find' or by some other word depends upon the database provider rather than the database itself. The database provider is also responsible for the facilities available for accessing the file. For example whether or not a truncation instruction is acceptable depends on the program used by the

**230**

## Fig. 8:6
### On-line searches

(1)    *Building Technology Database: using the controlled vocabulary facility.* The topic is 'straw as an insulating material in building'. Search terms chosen after consulting the thesaurus are: 'Straw' (with 'Plant products' as a related term), and 'Insulating materials'. 'Buildings' is a taken-for-granted term and will not be used.

| USER: | FIND | STRAW | *Notes* |
|---|---|---|---|
| PROG: | S/S 1 | PSTGS 2 | Searcher (user) command is |
| USER: | FIND | PLANT PRODUCTS | followed by computer (prog.) |
| PROG: | S/S 2 | PSTGS 10 | response. |
| USER: | FIND | 1 OR 2 | S/S = search statement. |
| PROG: | S/S 3 | PSTGS 10 | PSTGS = postings (number of |
| USER: | PRT | | items found). |
| | | | PRT = Print (to get citations of items). |

*Note* 'Straw' was used as the initial and key search term, on the grounds that it was likely to produce least postings, and therefore be economical in terms of computer search facility. The related term 'Plant products' produced 10 postings and the combined postings for 'Straw' and 'Plant products' were also ten. (This is because two of the items dealt both with straw and with plant products). As there are only ten postings for the key concept it is not worth while attempting a match with 'Insulating materials', since these ten items can easily be scanned for relevance.

(2)    *Building Technology Database. Using the uncontrolled vocabulary.* The topic is 'asbestos as an insulating material for buildings'. As before 'Buildings' is not chosen as a search term.

| USER: | FIND | ASBESTOS | |
|---|---|---|---|
| PROG: | S/S 1 | PSTGS | 64 |
| USER: | FIND | INSULAT: | |
| PROG: | S/S 2 | PSTGS | 79 |
| USER: | FIND | 1 AND 2 | |
| PROG: | S/S 3 | PSTGS | 15 |
| USER: | PRT | | |

231

database provider.

Much of the information regarding availability of databases and regarding facilities provided rapidly becomes out of date. Items 28 and 29 in the list for further reading provide useful information which can be updated by the reader. Item 29 (Henry et al.) provides excellent generalisable instructions on how to search; and indeed the instructions and discussion can be applied to manual searching.

## MAKING THE MOST OF WHAT EXISTS

It is obvious that a searcher must make the most of the facilities provided by a file, taking into account possible defects and idiosyncracies. At one extreme the file may be totally unorganisable and in this case the searcher must use clues which may not have been purposely provided. At this extreme the searcher is in the position of a police detective whose 'store' of suspects is not only unorganised, but may be purposely organised in order to deceive him. In such cases the police detective takes into account the 'natural history' of crime, just as the botanist takes into account the natural history of plants in searching for particular species. Whether searching in a totally unorganised document store is more or less difficult than looking for burglars or rare mountain plants depends upon a number of factors including the size of the store, the distinctiveness of the items in the store, and the time available for search. Fortunately the activity is not usually a dangerous one.

## FURTHER READING

Items 20, 22, 28, 29 and 60 from section B, p. 276 – 280.

## CHAPTER 9: DESIGN, ORGANISATION AND EVALUATION

The first section of this chapter outlines some considerations which are relevant for the information collection organiser faced with the task of setting up an information system. In many ways this is a fortunate situation; it gives the opportunity to plan, develop ideas and select the methods and tools regarded as optimal for the collection, without the necessity to attempt to improve on existing (and possibly unsuitable) procedures. The second section deals with the organisation of the tasks involved in the operation of information retrieval systems, whether in one-person contexts or in departments comprising several people. The third part covers the evaluation of an existing system; once an IR system has been set up and operated for a while, it is important to be able to judge how well it is performing and in which ways it may be improved.

## DESIGN

It is not the intention to deal here with physical design (use of space, type of shelving and so on), but rather to discuss the design of the IR system by identifying its separate components and highlighting some major decisions affecting them; nor does this section include a step-by-step guide to IR system design, seeking only to encourage an informed and thoughtful approach by indicating the factors to be taken into account.

The information retrieval system can be usefully thought of as consisting of a number of separate components, each of which may be subject to a number of choices and decisions. These components include:-

- the store of documents in the collection
- the group of actual and potential users
- the information staff
- the document description content
- the means of subject representation
- the means and method of searching
- the various bibliographical outputs
- the physical file.

First, though, the proposed system must be considered as a whole in relation to its purpose. Most collections are set up with a particular aim in mind; sometimes this is set out in a formal policy statement of objectives, but is often expressed (or understood) in a more general way, as the result of recognising a need. For example:-

- to protect and store for posterity a collection of 19th century political pamphlets and broadsheets
- to provide rapid access to the current trade literature of the furniture industry
- to keep a chronological record of all the activities and output of a professional or learned society
- to fulfil the recreational and leisure needs of the residents of a housing estate.

There may sometimes be more than a single aim in view and this may require a compromise in the setting up of the system, in

234

order that it may go some way towards meeting both or all of the aims (though probably not completely satisfying any of them), or alternatively, it may necessitate one aim being given priority over the others, or a rank order of priority for all aims being determined.

In the following summary (in which there is no implication of priority in the order in which the matters are treated) references are indicated to more detailed discussion of topics in earlier Chapters.

## Document Characteristics

Sometimes an organiser starts in a new post with no documents at all, sometimes a collection has already been assembled (albeit on a rather haphazard basis); in most cases it will be expected that there will be a need for additions to the collection and this requires that some kind of positive acquisitions policy (other than merely 'response to demand') is established. It will need to take into account:-

- the required subject coverage

- the possible sources of documents (departments within the organisation, government, official bodies, commercial publishers, independent research organisations, individuals, for example)

- the appropriate bibliographical sources of information about the documents

- the internal and external forms of the documents (standards, conference proceedings, bibliographies, theses, films, slides, books, maps, and so on)

- costs of acquisition

- the need for ancillary equipment such as microreaders.

Identification and acquisition may not be problems for those in charge of collections of documents generated within the organisation, such as reports, minutes and correspondence, as they should be received automatically and regularly through internal channels. The organiser's task is considerably simplified if the documents form a homogeneous group of this kind – all of the same physical form, all of the same internal form, all requiring the same level of description and indexing – since standardised procedures can be established for them, leading to easier processing; most collections, however, are not so constituted, and comprise a wide variety of materials from a number of sources. The internal form of documents is a factor which is likely to have implications for their description and indexing (taken in relation to the users of the collection) – some being deemed to require detailed treatment, others not (as mentioned in Chapter 3). The external (physical) form of the documents is also a matter for consideration, as this will affect shelving, housing, storage, location and level of accessibility.

A major decision which is affected by such document characteristics as are exemplified above, is whether to provide a completely open-access collection, to restrict direct access to staff only, or to have variable access to different parts of the stock. This, in turn, has implications regarding arrangement, guiding, the amount of document description provided and so on (as indicated in Chapters 3 and 4). The physical form of documents can sometimes be overemphasised, leading to a multiplicity of categories in the stock arrangement – on the grounds of using shelf space economically; as stated in Chapter 2, physical form by itself is rarely sought, a subject title or other element usually being the primary feature, therefore the stock should, as far as possible, be integrated rather than separated by what is, in many contexts, an irrelevant distinction. (Given access to the necessary apparatus, there may be no difference in utility between a hardback copy, a paperback copy, a cassette or disc of the spoken text, and a microform copy).

## User Characteristics

An organiser setting up an IR system sometimes knows fairly well who the users of the collection will be — the research staff of a laboratory, or the teachers from local primary and secondary schools, or the members of a learned society, for example, but in other situations the exact clientele may be more difficult to predict — such as the opening of a new branch library in an urban area with a mixed residential and (commuting) office population. Even when the system has been set in operation, and a group of actual users identified, there always remains a group of potential users whose needs should be considered, the intention being that they, too, should become actual users.

Once the identity of the user group has been established, its particular characteristics should be noted and analysed;  these help to determine the nature of the stock, description and indexing policies and physical design.  Once again, this is easier in a restricted context, such as a commercial firm's information collection open to the public at large.  The characteristics which may be of interest (and much depends on the context as to which of these are important) are:-

- educational level (including reading ability)
- professional and technical subject knowledge
- degree of familiarity with the use of documents, information collections and retrieval systems
- physical abilities (there is little point in acquiring microform documents if the collection is solely for the use of the partially-sighted, for instance)
- type of information need.

The last may be difficult to anticipate in the context of a new collection, but is nevertheless important;  the expression of information need by users is, in any case, dependent to a certain extent upon the information staff, since it is up to them to make users aware of the kinds of information which are available, and the needs which can be met — most people do not realise what information collections are able to provide for them, and therefore under-use them.

As with documents, users forming a homogeneous group — all professionally qualified members of an institute or society, or skilled technicians in a factory, or undergraduates in a university, for example — are easier to provide for than is a heterogeneous group of people with differing interests, educational and technical backgrounds, occupations, ages (from children to the elderly, perhaps), approaching the collection for a variety of purposes — leisure reading, fact-finding, formal study and so on. In order to plan for the best provision — whatever the nature of the users — it is necessary to know whether inquirers will always (or most frequently) need to seek reference to the full texts or forms of documents ('I need to look at the government report on rating reform', or 'I have to consult the plans for Dymshire County Hall'), or whether abstracts of texts will be required, or whether only certain information about the document will be needed ('On which date was the letter of acceptance sent to Maguire and Company?'). One also needs to know whether users will be interested only in current material ('current' being defined within the particular context) in order to keep up to date with the subject or activity, or whether access to older material will be needed for retrospective searching — and if so, how often this will be done, and how quickly answers will be needed. Inquirers may want immediate replies to their questions, or they may be prepared to wait for a few hours, days or even weeks. Material which is likely to be heavily used needs to be readily accessible, in an easily readable form, perhaps supplied in multiple copies, and suitably described and indexed — the catalogue of descriptions perhaps also requiring to be supplied in multiple copies.

238

## Staff

In most cases it is the information staff who are responsible for the interpretation of the system, ensuring that inquirers use it in the best possible way in the search for answers to their questions. The level of interpretation required varies according to the nature of the users and of the system. A policy decision has to be made as to whether users will themselves carry out the search for information, relying on the staff only for occasional guidance, or whether the information staff will act always as intermediaries, receiving inquiries, clarifying and checking details with inquirers, and then finding the required information and relaying it to the inquirers. The latter may be thought best in the use of on-line systems, when a certain level of technical information-handling expertise is required. Depending on the context, the number of information staff may vary between one and very many; the education, skills, abilities and aptitudes of the staff should be those which enable the fulfilment of the total information needs of the users of the collection.

## Document Descriptions

As has been indicated in Chapter 3, the content of a description can range from very brief to extremely detailed; the level of descriptions must be chosen to meet the requirements of the collection user, as interpreted by the information staff. Compilation of descriptions takes time and therefore it is most efficient to produce only the level of description which is required to satisfy the existing demands, rather than to provide great detail which is not used. In collections consisting of a variety of types of document, or with different levels of access, the amount of description needed is also likely to vary. A decision regarding the elements to be included in the description, and their form, must also be made; if a standard code of cataloguing rules is to be applied, the choice of the most appropriate code must be made — if, on the other hand, a set of rules is to be specially compiled for the collection, all the relevant features of the documents must be

**239**

recognised and provided for in the rules. Measures must then be taken to ensure the consistent application of the rules.

As indicated in Chapter 3, some bibliographical data is now available from commercial suppliers and by exchange through cooperative networks; when considering the possible benefits of subscribing to or cooperating with such systems, the organiser should ascertain what percentage of the material in his collection is covered by these data, by which standards and rules they are prepared, how full they are, how much modification will be required before use, in which physical form they are produced (and therefore which equipment may be needed), how quickly they can be supplied, and what the cost is likely to be. Involvement in cooperative schemes (as with other kinds of resource-sharing) can be beneficial, but care should be taken not to commit the organisation in such a way that freedom of operation is severely restricted.

Since documents may be requested by a number of features – author, title, series and so on (see Chapters 3, 4 and 6) – approaches using these elements must be catered for by provision of entries under such headings in the catalogue, taking into account the characteristics of the documents and of the users; it should be remembered also that some approaches to documents are very well provided for by published bibliographical tools which are readily available (abstracting and indexing publications, publishers' catalogues and the like) – it may not be necessary, therefore, to repeat these approaches in the collection's own catalogue. Once the entries have been produced and the basic file data assembled, the precise filing order must be decided on and applied (see Chapter 3), and staff and users informed as to the type of order observed. It is advisable to find out, before choosing, which order is used in other files within the organisation, or in other files in the same subject field or activity – if there is a clear preference for one order rather than another, it seems appropriate to conform to that, for the convenience of users.

240

## Subject Representation

Assuming that a subject approach is thought necessary – and in the great majority of situations it is – a choice of index language must be made. As has been seen (Chapter 4), index languages can be characterised in a number of ways, and a choice must be made from these: a natural or an artificial index language, alphabetical or systematic, precoordinate or postcoordinate, general or special, published or 'home-grown'.

This component of the IR system deserves more thought and study than it sometimes receives; a choice of index language should not be made without full consideration of the tasks which it is required to perform. If summarisation indexing is needed, the choice of one particular index language may be suitable, but that same index language may not be adequate in a situation requiring in-depth indexing. The organiser, therefore, needs to establish the level of indexing which is wanted (in the context of the documents and the users, and the type of inquiry to be dealt with), and then select a language which will provide that level most efficiently.

The varying requirements for precision and recall (see Chapters 4 and 8) must also be identified and borne in mind when considering index languages; as has been seen, languages differ in their ability to provide for high levels of these. The combination of indexing policy decisions, relating, for example, to the summarisation/in-depth indexing distinction, and the features of index languages, are influential in providing the best levels for the system.

The vocabulary used by inquirers should also be recognised, so that the index language selected can match as closely as possible the terms in currency in the collection, using the spellings and meanings and forms of words with which the inquirers are familiar. The index language chosen should reflect the subject coverage of the collection in a way which aids searching, giving easy movement from one topic to another related to it, by providing appropriate identification and arrangement of the classes which are to be found in the literature. Some fields of activity refer to topics drawn from more than one discipline and, as a result, a considerable number of composite classes (see Chapter 5) may need to be represented by the index language — some languages are poor in this respect.

In a collection representative of a quickly-developing subject field, it is vital that the index language is capable of matching the current concepts found in the literature — procedures for revision and updating should, therefore, be examined before making a choice. The existence of a user group for a particular index language is a sign of interest and activity, and involvement in such a group can be helpful in solving problems, developing the language and ensuring its stability and continuance; such groups are of particular value in relation to special index languages — which, because of their special nature, are used in small numbers of collections and do not possess many resources for revision and development.

As stated earlier, the business of selecting an index language must not be hurried. A careful examination of the required characteristics must be made, including any anticipated changes in the nature of the collection and its use, and all apparently suitable indexing languages considered and studied, in order to select the most appropriate. If none of the existing languages seems suitable, and it is decided to compile one, (see Chapter 5), it must be remembered that, although the language may be perfectly fitted to the collection, it takes time to develop it and therefore there will be a delay in application to the collection; the organiser must decide which consideration takes priority.

## Searching

(*see also* Chapter 8)

The means and method of searching for information are very

242

dependent on the types of document in the collection, the skills and abilities of the users, the index language employed and the physical form of the file. The matters which must be given consideration by the organiser include:-

- the kinds of questions which will be asked by inquirers
- the ways in which they may make their first look-up in the file
- what they will do if they find nothing at their first look-up
- what they will do if they find twenty (or a hundred, or more) apparently relevant documents or references to documents.

To a large extent, the search strategy is dictated (or at least influenced) by the arrangement and guiding of the documents, the sequence (or sequences) and guiding within the representation file, the number of approaches provided for, and the nature of the index language, the users may also employ their own idiosyncratic methods of searching, however, and the organiser should endeavour to become familiar with these, so that he can ensure that the document arrangement and the representation file sequences complement them.

**Bibliographical Outputs**

Users sometimes require to use the documents themselves, but frequently an inquiry requires only the identifying details, or one particular detail, of the document — this can lead to the document itself being needed later. The organiser needs to decide in what form this information is to be provided. An on-line system can enable almost any selection and combination of information elements to be supplied, in any order and in a variety of physical forms; it may, therefore, be possible to ask for a (hard-copy)

243

printout, in alphabetical order, of all report titles issued between June 1981 and May 1982. Other systems may be more restricted; given access to photocopying equipment, however, whole entries can be manually extracted from card and some other files, assembled in the required sequence and a copy made which the user can take away. Otherwise manual copying of selected details may be necessary; if this is required frequently, it may indicate that an additional sequence should be established as part of the file.

## Physical File

The types of physical file, and their characteristics, have been described in Chapter 7. The organiser must attempt to match the requirements of the collection and its use to the appropriate kind of file. On occasion, certain resources and tools are already available, either for the sole use of the information collection, or to be shared with others in the organisation. The ready availability of equipment and facilities can be a spur to their rapid adoption, but it is prudent to pause to consider whether they will, in fact, provide the service that is required. In particular, resources which have to be shared may not always be available at the time or in the form or quantity desired, causing delays and inadequacies in the information activities, or may suddenly be withdrawn, if their existence depends primarily upon their use by another department. With this proviso, it is always worth investigating to discover facilities provided centrally which could be utilised; organisations frequently have a central reprographic unit, for example, which is able to take responsibility for the reproduction of catalogue entries and other bibliographical outputs.

If starting from scratch, the organiser should make herself familiar with every kind of physical file, if possible seeing them in working environments, before coming to a conclusion which takes into account those features mentioned in Chapter 7 – amount of information and number of entries to be included, number of users, ease of use and so on.

**244**

## The Need for Modification

The initial design made for the IR system must include provision for change in line with changes in document and user characteristics, subject coverage, type of inquiry, amount of use, and provision of technical facilities. No system should be held back in its development by any feature of the original design, and improvements seen to be needed, following *evaluation* (see later in this Chapter), should be implemented as soon as is feasible.


## ORGANISATION

Once the IR system has been designed and set up, the requirements are:-

- that it processes incoming documents (giving them the appropriate attention and treatment)
- incorporates them into stock
- makes them (and information about them) available for use
- and exploits them fully in the answering of inquiries.

Ideally a steady flow of work should proceed through the system without unacceptable delay and without stress to any component of the system.

The size of the 'department' having responsibility for the work varies from one person (or in some situations, part of one person — since he may have other responsibilities) to many people (perhaps coordinated as 'technical services' and 'reference inquiry' teams), depending on the circumstances within which the IR system operates. Whether few or many people are involved, a number of skills, aptitudes and abilities are necessary in order to deal satisfactorily with the combination of tasks to be performed. Efficient and consistent processing is aided by the compilation and consultation of a procedures manual which sets out clearly, and in the appropriate sequence, the operations which are to be performed in the receipt, processing and integration into stock of a document and the answering of inquiries, and analyses each operation into its constituent steps. These procedure descriptions should be compiled during the actual processing of documents and inquiries, preferably by the person or persons carrying out the tasks, so that no step is omitted; once described, the events and decision points are best translated into diagrammatic form − if properly done, this is more readily comprehended than several lines or paragraphs of text, though footnotes may be added for anything not easily represented diagrammatically. (Examples of flow-charts relating to technical services operations are given by Gilchrist, 1982). This kind of record is of great value in ensuring that every document and every inquiry received gets consistent and necessary treatment and that nothing is forgotten; additionally, new members of staff can gain from it an initial overview of the activities of the department and can become familiar with the tasks for which they are appointed.

## Document Handling

The twin aims of the technical services 'department' (regardless of its size) − accurate and appropriate description and indexing, and speedy processing − need to be balanced against each other. The need for quick transit of a document through the various stages should not overrule that for careful attention to its particular features and for accurate description and indexing at the appropriate level; time skimped in processing may result in inadequate records, leading to the document being overlooked in connection with an inquiry for which it is particularly relevant. On the other hand, particularly in specialised environments, there is frequently a need to give urgent treatment to a document whose receipt has been anxiously awaited by an inquirer; in such cases, it may be necessary to release the document after initial recording, on a provisional basis, ensuring that it is returned in due course for completion of its treatment. In a single-person department, it

246

may be possible for documents as a matter of course to be passed through all stages of processing in one day, but in a larger department with a number of people performing separate tasks, documents are normally likely to take longer to complete all the stages, being passed from one point to another and awaiting their turn.

Apart from the number of staff, their skills and experience, and the division of labour, speed of processing is affected by several other factors:-

— the number of documents received per day, week
  or month

— the variety of document types received (as stated
  earlier, if the documents received are all of one
  physical form, or one internal form, standardised
  procedures can lead to faster progress)

— the percentage of documents that is to be represented in the catalogue

— the amount of description required

— the level of subject indexing needed

— the proportion of catalogue data acquired from
  external sources (bought in or received by exchange)

— the amount of necessary modification of such external
  data

— the physical form of the file and the processes involved
  in producing and reproducing the entries for it

— the number of checks which are carried out during
  processing.

Data relating to the time taken in processing, and related costs, are sometimes published in the library and information literature, and at first sight these may appear useful in assisting the planning and operation of technical services. Such data, however, must be treated with caution, as they frequently refer only to one set of circumstances, perhaps to a large academic library with a substantial daily intake of several different types of document, a considerable division of labour, a low percentage of urgently-required material, providing medium document descriptions, receiving 50% of its catalogue data from external sources, practising summarisation indexing and producing entries for a card file. It should not be assumed that the data will apply to another set of circumstances. As has been seen, a number of variables can affect the times taken and the resultant costs; it is necessary, therefore, before making a judgment and applying the results to one's own situation, to ascertain the nature of the documents, the staff, the tasks performed (what passes for 'cataloguing' or 'indexing' in one environment may be very different from that in another place). Inappropriate application of published data can result in staff being expected to process impossible numbers of documents and inquiries in a given time; such a situation is often the consequence of target-setting by managers who are unaware of the nature of technical services operations and information handling and of the differences in practice which can exist between information environments.

As far as possible, it should be arranged that documents start their path through the system as soon as they are received. The precise number or nature of stages to be undergone varies according to the circumstances, but is likely to include as a minimum:-

— some sort of check against a file of ordered or expected documents

— sifting out of unwanted items (most collections receive some unsolicited material)

— stamping or other indication of ownership

248

- making out of a record of some of the document's details (or retrieval of details from data supplied by an external source)

- entry of those details in a file

- location of the document in a sequence of other documents.

In reviewing the remaining documents (after removal of unwanted material), these may be divided into groups on the basis of their form (external or internal) for batch processing, perhaps by different members of staff; or, on the other hand, staff may prefer the constant change from one form to another in their day's work. Description and subject indexing may be carried out by the same or by different people; if the same people are responsible for both, there is a decrease in the necessary 'familiarisation' time per document, but if different people are responsible, they can become specialists in their activity, developing their particular aptitudes, and (not having to switch from one task to another for each document) may thereby find greater satisfaction.

As stated in Chapter 7, the existence of a variety of forms of physical file means that the ways in which catalogue data are produced and reproduced also vary. The facilities provided by other departments, (typing, reprography, preparation of data for computer processing, and so on) may be utilised, or the data may be handled entirely within the 'home' area. If other departments are involved, this introduces another element to the system,

Frequently there are several other stages, but no activity should be included unless it is established to be necessary; the compilation of procedure diagrams − mentioned earlier − can be helpful in this respect, as the necessity to analyse an activity into its components can prompt the question 'Why do we do this?' and, if no satisfactory answer is found, the activity (or one or more of its components) may be discontinued.

**249**

one which is not altogether within the information organiser's control; it is important, therefore, that there is a clear understanding (by the information organiser) of the capabilities and limitations of the other service facilities, and (by the managers of the other services) of the requirements (layout, physical form, degree of accuracy, tolerable delay) of the IR system. If bibliographic data are bought in, or received by exchange through cooperative systems, they must be matched with the documents they represent, and any necessary modifications made to conform with house practice (the more of these which are necessary, the more delay in the data reaching the file).

Once the data have been prepared from the document, then document and data can proceed on their separate ways. The amount of preparation needed by documents prior to being filed in their allocated places is dependent upon the type of document, the use to which it is to be put (closed-access, confidential, reference only or open-access, available for borrowing, for example) and the degree of processing already carried out by the suppliers or originators of the document. Some books for public library use, for instance, are supplied jacketed, labelled and stamped, and some photographs, films, slides and other easily-damaged materials may be provided in appropriate coverings and containers. Whatever has not been done by the suppliers or originators, and needs to be done, must be carried out by the technical services staff, and this may involve the use of specially-purchased tools and materials. The finished document should be able to withstand wear and tear for whatever is regarded as the required period of time and should, in most cases, carry some kind of symbol (shelfmark, notation or other mark) indicating its place in the collection – a number of processes exist for this purpose, including some using embossed plastic labels, adhesive lettering, typewritten labels, electric stylus and tape, or pen and ink.

Because of the time taken for reproduction of entries in some forms of file, documents frequently take their places in the collection before their matching representations appear in the file. This is unfortunate, as it means that material is available for use, but that potential users are unaware of it; other means of publicising new material should be sought, such as a 'newly-received' shelf, or a brief typed listing of titles and locations. Every effort, though, should be made to keep to the minimum the delay in integrating file data — in many environments, it is, after all, the newer material which is the most heavily used and its existence and location should, therefore, be made known as soon as possible.

The design of the IR system may include checking stages, at which the finished product of a particular operation, or series of operations, is examined by a member of staff other than the one who produced it, perhaps on the basis of colleagues working on the same operation checking each other's work. Bearing in mind the desirability (and sometimes the absolute necessity) of having accurate records and the correct level of representation for documents, checking at some stage seems prudent; the interposition of any check, and any consequent alteration, adds to total processing time, but this must be weighed against the inconvenience (or worse) of incorrect, incomplete or insufficient numbers of records. The number and timing of checks, therefore, must be decided in relation to the conditions within which the IR system operates. It should be noted here that few tasks in the IR context are suitable for entrusting without checks to a new, uninstructed member of staff. The filing of documents and of catalogue entries are often thought to be such tasks, but in fact instruction and guidance — sometimes very detailed — are required in relation to the nature and number of sequences, the kind of alphabetical order observed, the characteristics of shelf notation and so on; failure to understand or observe these instructions may result in documents being permanently misplaced, thereby negating all the work previously done in relation to them.

Provision for maintenance (as well as updating) of the file and the document sequences must be made; changes requiring reprocessing of documents and catalogue entries (due to relocation, or to additional information becoming available) occur more frequently than is sometimes anticipated and this element of technical service responsibilities is sometimes, therefore, overlooked or under-resourced. After a period of time in operation, and after evaluation, there may be a need for a more radical revision involving recataloguing, reclassification or re-indexing; this may be due, for example

- to a change in the aims of the collection, or in the characteristics affecting it

- to the issue of a revised edition of the subject index-ing system used, or a decision to change from one indexing system or from one code of rules of descrip-tion to another.

In such circumstances the existing staff may be insufficient in number to deal with the load and it will be necessary to recruit temporary staff with the right mix of skills and aptitudes to complete the revision in a reasonable time and with the least possible inconvenience to users and to the permanent staff (who still have to deal with their normal everyday activities during this period). Organisers contemplating revision of this kind should plan the operation carefully well in advance, and should seek guidance from those who have carried out similar operations, and from the published literature on the subject.

**Inquiry Handling**

As already stated, it is helpful to have a planned procedure, or set of procedures, for the handling of inquiries, to ensure that no step of investigation is overlooked, and that inquirers receive com-plete and accurate answers to their questions. Inquiries, as has been seen, may vary in their requirements, extent and complexity; some information environments deal with only one kind — requests for statistics, for example — while others handle many types. The likely set of inquiry types must be anticipated and the appropriate procedures established; clarification of the question is necessary, and specification of the precise form of information required (documents, citations, 'facts'), the currency of the information needed (within the last five years, up-to-date today), how quickly the answer is needed, how much information must be supplied (all references available, one document), the appropriate physical and internal forms (photograph, specification), the level of information (introductory, advanced) and so on. Standard inquiry forms overprinted with brief questions are useful in reminding the inquiry handler of the background to be established; addition of the identifying details of the inquirer and how and where she may be contacted, completes the 'dossier'. If the inquiries are all of one kind, always requiring the consultation of a succession of standard reference books or files, the titles of these may also be printed on the form and checked off as the inquiry proceeds, with brief notes of terms used for searching and of the results. Whether the forms are retained after completion of the inquiry depends on whether an analysis of inquiries is intended, and whether it is thought useful to have the record available if there should be a further, related inquiry, or if the same inquiry is received later from another person. Analysis of inquiries can be useful in providing feedback for evaluation of the utility, structure and content of collections and files, in assisting the selection of reference materials and subscriptions to other information services, and in allocating staff time to, and costing, inquiries.

As with the handling of documents, the two aims of accurate and comprehensive treatment and quick processing must each be borne in mind. Inquiries may have to be arranged in order or priority, but each one, regardless of rank order, must be given its due attention and appropriate treatment. Speed of processing is affected by some of the factors already mentioned:-

— number of inquiries received and their nature

— the number of staff available to deal with them and

253

their skills and experience

- the form in which the answer is required

- the number of sources, files and so on to be consulted

- the need for reference to outside sources.

Adequate resources must be available for the accurate and speedy processing of inquiries, in terms both of staff and of materials and services. Some inquiries may be answered comprehensively by the internal resources of the department, others require the use of external services; staff responsible for the handling of inquiries must be knowledgeable about the contents and potential of their own collection and about the locations, contents and potential of other collections and services. (More detailed guidance on the handling of inquiries can be found in Finer, 1982).

**Workspace**

Having identified all the necessary steps for processing documents and inquiries, and for matching them, the workspace should be arranged so that the material can proceed easily from one stage to the next, without the need for constant carrying or moving from one location to another. Much depends on the total size of the technical services and inquiry-handling operations; one person may be able to deal with all the necessary tasks within the area of her own desk while a larger department may require a series of interconnected work stations. In any situation, the materials and tools required for processing (including cataloguing codes, classification schemes, thesauri, dictionaries, bibliographies, typewriters, stationery, copiers and so on) should be within easy reach and arranged so that staff can work in comfort and safety.

**EVALUATION**

After the system has been in operation for some time, it may

254

become apparent that, in one respect or another, it is performing less well than expected. It may be that:-

- the success rate in finding answers to inquiries is low

- the number of inquirers falls steeply

- it takes longer to deal with inquiries than anticipated

- documents which are known to be in stock cannot be traced

- the details given in document descriptions are found to be inadequate for the assessment of document utility.

If deficiencies of this kind are observed by staff, or commented on by users, then – assuming that the information is fed back to the organiser – it should be possible to examine the appropriate component of the system, make the necessary modifications (increase the number of staff engaged on a particular process, upgrade or service the apparatus used, acquire more up-to-date and relevant documents, move to a fuller level of description of subject representation, or whatever else is needed) and observe a subsequent improvement.

It should not be assumed, however, that if no fault is apparent, the system must be operating at the optimal level. Casual feed-back from users, although helpful, is not likely to be a reliable guide to performance; if users are unaware of the full range and power of information services, they will not complain if they do not receive the best. It is incumbent upon the organiser, there-fore, to discover those parts of the system which may be operating inadequately at any time and to attempt to provide a solution to the problem. This requires either the continuous monitoring of the system so that any fluctuations show up immediately or frequent spot checks and inspections to identify changes which occur in a component.

Lancaster (1979) distinguishes four levels at which an information service may be evaluated:-

(i)     the evaluation of effectiveness (the extent to which the service satisfies the information needs of its users)

(ii)    the evaluation of benefits (the impact an information service has on its users)

(iii)   the evaluation of cost effectiveness (relation of measures of effectiveness to measures of cost)

(iv)    the evaluation of the cost-benefit relationship (relation of the costs of providing some service to the benefits of having the service available).

He provides a detailed description and analysis of the functions of IR systems and the techniques of evaluation.

In order to assess the performance of a system, there has to be a criterion, or criteria, against which to measure; the original design may have included a statement of objectives and some standards around which the system was planned, which may be used for initial comparison in ascertaining whether the system is doing what it was intended to do, and what the organiser thinks it is doing. Evaluation may be made of the system as a whole, at the levels indicated by Lancaster, or of any one of its parts. In considering an individual component, attention must be paid to its original purposes and it must be established whether its characteristics and circumstances have changed: Were 200 regular users anticipated and are there now 800? Was the collection equally made up of print and non-print materials? Is there now a preponderance of one over the other?; and whether the system needs to change in line with them.

256

Objectives may be stated in general or specific terms, but are unlikely at the outset to have been expressed quantitatively, unless the system being set up was similar in most of its characteristics to one already established and running, in which case data from that system may have been used as a measure of the expected use of the new system. The objectives formulated may be related more to the kinds of service to be offered, than to the numbers of transactions expected, as indicated at the beginning of this Chapter. These basic objectives may be fulfilled and yet the organiser may still subjectively judge — on the basis of previous experience or discussions with opposite numbers — that the service could be improved. Another reason why reference to original objectives is sometimes not very helpful is that once any kind of information system is set up, and it becomes relatively well known, there may be an expectation on the part of those users who already know the potential of such systems, and who have had experience elsewhere of information services, that additional services to those planned will be provided; if gradually (in response to this pressure) some further activities are undertaken, evaluation against the original objectives is more difficult, since the priorities given to the various parts of the service may have been adjusted.

**Methods of Gathering Information**

Despite the slight difficulties mentioned above it is essential that the organiser keeps a watch on the activities and performance of the system in order to be aware of the stresses and strains affecting it, and also to be able to justify and give an account of it when the occasion demands. The quantitative and qualitative aspects of evaluation must both be attended to and require different methods for assessment. The mere recording of numbers of inquiries received or calculation of an average time for answering an inquiry does not provide an adequate picture of an information service; it is necessary also to know what was involved in the answering of inquiries, what kind of answers were provided, whether they were complete answers, and whether users were satisifed. The problem for the organiser is that the more time and effort is expended on the examination of past work done, the less is available for the handling of current inquiries; the proportion of resources to be devoted to checking and monitoring must not, therefore, be too great. Ideally, what is required is a method, or methods, of gathering information which can be incorporated into the system without disturbing it and which will constantly feed back to the organiser most of what she needs to know, requiring the addition of occasional (but regular) sampling to gain greater detail. Failure to maintain any kind of performance record may result in the imposition by higher management of an external monitoring team to check the activities of the system; this is a situation which organisers may wish to avoid, since the criteria chosen for assessment may not be those which the organisers consider most appropriate (though, on the other hand, there may be value in the more detached viewpoint of an outside group).

One of the simplest means of measuring performance is the counting of the various transactions — number of inquiries received, number of documents catalogued, number of literature searches carried out and so on. Such data can be gathered by recording a mark on a work-sheet, or by pressing a digital counter, for each item as it passes through a particular operation, or by counting the number of accumulated items and recording the total after a particular stage has been completed. If standard inquiry forms, work-sheets or other papers are generated by a process, these can sometimes be more conveniently counted than the items to which they refer. The exact point at which counting is done must be agreed, so that duplication and omission are avoided.

It may be of interest to count not just items and transactions but other elements which may give some indication of intellectual activity — the average number of index terms allocated to documents for subject representation, for instance. This kind of datum is useful as it not only gives information about work done,

258

but may tell something about the level of indexing being performed, and the effectiveness of the index language being used (a high number of index terms per document may imply a high level of exhaustivity in indexing, or that the index language used is not adequate, the indexer being forced to allocate several approximate terms in an attempt to cover the subject.

Whilst it is certainly essential to maintain a numerical record of IR activities, it is necessary also to ensure that the quality of response is kept to an appropriate level. In order to make any kind of judgment it is first necessary to decide what that 'appropriate level' is; the minimum level is presumably that at which no user complaints are received, but this is barely satisfactory. From experience, the organiser must establish what is to be the required level of performance, and must then assess the system's actual performance by methods such as observation, questionnaires and interviews. No evaluation should be based entirely on the information staff's assessment, nor only on that of users; both must be incorporated. Observation can be helpful in gathering data on the use of files — revealing that there are frequently several people waiting to use the catalogue, for instance, or that one sequence of material is much less often referred to than another, despite being more prominently displayed, or highlighting a tendency of inquirers to give up their search if they do not find anything relevant at their first look-up in the file (perhaps because they find the system difficult to use). It is unlikely that observation can be practised on other than an occasional sampling basis, since continuous observation (if the users are aware of it) is likely to affect the activities being observed. Its value is that it can reveal what is actually happening (so long as the observer correctly interprets what he sees) rather than what people say is happening.

Questionnaires and interviews, on the other hand, asking users (and perhaps non-users, too) about their information needs, use of services and opinions of them, rely on very careful formulation of questions and prompting remarks and on the willingness of

**259**

respondents to give answers and opinions (which may be seen as criticisms or indictments of the services being offered, or as admissions of their own inadequacies in failing to make the most of the system). The compilation of questions and structuring of interviews should only be undertaken by those who have had some instruction in the appropriate techniques, otherwise ambiguity and unreliable data may result. Data gathered by qualitative methods should be matched against those obtained quantitatively to seek some confirmation of the information received.

The information activities which may be the most resource-intensive are the preparation of document descriptions and the representation of subjects through an indexing language; the results of these activities may also be more difficult to assess, as users may not be sufficiently aware of what is involved to provide many insights into the problems and information staff may not be able fully to appreciate the users' situation. In the case of document descriptions and catalogues generally, the organiser may be able to benefit from the published results of research done in other information environments (such as those quoted by Bryant, 1980), in which, for example, the utility of brief and full entries has been investigated and user responses elicited to certain physical forms of catalogue. (The dangers of too literal a transfer of data from one situation to another have already been stressed). It may be possible for some comparisons to be made within the organiser's own environment, perhaps by providing two files – in different physical forms, containing different levels of description, or supplying different approaches – and observing the results in terms of actual usage, questioning users to discover subjective attitudes and so on; the possibilities for experiments of this kind in many information environments are limited, since they either involve regular staff in work additional to their normal duties or require the recruitment of additional effort.

As far as subject representation and information retrieval are

260

concerned, the use of the recall and precision measures mentioned in Chapters 4 and 8 are appropriate, the recall ratio being:

$$\frac{\text{number of relevant documents retrieved}}{\text{total number of relevant documents in the collection}} \quad \text{x} \quad \frac{100}{1}$$

and the precision ratio:

$$\frac{\text{number of relevant documents retrieved}}{\text{total number of documents retrieved}} \quad \text{x} \quad \frac{100}{1}$$

Lancaster distinguishes further between relevance (the relationship between a document and a request statement) and pertinence (the relationship between a document and a particular information need, as assessed by the inquirer). It must be remembered that there are varying requirements for recall and precision (an inquirer may on one occasion want everything ever published on a topic, and on another only one document which tells him all he needs to know on that topic) and that the available levels of recall and precision are influenced by the nature of the index language and the indexing policy adopted. Evaluation must therefore attempt first to discover whether the levels which are actually required are capable of being achieved by the system as constituted, and then to find out whether they are in fact being achieved.

It is worthwhile for collection organisers to maintain an interest in activities outside their own environments. Except in circumstances where organisations are in straight-forward competition with each other, and therefore unwilling to tell each other anything, it is possible to make contact with workers engaged in information activities in the same area of interest in order to exchange ideas, pass on information and so on. This can be a useful way of receiving informal comments on the effectiveness and value and performance of particular systems, machines,

261

indexing languages and the like. Apart from the user groups which are sometimes established around indexing languages and systems, there are also interest groups within larger organisations, such as the Economic and Business Information and the Biological and Agricultural Sciences Groups of Aslib, and the Community Services and Industrial Groups of the Library Association. It also helps to keep up to date with the literature of information retrieval (through abstracting and indexing publications and through periodicals which contain reviews, descriptive articles, correspondence, advertisements, state-of-the-art reports and other features). Those organisers who have devised new systems or produced new solutions to old problems may also consider publishing accounts of their activities for the benefit of fellow-workers.

## Presentation and Application of the Results

In most cases, the data gathered in evaluation are seen only by the information staff, who interpret them and may subsequently modify the system. The preparation of some of the data in a form suitable for release to users, or for wider publication, should be considered, as this can provide publicity for the service, enhance the volume of usage and improve user performance; this kind of presentation should consist not of numerical data alone, but should be amplified, perhaps by examples of inquiries dealt with, sources exploited or services offered. Sometimes data are needed for inclusion in a statement to management — perhaps to indicate the work-load being carried — and in this case the quantitative information is likely to be more pertinent than the qualitative (regrettably).

It is important not to react too quickly to changes in data; it is better to wait and see whether a permanently changed pattern has emerged, rather than just a temporary fluctuation, before making modifications. Once the modifications have been carried out, the effects should be monitored, to see whether the desired outcome has been achieved.

262

# REFERENCES

Bryant, Philip. (1980) Progress in documentation: the catalogue. *Journal of documentation,* vol. 36, no. 2, June, p. 133-163.

Finer, Ruth. (1982) Reference and enquiry work. In: *Handbook of special librarianship and information work.* 5th ed. Editor: L J Anthony. Aslib. (Ch.12, p.307–324).

Gilchrist, A. (1982) System design and planning. In: *Handbook of special librarianship and information work,* op. cit. (Ch.2, p. 9–35).

Lancaster, F Wilfred. (1979) *Information retrieval systems: characteristics, testing and evaluation.* 2nd ed. New York; Chichester: Wiley.

## FURTHER READING

Items 5, 6, 7, 10, 14, 20, 21, 22, 37, 47, 48, 50, 52, 53 and 61 from section B of further reading on p. 274 – 280.

# CHAPTER 10: INDEXES FOR INDIVIDUAL DOCUMENTS

The main concerns of Chapters 1 to 9 have been the appropriate description, representation and processing of the documents in a collection, and the construction of related files so that documents may be identified and retrieved when needed. This final chapter deals with the provision of an index to the contents of an individual document, to enable items in the text to be traced. Much of what has already been treated in Chapters 4, 5 and 8 is relevant to the informed and methodical compilation of such an index, and that will not be repeated here. The intention is to provide guidance for those who set out to construct an index, perhaps to books which they themselves have written, or to publications such as company histories, brochures and other publicity material produced by the organisations within which they operate.

There should be no need here to emphasise the importance of providing an index to a text; the difficulty of tracing a 'piece' of information in a document without an index is easy to appreciate. It is perhaps necessary, however, to exemplify the reasons why some indexes are inadequate: omission of sought terms — perhaps due to lack of the identification of synonyms; inclusion of unsought terms; presentation of terms in unusual forms; lack of distinction between major and minor references; lack of distinction between references to different kinds of content; mixing of terms from different languages in a single, undifferentiated sequence; lack of an established alphabetical order; lack of context provision for words with more than one meaning (homographs).

The aim of the index, or indexes, to a text is the supply of references, in self-evident order, from terms (usually words or phrases) sought by users in trying to trace particular items of information, including related items scattered throughout the text. It follows that each index is unique, including those terms, and only those terms, which are relevant to that text and to the anticipated users of that text, the terms being generated in relation to the text itself, not by reference to a classification scheme of knowledge for the appropriate subject field. (A book on zoology which does not specifically mention gorillas will not require an index reference 'Gorillas . . . ', whereas a classification scheme for zoology must include a class for those animals). The index is required to show, against the chosen terms, those places (usually page numbers, but sometimes frame, column, section, paragraph or line numbers) where information related to the particular concepts is to be found. The more information which can be given to distinguish one kind of reference from another, the easier it is for the user to decide where to turn.

In many cases, a single sequence containing all the index terms is entirely satisfactory, and constitutes an obvious and straight-forward searching tool, but in other situations it may be appropriate to provide two, or even more, sequences. A text dealing with flowering plants may be judged to need an approach by both popular and botanical (Latin) names – 'Dandelions . . . ' and 'Taraxcum officinale . . . '; it may be more convenient for users (each of whom is likely to employ only one set of names – either popular or botanical) if two separate sequences are provided. If only a single listing is possible, for reasons of space, or is thought more useful, then one set of names could be presented in a different type – *italic*, perhaps – to differentiate them. Another case for separate indexes might be a history in which events, places, institutions, and people feature; if it is thought that the major approach is likely to be by names of persons, these could be listed separately. Since separate listing takes up rather more space than a single listing, there must be a real justification for this kind of arrangement; the space allocated for indexes at the end of texts

266

is often restricted and must be used to the best possible effect.

It is possible to produce a natural language index using significant terms taken unaltered from the text and arranged in alphabetical sequence with accompanying page numbers; if the text itself is computer-stored then, once a stop-list of non-index terms has been established, the index can be generated automatically. As explained in Chapter 4, this kind of index language does not provide for contexts for homographs, supply links between synonyms or indicate hierarchical relations between terms, nor does an index compiled by this method provide more than a sequence of undifferentiated page references against an index term, though greater refinements are possible as a result of additional input. For certain kinds of document — with a short text, in circumstances where the users are totally familiar with the vocabulary used and are able to predict the context and appropriate terms, and where the lack of subdivision under terms is not disadvantageous — this method can provide a suitable index.

In other cases, though (perhaps the majority) the intellectual activities of selection of terms and vocabulary control (and therefore the use of an artificial index language) must be practised. Clearly it is necessary for the indexer to familiarise herself with the text; if it is her own, then she can start indexing immediately, otherwise ample time must be allowed for the reading of the text. There is a continuing debate as to whether the author is the best person to index her own work — having greater knowledge of the subject, but not necessarily knowing anything of the techniques of indexing or being able to anticipate users' search behaviour — or whether someone skilled in indexing though less familiar with the subject, is likely to produce the best result.

Opinions also differ as to the thoroughness of reading required at this stage; much obviously depends on the nature of the text and the indexer's knowledge of the subject field (which can be aided by consultation of reference material and appropriate classification schemes and thesauri). At the least, a detailed scanning of the document is likely to be needed if an effective and comprehensive index is to be constructed. The first read will also provide some indication of the likely extent of the index, the number of terms, whether subheadings are likely to be needed, and how many sequences should be envisaged. (The text used should of course be a final copy, not subject to alteration, though actual page numbers may be added at a later stage).

The second examination of the text can be the starting point for index compilation; there are several methods of recording the terms selected, ranging from those using slips of paper, one for each term, in a box, to those employing word processors, into which terms can be entered, amended and rearranged in sequence. (Several of the manual methods are described by Knight, 1979). Indexers will choose whichever method suits them best and use resources which are readily available.

The terms chosen, as stated earlier, must reflect adequately the content of the text, with the indexer amplifying the text terms from his knowledge of language and the search behaviour of the users. Terms selected are to be regarded as provisional at this stage, subject to alteration and expansion in the light of the number of page references found for each term. The significant terms chosen may — depending on the type of text — include names of manufactured objects ('Motor cycles'), natural elements ('Aluminium'), abstract concepts ('Freedom'), people ('Brezhnev, Leonid Il'ich'), places ('Harare, Zimbabwe'), events ('Edinburgh film festival, 1979'), periods of time ('Nineteenth century'), and so on, and may consist of single words or combinations of words. Short index terms are easier to consult, but lengthy combinations may sometimes be necessary ('Antibiotics, use of in animal husbandry, medical opinions towards', 'Hashimoto, S., Fourviere, T. and Bulgheroni, R. Research on art forgeries' and 'Rivas, Angel Saavedra y Ramirez de Baquedano, duque de, 1791–1865, Spanish poet and diplomat').

268

The problems to be resolved by vocabulary control have been discussed in Chapters 4 and 5; in the context of individual document indexing, the most common are: nouns – singular or plural forms; noun and adjective combinations – direct or inverted entry; institutional names – full or acronymic form; personal names – full, abbreviated, best-known or other form; homographs – need for context; synonyms – choice from several; spelling differences. Nouns of which the plural form requires the addition of 's' or 'es' can be represented in indexes as 'Turbine(s)', if access to both singular and plural forms is required; while for noun and adjective combinations the direct form 'Diesel engines' is usually preferred to the inverted 'Engines, diesel', though there are occasions when the latter can be useful. The form of personal and institutional names chosen should be that most likely to be used by the searchers, with additional references under other forms, or *see* references from them to the form chosen; thus either

'OPEC . . . . . . . . . 36, 45, 67
Organisation of Petroleum-Exporting Countries . . 36, 45, 67'

or

'OPEC . . . . . . . . . 36, 45, 67
Organisation of Petroleum-Exporting Countries *see* OPEC'

Very detailed references for personal names are sometimes required with titles and dates – as in the example given above for 'Rivas . . . '. The choice of one index term from two or more synonyms should also be made in accordance with user practice, with double entry, or use of *see* references, as just indicated. Contexts for homographs help to clarify meaning, as in : 'Cables (hawsers)' and 'Cables (electric)'; if a word, in the context of a particular text is readily understood to have only one meaning, then such clarification is unnecessary. In considering different spellings, the indexer should normally favour the spelling in the text, but if there are irregularities – such as the misspelling of names or other words in diary entries quoted in the text – the

**269**

correct spelling should be used in the index, with the textual version beside it: 'Corleigh ['Corley'], Frances . . .'.

There are various conventions for the presentation of page references (see, for example, British Standards Institution, 1976). For a sequence of pages, the first page only may be quoted ('Textiles . . . 89'), but it is more helpful to give the first and last pages ('Textiles . . . 89–94') or the first page and an abbreviation indicating later pages ('Textiles . . . 89 et seq' or '. . . 89ff' or '. . . 89+'). When a term has several references against it, those which are considered to be the principal sources of information, as opposed to minor mentions, may be highlighted in some way; perhaps by the use of bold type ('Ross and Cromarty . . . 48, 61, 75') or by underlining (' . . . 48, 61, 75'). References to text should be distinguished from those to illustrations, glossary terms or definitions, footnotes and bibliographical entries, again by the use of type or by the supply of additional information ('Eisteddfod . . . 3 G1, 67, 125 ill, 242n, 476 bib').

Long lists of page numbers, even if the major references are differentiated, are tedious for the user to consult; terms which have accumulated many references to text pages during index compilation should be considered for the addition of subheadings. This involves checking back to the appropriate pages of the text and identifying subthemes and relationships which may be added to the original index term; instead of

'Infra-red photography . . . 16, 24, 38, 243, 716, 934 . . . '

it may be possible to provide

'Infra-red photography: apparatus          934
                     : crime detection     24
                     : medical uses        38
                     : military uses       16
                       and so on.

Subheadings are clearer to read if set out as above, with each one starting a new line, but space may be used more economically if they are run on: 'Infra-red photography: apparatus 934; in crime detection 24; medical uses 38; military uses 16; . . .'. A range of punctuation symbols may be used to help to clarify and separate parts of index references, the aim being to present as much information as precisely and as clearly as possible.

The use of *see* references for synonyms and near-equivalents has already been mentioned; *see also* should be employed to link related terms when this is held to be appropriate, as in 'Taxation . . . 167; *see also* Capital gains tax; Capital transfer tax; Income tax . . .' and 'Political parties . . . 567; *see also* names of particular parties'.

Ideally, the compilation of an index should be an unhurried, methodical process, allowing ample time for reflection upon the completed product, before sending for printing or other reproduction. It often happens, however, perhaps because more time has been taken than expected in the preparation of the text, that the index is wanted very quickly, so that a publishing deadline may be met. The indexer, therefore, may find himself pressed both for time and space; negotiations may slightly increase the allowance for both, but he must always be prepared for rapid action and must endeavour to produce a high-quality result despite the constraints under which he works. The final task, after production of a good typed or clearly written copy for the printer and checking for accuracy, consistency, correct punctuation, capitalisation and filing order, is to prepare an introductory paragraph or two explaining the construction of the index(es) to the users; this should include statements indicating which parts of the text have been indexed and which have not (appendixes and preliminaries may have been excluded, for example), which kinds of terms have been indexed, the type of alphabetical order used (word-by-word or letter-by-letter), the method of treating unusual,

**271**

compound or transliterated names and acronyms, the conventions used (bold type, italic, underlining), abbreviations employed and differences between sequences.

The value of good indexes to documents is increasingly recognised and the Society of Indexers, through its journal *The Indexer*, and the maintenance of a professional register of, and training for, indexers, seeks to improve the standard and level of provision of indexes generally. Index compilers wishing to better their technique may gain useful guidance by consulting those book indexes which have been awarded the Wheatley Medal (given annually for an outstanding index to a book or periodical) and comparing them with other indexes which they know from using them to be inadequate.

## REFERENCES

British Standards Institution (1976) *Recommendations: the preparation of indexes to books, periodicals and other publications*. British Standards Institution. (B.S. 3700:1976).

Knight, G Norman (1979) *Indexing, the art of: a guide to the indexing of books and periodicals*. Allen and Unwin.

## FURTHER READING

Items 3, 16, 19, 22, 33, 40 and 58 from section B of further reading on p. 274 – 280.

## FURTHER READING

**A)** Periodicals which regularly include feature articles and other material of interest to those involved in information retrieval include:

*Aslib Proceedings.* Aslib. (Monthly).

*Audiovisual Librarian.* Library Association. (Quarterly).

*Business Archives.* Business Archives Council. (Annual).

*Catalogue & Index.* Cataloguing and Indexing Group of the Library Association. (Quarterly).

*Indexer.* Society of Indexers. (2 issues p.a.).

*International Journal of Micrographics and Video Technology.* Pergamon. (Quarterly).

*Journal of Information Science.* North-Holland for Institute of Information Scientists. (Five issues per year).

*Library Resources and Technical Services.* American Library Association, Resources and Technical Services Division. (Quarterly).

*Program: automated library and information systems.* Aslib. (Quarterly).

*Records Management Quarterly.* American Records Management Association. (Quarterly).

*Special Libraries.* Special Libraries Association. (Quarterly).

**B)** Some related books, parts of books, and periodical articles are listed here, and are referred to by their numbers at the end of appropriate chapters in this book.

1. J Aitchison. Indexing languages: classification schemes and thesauri. In: *Handbook of special librarianship and information work.* 5th ed. Editor: L J Anthony. Aslib, 1982. (Ch.10).

2. J Aitchison and A Gilchrist. *Thesaurus construction: a practical manual.* Aslib. 1972.

3. M D Anderson. *Book indexing.* Cambridge University Press, 1971. (Cambridge authors' and printers' guides).

4. D Austin. *PRECIS: a manual of concept analysis and subject indexing.* Council of the British National Bibliography, 1974.

5. K G B Bakewell. *Classification and indexing practice.* Bingley, 1978.

6. K G B Bakewell and E J Hunter. File creation: cataloguing and indexing. In: *Handbook of special librarianship and information work.* 5th ed. Editor: L J Anthony. Aslib, 1982. (Ch.11).

7. K G B Bakewell. *Manual of cataloguing practice.* Pergamon, 1972.

8. *Bath University Comparative Catalogue Study. Final report: papers 1 to 10.* Bath University Library, 1975.

9. C D Batty. *An introduction to the nineteenth edition of the Dewey Decimal Classification.* Bingley, 1981.

10. J F Blagden. Financial management. budgeting and costing. In: *Handbook of special librarianship and information work.* 5th ed. Editor: L J Anthony. Aslib, 1982. (Ch.4).

11. A G Brown. *Introduction to subject indexing: a programmed text* (with D W Langridge and J Mills). 2nd ed. Bingley, 1982. Vol.1. Subject analysis and practical classification. Vol.2. UDC and chain procedure.

12. B. Buchanan. *A glossary of indexing terms.* Bingley, 1976.

13. B. Buchanan. *Theory of library classification.* Bingley, 1979. (Outlines of modern librarianship).

14. J Burkett. Library and information networks. In: *Handbook of special librarianship and information work.* 5th ed. Editor: L J Anthony. Aslib, 1982. (Ch.15).

15. T W Burrell and K J McGarry. *Introduction to logic and semantics: a programmed text.* Bingley, 1972. Biased towards the needs of librarians and information workers.

16. G V Carey. *Making an index.* 3rd ed. Cambridge University Press, 1963. (Cambridge authors' and printers' guides).

17. *Cataloguing and classification of non-western material: concerns, issues and practices.* Editor: M M Aman. Phoenix, Arizona: Oryx Press; London: Mansell, 1980. (Neal-Schuman professional book).

18. E J Coates. *Subject catalogues: headings and structure.* Library Association, 1960.

19. R L Collison. *Indexes and indexing: guide to the indexing of books.* 4th ed. Benn, 1972.

20. M Cook. *Archives and the computer.* Butterworths, 1980.

21. *The design of information systems for human beings: Informatics 6.* Editors: K P Jones and H Taylor. Aslib, 1981.

22. A C Foskett, *The subject approach to information.* 4th ed. Bingley, 1982.

23. A C Foskett. *The Universal Decimal Classification.* Bingley, 1973.

24. D J Foskett. *Classification and indexing in the social sciences.* 2nd ed. Butterworths, 1974.

Includes samples of faceted schemes.

25. *General classification systems in a changing world: proceedings of the FID classification symposium held in commemoration of the Dewey Centenary, Brussels, November 1976.* The Hague: Federation Internationale de Documentation, 1978.

·26. A Gilchrist. *The thesaurus in retrieval.* Aslib, 1971.

27. M Gorman. *The concise AACR2.* 2nd ed. Library Association, 1981.

28. J L Hall. *On-line information retrieval sourcebook.* Aslib, 1977.

29. W M Henry. *On-line searching: an introduction* (with J A Leigh, L A Tedd and P W Williams). Butterworths, 1980.

30. R Hindson. UDC in the UK: a report on the 1979/ 1980 survey. *Aslib Proceedings,* vol.33, no.3, March 1981, p. 93–101.

31. J Horner. *Cataloguing.* Association of Assistant Librarians. 1970.

32. J Horner. *Special cataloguing with particular reference to music, films, maps, serials and the multi-media computerised catalogue.* Bingley, 1973.

33. R F Hunnisett. *Indexing for editors.* British Records Association, 1972. (Archives and the user: no.2).

34. E J Hunter. *AACR 2: an introduction to the second edition of the Anglo-American Cataloguing Rules.* Bingley, 1979.
A programmed text.

35. E J Hunter and K G B Bakewell. *Cataloguing.* Bingley, 1979.

36. W J Hutchins. *Languages of indexing and classification: a linguistic study of structures and functions.* Peter Peregrinus, 1975.
Deals with basic linguistic processes.

37. *Information retrieval experiment.* Editor: K Sparck Jones. Butterworths, 1981.

38. F W Lancaster. *Vocabulary control for information retrieval.* Arlington, Va.: Information Resources Press, 1972.

Includes samples of thesauri.

39. D Langridge. *Approach to classification for students of librarianship.* Bingley, 1973.

Deals with basic logic biased towards the needs of librarianship.

40. D Langridge. Classification and book indexing. In: *Sayers memorial volume* . . . edited by D J Foskett and B I Palmer. Library Association, 1961. (Ch.13).

41. D Langridge. *Classification and indexing in the humanities.* Butterworths, 1976.

42. S M Malinconico and P J Fasana. *The future of the catalog: the library's choices.* White Plains, N.Y.: Knowledge Industry Publications, 1979.

43. A Maltby and L Gill. *The case for Bliss: modern classification practice and principles in the context of the Bibliographic Classification.* Bingley, 1979.

44. K J McGarry. *Communications, knowledge and the librarian.* Bingley, 1975.

45. J Marshall. *On equal terms: a thesaurus for nonsexist indexing and cataloguing.* New York: Neal-Schuman, 1977.

Designed to be interfilable with Library of Congress Subject Headings.

46. *New trends in documentation and information: pro-ceedings of the 39th FID Congress, University of Edinburgh, 25–28 September 1978,* edited by P J Taylor. Aslib for FID, 1980. (FID Publication 566).

47. C M Overton and A Seal. *Cataloguing costs in the UK: an analysis of the market for automated cataloguing services . . .* Bath University Library, 1979. (British Library research and development report 5477).

48. A S Pollitt. Planning for new information systems. In: *Minis, micros and terminals for libraries and information services . . .* Edited by A Gilchrist. Heyden, 1981. (Ch.2).

49. S R Ranganathan. *Elements of library classification . . .* 3rd ed. Bombay: Asia Publishing House, 1962.

50. *Reclassification: rationale and problems: proceedings of a conference on reclassification . . .* April 1968. Editor: J M Perreault. College Park, Md.: School of Library and Information Services, 1968.

51. M Rigby. *Automation and the UDC 1948–1980.* 2nd ed. Hague: Federation Internationale de Documenta-tion, 1981. (FID publication 565).

52. A W Seal. *Automated cataloguing in the UK: a guide to services.* Bath University Library, Centre for Cata-logue Research, 1980. (British Library research and development report 5545).

53. A Seal and others. *Full and short entry catalogues: library needs and uses.* Bath University Library, 1982.

54. J R Sharp. *Information retrieval: notes for students.* Deutsch, 1970. (Grafton basic texts.)

55. J R Sharp. *Some fundamentals of information retrieval.* Deutsch, 1965.

56. M Shaw and others. *Using AACR2: a step-by-step algorithmic approach to part II of the Anglo-American Cataloguing Rules.* Library Association, 1980.

57. J A Shinebourne. A critique of AACR. *Libri*, vol.29, no.3, October 1979, p.231–279.

58. Society of Indexers. *A select reading list on indexing.* Society of Indexers, 1978.

59. D Soergel. *Indexing languages and thesauri: construction and maintenance.* Los Angeles, Cal.: Melville, 1974.

60. L Tedd. Computer-based information retrieval services. In: *Handbook of special librarianship and information work.* 5th ed. Editor: L J Anthony. Aslib, 1982. (Ch.13).

61. H Townley. *Systems analysis for information retrieval.* Deutsch, 1978. (Institute of Information Scientists monograph series).

An introductory text biased towards the needs of information workers.

62. H Townley and R D Gee. *Thesaurus making: grow your own word stock.* Deutsch, 1981.

63. B C Vickery. *Classification and indexing in science.* 3rd ed. Butterworths, 1975.

Includes samples of faceted schemes and a discussion of fundamental categories.

64. B C Vickery. *Faceted classification: a guide to the construction and use of faceted schemes.* Aslib, 1960 (reprinted 1970 with additional material).

65. B A J Winslade. *Introduction to the Dewey Decimal Classification for British schools.* 3rd ed. Albany, N.Y: Forest Press for the School Library Association, 1977.

66. B S Wynar *Introduction to cataloging and classification.* 6th ed. Littleton, Colo.: Libraries Unlimited, 1980.

# INDEX

# INDEX

The index provides references to topics treated in Chapters 1 to 10, and to persons, institutions and selected titles of works treated in those Chapters and in the Further Reading lists. (The preliminaries — introduction, acknowledgement, about the authors and so on — have not been indexed).

References are arranged alphabetically using letter-by-letter order (see p.55); spaces and punctuation symbols between words are ignored in the filing order.

Organisations, systems and objects having both full and acronymic or abbreviated forms are listed under both forms, but full details of page references appear under what is judged to be the best-known form, with a *see* reference from the other form.

Where there are several page references for a term, the major references, including those carrying a definition or illustration of a term or topic are given in bold type — **43**; references to full bibliographic citations are given in italic — *277*. Titles of publications are given in italic — *Program*.

P.F.B.

**287**

288

**291**

Jones, K Sparck *see* Sparck Jones K
*Journal of information science. 273*

Key Word And Context indexing
(KWAC) *see* KWAC
Key Word In Context indexing
(KWIC) *see* KWIC
Key Word Out of Context Indexing
(KWOC) *see* KWOC
Key words . . . . . . 60,171,181,209
Knight, G. . . . . . . . . . . . 268,272
KWAC Indexing (Key Word And
Context) . . . . . . . . . . . . . .64
KWIC indexing (Key Word In
Context) . . . . . 61–63,130,171
KWOC indexing (Key Word Out of
Context) . . . . . . . . . . .63,171

Labelling *see* Guiding of files
Headings
Lancaster F W. . . 256,261,*263*,278
Langridge, D W . . . . . . . . *275,278*
Language
of documents . . . . . . 160–161
of computers *see* Command
languages
Language (common concepts)
representation in notation. . . . .
83,84,86
Lang, V . . . . . . . . . . . . .80,*89,92*
*LC classification see Library of*
*Congress classification*
*LCsh see Library of Congress*
*subject headings*
Learning resource centres (educa-
tional resource centres, media
resource centres) . . . . . .23,161
Legibility of file entries . 193–194
Leigh, J A . . . . . . . . . . . . . *277*
Letter-by-letter order . . 55,170,207
Libraries *see* Document collections

*Library and information science*
*abstracts (LISA)* . . . . . . .*79,91*
Library Association . . . .77,86,262
*Library literature.* . . . . . . . .*79,91*
Library of Congress . . . . . .44,183
*see also Library of Congress*
*classification; Library of*
*Congress subject headings*
*Library of Congress classification*
*(LC)* . . . . . . . .81,*87–88,91*
*additions and changes.* . . *88,91*
*Library of Congress subject head-*
*ings (LCsh).* . . . . . .*78,91*,135
*Library resources and technical*
*services* . . . . . . . . . . . . . *273*
Life of files . . . . . . . . . . . . 201
*LISA see Library and information*
*science abstracts*
Literary form of documents *see*
Internal form of documents
Local Catalogue Service (LOCAS)
*see* BLAISE/LOCAS
LOCAS (Local Catalogue Service)
*see* BLAISE/LOCAS
Lockheed Corporation . . . . . . 230
Logic in relation to index language
construction. . . . . . . .93,118
*see also* Boolean logic;
Logical division
Logical differences ('NOT' opera-
tors) . . . . . .215,217,219,223
Logical division. . . . **102–106**,107
Logical operators. . . . . . 215–221
*see also* Logical differences
Logical products
Logical sums
Logical products ('AND' operators)
215,216,219,220
Logical sums ('OR' operators)
**215,218**,219,221,223-225,227,231

293

294

300